ETHICS AND CAPITALISM

Edited by John Douglas Bishop

Despite the great economic advantage of capitalism – that it is an efficient system of production and distribution – capitalist societies
struggle with its by-products of poverty, exclusion, corruption, and
environmental destruction. The essays in *Ethics and Capitalism* address
the challenge of ensuring ethical and just societies within a capitalist
system without sacrificing productivity.

The introductory essay is a guide to the issues in the emerging field
of ethics and capitalism, and refers to recent contributions from several
disciplines. The collection as a whole evaluates the morality of capitalism by looking at its foundation in property theory, its relationship to
democracy, the problems of corruption and globalization, as well as
the impact of capitalism on non-European cultures and the environment. Contributors consider various ideological and cultural biases
that affect our understanding of capitalism. It is the aim of the collection to defend the practical merits of capitalism while raising concerns
about its ethical problems. In conclusion, the volume considers the
possibility of a mitigated form of capitalism that would ensure
economic efficiency and productivity while avoiding ethical pitfalls.

JOHN DOUGLAS BISHOP is Associate Professor in the Administrative
Studies Program at Trent University.

EDITED BY JOHN DOUGLAS BISHOP

Ethics and Capitalism

UNIVERSITY OF TORONTO PRESS
Toronto Buffalo London

© University of Toronto Press Incorporated 2000
Toronto Buffalo London
Printed in Canada

ISBN 0-8020-4689-4 (cloth)
ISBN 0-8020-8273-4 (paper)

Canadian Cataloguing in Publication Data

Main entry under title:

Ethics and capitalism

Includes bibliographical references.
ISBN 0-8020-4689-4 (bound)   ISBN 0-8020-8273-4 (pbk.)

1. Capitalism – Moral and ethical aspects.   I. Bishop, John Douglas.
HB501.E84 1999   330.12'2   C99-932816-6

University of Toronto Press acknowledges the support of the Canada
Council for the Arts and the Ontario Arts Council to its publishing
program.

University of Toronto Press acknowledges the financial support for its
publishing activities of the Government of Canada through the Book
Publishing Industry Development Program (BPIDP).

Canadä

Contents

Acknowledgments

The editor of these chapters wishes first to thank the contributors to this volume for their ideas, encouragement, and patience. The encouragement of Wesley Cragg was especially valuable at crucial times.

The idea for this book originated in the 1996–7 Bank of Montreal Distinguished Speaker Series at Trent University which explored many issues in the area of ethics and capitalism. Some of the chapters in the current volume began life as public talks in that series. I am grateful to the Bank of Montreal for their sponsorship of the Distinguished Speaker Series and this project on Ethics and Capitalism. The bank, of course, had no input into the content of the current volume, and none of the ideas in the current volume are necessarily those of the bank.

Much of the work on this volume, and the writing of my own contribution, were done while I was on sabbatical from Trent University. I was at the time Research Fellow at the Schulich School of Business at York University, and I wish to acknowledge lively discussions there especially with Professor Wesley Cragg and students Jim Lyttle, Mark Schwartz, and Neil Shankman.

During my sabbatical I enjoyed the traditional collegiality of that jewel in the academic crown of Canada – Massey College. Thanks are due to everyone at Massey who questioned my ideas, especially to the early morning breakfast clique.

Many colleagues have helped with this whole project. Thanks are especially due to Kathryn Campbell, Bernard Hodgson, Peter Lapp, David Newhouse, Frank Rotering, and an immensely thorough anonymous reviewer with the University of Toronto Press.

Introduction

Capitalism is the only economic system viable for the foreseeable future. There are no workable alternatives.

The great merit of capitalism over other economic systems is its efficiency and productivity. If resistance to capitalism is futile, as David Newhouse argues later in this volume, its inevitability is solidly based on the attractiveness of its immense productivity, its immense output of desired goods and services.

But accepting capitalism because of the lack of alternatives, or because of its desirability, or even because of its inevitability, leaves many issues unresolved. Some or these unresolved issues are precisely the kinds of issues that can only be discussed with a thorough grounding in ethics.

Most fundamental is the question of whether the bases of capitalism – private property and free markets – are morally acceptable. Since even a productive economic system will be morally suspect if it rests on questionable foundations, the moral justification of the defining institutions of capitalism needs thorough discussion.

Accepting capitalism leaves unresolved the question of which of the many possible forms of capitalism is morally best. Even though the specific outcomes of a capitalist free market cannot be planned, the laws, policies, and regulations which create and sustain free markets and private property are intentional social creations. How best to structure capitalism is a suitable, indeed crucial, subject for ethical reflection.

Capitalism is only an economic system. It is not a complete social and cultural world. What are the limits of capitalism? Is capitalism compatible with democracy and civic virtue? Is capitalism compatible with the many other things we value such as family, community, beauty, truth, friendship, and the natural environment? Is capitalism compatible with virtue – do free markets allow and encourage human and institutional behaviour which is ethical? Asking such questions is vital to deciding if capitalism is a just economic order. We must ask how we can structure capitalist institutions that are just, how we can mitigate the known harms of capitalism, and how we can preserve and express our non-economic values under capitalism.

The well-established efficiency and productivity of capitalism cannot in themselves answer any of these questions. The ethical assessment of an economic system must be conducted at a more fundamental level than the assessment of its efficiency. Economic models of free markets assume people's preferences are given prior to and independently of the economic system being modelled. Since ethics concerns and affects the formation of these economically 'exogenous' preferences, ethical discussions of capitalism are logically more fundamental than economic analysis. Discussion of ethics can influence how people behave within capitalism, which will dramatically affect the nature of the capitalism we live with. For example, the level and nature of interpersonal trust in a society greatly impacts the economic structures of that society even within free markets.

There is a spectre haunting the discussion of capitalism. For more than a hundred years, most ethical assessments of capitalism were written from within a debate about whether capitalism was morally superior to socialism, and whether the results of free markets were more ethical than the results of planned economies. The collapse, along with that of the Berlin Wall, of one of the terms of this debate means that the ethical assessment of the other can be reframed. With the death of socialism, we need no longer view every moral criticism of capitalism as a defence of socialism, and we should no longer hesitate to advocate moral improvements to capitalist structures for fear of advancing the socialist agenda.

Reframing the debate about ethics and capitalism yields a group of discussions about capitalism itself – its nature, structures, effects, varieties, and possibilities. The purpose of this volume is to present essays that contribute to one or more of the discussions which constitute the ethics and capitalism debate. Collectively these essays help reframe this debate.

The study of ethics and capitalism is a huge field because it involves many aspects of capitalism, and because contributions have been made to it from the viewpoint of many different disciplines. The first essay in the present volume is a guide to the issues in this field, and refers to key recent contributions from several disciplines. The remaining essays are original contributions to a variety of issues that surround the moral assessment of capitalism. They are written by economists, philosophers, and others using approaches and styles appropriate to their various disciplines. Together they reflect the reframing of the ethics and capitalism debate made possible by the death of socialism.

Capitalism produces goods and services beyond the wildest fantasies of most of humanity for most of human history, but capitalist societies also still struggle with unresolved issues of poverty, exclusion, violence, and environmental destruction. Before people suffer the despair of fatalism or the indifference of overconfidence, let us accept the challenge of making capitalism ethical while maintaining its productivity.

ETHICS AND CAPITALISM

1

Ethics and Capitalism:
A Guide to the Issues

JOHN DOUGLAS BISHOP

For the past three hundred years or more, writers from a multitude of disciplines and perspectives have addressed issues relating to ethics and capitalism. Capitalism was defended on moral grounds by Adam Smith in the eighteenth century and criticized on moral grounds by Karl Marx in the nineteenth. The moral beliefs that are prerequisites to capitalism were examined by Max Weber and have been criticized by Tawney, Galbraith, and others. Consumer values were defended as early as 1714 by Bernard Mandeville, but today are criticized by feminists, environmentalists, and sages such as Marshall McLuhan. Lately, the field of business ethics has exploded: theorists and politicians have debated government regulation of capitalism; environmental ethicists have discussed capitalism; and many cultures have faced the bittersweet choice of whether they ought to adopt capitalist values. Even economists have started serious discussion of ethics and economics; the work of Amartya Sen is particularly striking.[1]

Are there any themes, methodologies, paradigms or even issues that might unify these writings? The first step to seeing themes that might run through such diverse viewpoints is to construct a guide to the ethical questions these writers on capitalism see themselves as addressing. The guide will help clarify the issue each writer is discussing, and show how various writers and debates relate to one another.

The present guide identifies and distinguishes from each other the ethical issues that capitalism gives rise to. Some of the key writings, especially recent writings, which contribute to these various ethical debates are placed in the context of the issues they address. No attempt is made to completely survey recent or current writing; the field of ethics and capitalism is far too large and various for that. It is sufficient at this stage to identify the key issues and debates. In future, once these are laid out, unifying themes or methodologies may emerge, or at least there may emerge some understanding of how all these approaches and issues are interrelated.

Definitions

Capitalist economic systems are characterized by the private owner-ship of property and the consensual exchange of goods and services in a free market. The word 'capitalism' is sometimes used in the broader sense of any economic system that includes the accumulation of capital, which might include, for example, state capitalism; but in this book capitalism will refer to economic systems with the two essential features of private property and free markets.

Private Property

Private property is the ownership of productive resources, that is, the means of production, distribution, and exchange, by individuals who control the use of their resources for their own benefit. Private property should not be confused with personal property. The non-productive things which individuals own such as their clothes, furniture, house, and car are personal property. Private property is the ownership of productive resources such as mines, factories, companies, stocks, bonds, patents, and trademarks. Individuals invest in owning private property with the intention of making a profit. Individual ownership of personal property is a characteristic of most economic systems; private property is a characteristic of capitalism.

The ownership of private property confers on individual owners certain rights over the resources they own. This is often phrased as 'the right to private property,' but that is an awkward phrase for two reasons. First, the phrase could be interpreted as meaning that everyone has the right to own some property, as though this were the kind of right that would be violated when some or most people are not property owners.[2] In existing capitalist systems, most people do not own any or much private property except the productive resource of their own labour, and, late in life, savings from their labour earnings in the form of pensions. Such people may own a lot of personal property, but a few 'capitalists' tend to own most of the productive resources. This failure of most people to own any or few productive resources is not a violation of the right to private property as the phrase is usually used.

Second, the phrase 'the right to private property' seems to imply that owning private property confers only a single right. In fact, ownership of property under capitalism confers on the owner several rights, including the rights of profit, control, exclusion, sale, giving, bequeathing, and possibly other rights depending on what sort of property is owned. There are ethical and other issues involved in deciding which rights make up the bundle of rights conferred by owning private property; there is no specific bundle which is 'correct' for capitalism, though the rights to profit, control, and exchange are basic. The question of which rights are conferred by ownership is discussed in the section on 'Variations in Property Rights.'

Free Exchange

The idea of free exchange of property and services is more complicated and less obvious than might be thought. When Adam Smith claimed that a propensity to barter was fundamental to human nature, he was unaware that many societies did not barter but distributed goods by tradition or by gift-giving ceremonies such as potlatches, and that many traded by reciprocal gift-giving. The Huron, for example, when they first began to trade furs with the French and English were horrified at the European practice of haggling over prices.[3]

The concept of free exchange that underlies the notion of free markets is a sophisticated idea. It presupposes a belief that society is composed of a collection of separate individuals, each with their own utility based on their own preferences and each free to choose which exchanges to consent to in pursuit of their own utility. These individuals are assumed to be equal, not in the sense of owning equal amounts of property, but in the sense of having equal legal access to the market (see the section on 'Unequal distribution').

The notion of a free market, therefore, is based on several other concepts including a particular concept of the individual, plus specific concepts of consent, choice, preference, utility, rational behaviour, and legal equality. Each of these concepts has provoked many debates;[4] for example, questions have been raised about the accuracy of these descriptions of people and society, and whether such descriptions misconceive moral reality. If the concepts we use to understand free markets are biased or misleading, our moral assessment of capitalism may be inadequate. For example, in her contribution to the present volume, Julie Nelson argues that the view of individuals presupposed by free exchange, which she calls the 'separative self,' biases our understanding of capitalism.

Capitalism

One of the problems in discussing ethics and capitalism is agreeing on whether to discuss ideal capitalism, abstract models of capitalism, or actual existing capitalist systems. The abstract models that economists develop are often thought to be morally neutral, but the instant they are used to guide policy the abstractions are suffused with normative values.[5] Are the abstractions really neutral or are they biased? Is Pareto optimality morally desirable? Should 'economic man' be encouraged or restrained? The field of ethics and economics is fast developing and for good reason.[6]

Studying economic models may lead to a belief that pure free markets can actually be approximated, or to the belief that we should strive to approximate them as closely as possible. That we should so strive for ideal or theoretical capitalism is itself a moral belief, and one that needs careful examination. Libertarianism offers one such moral defence of free markets.[7]

But there are many who think that the moral assessment of capitalism should be concerned with actual existing capitalist systems, not theoretical models or pure ideals.[8] As David Copp points out in his chapter, no existing economy is an example of 'pure' capitalism; all have intentional or historical impurities. And since existing capitalist systems vary widely, which one we are assessing becomes relevant. Nor should we assume that capitalist systems are defined by national boundaries; capitalism can have local forms as well as extend across national boundaries in trading blocs like the European Union or the North American Free Trade Agreement. Increasingly, the free flow of capital and the development of transnational corporations is creating a global capitalism. What these various actual capitalisms show is that capitalist systems can be structured in various ways; how to structure property rights and free markets is an appropriate subject for moral discourse.[9] This is clearly the basis of Leo Groarke's assessment of the strengths and weaknesses of capitalism in the concluding chapter in the current collection and of his proposal for an ethically legitimate mitigated capitalism.

Theoretical models of free markets, ideal capitalism, and existing capitalisms can all be used legitimately in discussions of ethics and capitalism; however, identifying which of them we are talking and thinking about is essential.

Ethics

Ethics can be either descriptive or normative. Descriptive ethics describes the moral beliefs people do in fact have; this is not a significant concern of most of the papers in this book. Normative ethics is the passing of value judgments on human actions, policies, or social structures. Capitalism raises ethical concerns and calls for normative assessment on all three levels – actions, policies, and structures. The rest of this guide sketches these key ethical concerns; the other papers in this book investigate some of them in more depth.

Bias in Understanding Capitalism

All of the ethical issues we will consider – the justification, criticism, structure, and regulation of capitalism – presuppose that there are not serious ethical problems with our understanding of capitalism. If the understanding of capitalism on which we base our moral assessment is itself biased, then the value of those assessments becomes questionable. Is there evidence of biases in our understanding?

Some economists and philosophers say there are such biases, including biases in the concept of 'economic man.' It has been pointed out that economic man is an idealization, not an abstraction, and that one should not base moral judgments on idealizations.[10] Other philosophers (such as Beaudrillard, Derrida, Habermas) criticize the failure of economists to recognize that people's lives are embedded in cultural, symbolic, and communicative systems.

Feminists criticize our economic understanding of capitalism for failing to capture several important aspects of people's lives – economists, they say, fail to recognize that people are embodied, caring, related, dependent (including completely dependent during childhood), and self-creative. The chapter by Julie Nelson in this book considers the impact of this bias on economic thinking. These and like biases in our understanding of capitalism need to be kept in mind when assessing the ethical issues raised by capitalism.

The Moral Justification of Capitalism

Alternatives to Capitalism

Often the first question that comes to mind when thinking of ethics and capitalism is whether capitalism is morally justified.[11] This ethical assessment of capitalism as a complete economic system is often, and quite rightly, conducted by comparing capitalism with alternative economic systems. The most common alternative for comparison is socialism (or its dictatorial version, communism), a system which abolishes private property and replaces the free market with central planning.

The comparison of socialism with capitalism has been going on for most of the past two hundred years; many people now think the question has been resolved in favour of capitalism, others are not so sure. In terms of the moral assessment of the two systems, a lot depends on whether ideal or actual versions are compared. The ideals of socialism, which include an all-inclusive classless society in which everyone's needs are fully met by cooperative production, appear to have considerable moral merit. Actual socialist societies seem less morally praiseworthy, and some have been blatantly evil. The problem seems to be that centrally planned economies do not work, perhaps because, as Hayek tried to show, central planners cannot have adequate information without a free market price mechanism. However, it is not the purpose of this book to enter into the debate between socialism and capitalism.[12] Our concern is with the ethical issues of capitalism itself. These ethical issues remain, indeed they come to the fore, for anyone who does not consider socialism a viable alternative. If capitalism is the only sensible economic system in the postindustrial global context, it becomes morally vital that capitalism be structured and implemented in a morally defensible way.

Historically, socialism was not the only alternative to capitalism. When capitalism first arose in Europe, it replaced feudalism, a socio-economic system in which most property was privately owned but was not exchangeable on a free market. People had legally enforced inherited social positions which determined the exchange of goods and services. Equal access to a free market based on consensual exchange is usually thought to be morally superior to feudalism. This feudal background needs to be remembered when assessing the moral merits of equality under capitalism; free markets never distribute property equally, but they are not based on an unequal hereditary social hierarchy like feudalism is.

Currently, global capitalism is encountering other economic systems. None of these at the moment seems likely to withstand capitalism's tendency to absorb smaller cultures. David Newhouse's chapter looks at the impact of capitalism on Native Canadian cultures, many of which were historically based on communal production, tradition-based distribution, and reciprocal gift-giving, rather than private property and free markets.

Justifying the Basis of Capitalism

Besides comparing capitalism with alternative economic systems, a second approach to the justification of capitalism might be to justify morally its two components – private property and free exchange. If it can be shown that each component has great moral value, then it would follow that capitalism, since it is the only economic system which ensures private property and free exchange, would have moral merit. It would remain to be shown that the moral merits of capitalism are superior to the merits of other economic systems.

Arguments which provide a moral grounding of private property are of two types: those which argue that people have a moral right to own private property, and those which argue that the private ownership of property is useful because it helps support other morally valuable social institutions such as democracy, freedom, or the rule of law. The merits of the rights and the utility approaches to the moral justification of property are considered by Dan Usher in his chapter entitled 'The Justification of Property Rights.' He concludes that rights arguments are inadequate and that the institution of private property is best justified by its usefulness.

The moral justification of free exchange is often based on claims about the moral importance of human freedom, and the claim that the free exchange of goods and services promotes or is a form of freedom. Hayek has argued this in *The Road to Serfdom*, and the case has been forcibly argued by Milton Friedman in *Capitalism and Freedom*.

Free exchange has also been justified by its usefulness. Free exchange creates prices, which in turn convey information (including information about people's preferences) that allows the efficient allocation of resources to production. Without free exchange, price information is unavailable to investors, and efficiency is impossible.

Arguments are made, therefore, that purport to morally justify each of the two defining characteristics of capitalism – private property and free exchange. But there have also been attempts to justify capitalism as a complete socioeconomic system. The most important of these is the invisible hand argument.

The Invisible Hand Argument

References to the 'invisible hand' are ubiquitous in both technical and general writings on capitalism. Frequency of use in varied contexts makes it difficult to know exactly what is intended by the phrase, but there is a core of common meaning in most uses. Generally, the invisible hand refers to the mechanism by which, in a free market, the self-interested actions of many individual people have the unintended result of promoting the common good. From this concept, people often draw two moral corollaries: first, since free markets promote the common good, they conclude that free markets are morally justified. Second, since self-interested actions promote the common good, they conclude that self-interest is morally acceptable, perhaps even morally obligatory.

Since the invisible hand argument is so common, the concept is worth examining closely to understand its moral implications. First, it should be emphasized that the argument applies only to economic behaviour inside free markets; it does not follow that people ought to pursue their self-interest in other areas, such as within the family or when voting or running for elected office. It also does not follow that a person is justified in pursuing her self-interest by non-market means such as tax evasion, fraud, or violence. The invisible hand argument is strictly constrained to the honest pursuit of profit within free markets.

In its more technical forms, the invisible hand argument raises a couple of other issues. What is a free market? The phrase 'invisible hand' comes from Adam Smith's book *An Enquiry into the Nature and Causes of the Wealth of Nations* (1776); as this title suggests, Smith was writing about national economies. In the passage in which he refers to the invisible hand (and there is only one such reference in *The Wealth of Nations*), Smith says that because 'every individual' tends to invest in his own country he unintentionally promotes the 'public interest' as though by an invisible hand.[13] For Smith, the free market was a national market, and because capital was not internationally mobile the invisible hand argument worked. In today's global economy, capital moves freely, instantly, and in huge quantities across international borders. Investors can, with an acceptable degree of security, seek and get returns by investing abroad. In this situation, Smith's argument for the invisible hand cannot apply.

The invisible hand may still operate in a global economy, and indeed global capitalism does seem to be so productive of goods and services that it can sometimes significantly raise standards of living, but reliance on the invisible hand in a global context will need new and convincing arguments to replace Smith's. Are there other reasons for thinking a global invisible hand will transform the individual pursuit of profit into the common good? This issue is very problematic because today's global economy is clearly not a free market in Smith's sense. Capital can indeed move freely worldwide, but labour for the most part can only move within nations (or within regions such as the European Community). With capital mobile and labour restricted, the global economy may not allow the invisible hand to work its magic. Many modern economic arguments also cast doubt on whether the common good is promoted by profit seeking in global markets. For example, the notion of comparative advantage, often the basis of claims that international free markets benefit everyone, assumes that capital is not internationally mobile.[14] Whether the global equivalent of Smith's invisible hand works in today's global economy remains to be shown.[15]

The invisible hand argument and its moral corollaries have a further problem. When Smith wrote that the pursuit of profit promoted the 'public interest,' he thought that profit seeking would result in the greatest annual revenue for society. In fact, there is no theoretical reason to believe this. In a theoretically pure competitive market, if every individual pursues her self-interest by maximizing her own utility, the result is not maximum total revenue, but merely an efficient allocation of resources to produce a Pareto optimal distribution of goods and services. A Pareto optimal distribution means only that no one can be made better off without someone else being made worse off. Is Pareto optimality in the public interest?[16] The section on distribution suggests that in itself Pareto optimality has little or no moral significance. Furthermore, since there are always an infinite number of Pareto optimal results depending on original endowments, all of which are Pareto non-comparable with each other, there is no reason to believe that any particular Pareto optimal result promotes the common good more than others. Finally, Pareto optimality of economic models applies to human utility, not to human welfare. When utility is defined in terms of satisfaction of a person's preferences, there are many reasons for thinking that human welfare is not solely dependent on utility. For example, the view that welfare is dependent on utility seems to assume that a state of affairs will enhance my welfare if I prefer that state. But surely this is backwards; surely my belief that a state of affairs will enhance my welfare is the reason for my preferring it, not the result of my preference. Also, the identification of welfare with preference satisfaction preempts all discussion of preference formation, the impact of economic activity on preferences, and the rational and ethical preferring of some preferences to others. The ancient Stoics, some religions, and some modern philosophers,[17] have all argued that the essence of morality lies precisely in having or not having various preferences. The economists' identification of welfare with utility and preference satisfaction disallows all discussion of whether a person would be better off by not having a preference than by having it satisfied.[18]

For these reasons, it is not clear just what kind of common good, if any, is promoted by the invisible hand of the free market. The invisible hand argument is used far too freely, and moral conclusions are drawn from it too rapidly. On closer examination, we see that at best the argument applies only to a very restricted set of economic behaviours, that the argument may not apply to today's global markets, and that the notion of the 'public interest' that the argument relies on may have little moral significance.

Moral Criticisms of Capitalism

Although criticisms of capitalism are legion, we will here briefly discuss only a few which raise significant moral concerns. The most important of these is the claim that capitalist systems violate ethical principles of distributive justice, but people have also argued that capitalism violates or threatens other morally worthwhile values as well; some have claimed, for example, that it causes alienation or threatens human autonomy and integrity, others that it tends to undermine democracy. Finally, there have been suggestions that capitalism harbours contradictions that cause moral confusion and create a tendency for capitalist systems to undermine themselves.

Unequal Distribution

The most frequent moral objection to capitalism is that it involves vast inequalities. To assess this criticism, we must distinguish between inequality in the distribution of property (both personal and private), and other forms of inequality such as social, political, and legal inequality. It is undeniable that capitalism involves vast inequalities of wealth; the status of other forms of inequality is less clear, and we will discuss those first.

In theory, although capitalism does not assume equal distribution of property, any morally defensible capitalism does assume equal access to the market for everyone in the economy. Exclusion of a group of people such as women from the market has happened in actual capitalisms, but such exclusion means the market is neither theoretically pure nor morally defensible. Equal access implies that social and legal inequalities do not have an impact on the environment of free exchange; bargaining depends only on the goods and services a person has to offer, not on a person's inherited privileges or social status. Capitalism is theoretically incompatible with feudal hierarchies, slavery, apartheid caste systems, and the exclusion of any group (such as women) from property ownership and the labour market. Free exchange is exchange free from constraints based on the legal and social status of the people who bargain.

In practice, the rise of capitalism was the key cause of the end of feudal hierarchies in Europe, and it can be argued that capitalism contributed to the end of slavery and apartheid and that it is tending to undermine caste systems. On the other hand, it can also be argued that capitalism financed the slave trade and apartheid, and that it perpetuates the oppression of such groups as Native populations in South America. The position of women in capitalism is equally two-sided. Denying women social and legal equality is inconsistent with any morally defensible capitalism, yet inequality persists in existing capitalist systems. Is capitalism simply slow in undermining these forms of unequal access to the market? Or does capitalism tend to perpetuate patriarchal control? Both sides have been argued.

Political equality can only be achieved in democratic political systems, so the compatibility of capitalism with democracy is an important issue. Dan Usher, in his chapter, argues that the political and legal freedoms of democracy depend on private property and free markets. On the other hand, David Copp, in his chapter, argues that the unequal distribution of wealth under capitalism can threaten democratic equality and that steps need to be taken to restrict the power of money in the political arena. Both Copp and Usher have compelling arguments.

What is never distributed equally under capitalism is property; this is true of both private property and personal property. In the case of personal property, that a fair distribution is necessarily an equal distribution is not obvious. The primary moral issue with respect to personal property would seem to be making sure no one lives in abject poverty without enough to meet his basic needs. Beyond this minimum, a fair distribution of personal property might involve considering such issues as desert, incentives, and non-interference in current ownership, and it might view those considerations as more important than the principle of equality of distribution. In the case of private property in productive resources, the principle of equality seems to have considerable moral weight, though not necessarily absolute moral decisiveness. Inequality of private property is more important than inequality of personal property because the former involves unequal access to productive resources and hence unequal opportunity for productive labour. The issue of unequal distribution of property needs to be approached both theoretically and in terms of actual capitalist economies.

Theoretical models of purely competitive economic systems show that the distribution of goods in free markets is entirely dependent on the distribution of original endowments.[19] It is vital that distribution, that is, who owns goods and resources, should not be confused with the allocation of resources to productive activities. Pure free markets tend towards an equilibrium in which allocation of resources is Pareto optimal, but this is only one of an infinite number of such Pareto equilibriums; which equilibrium is reached depends on original endowments. In other words, various *distributions* of goods are compatible with efficient allocation of resources and Pareto optimal equilibrium; from *any* starting point of endowment distribution, free markets will allocate efficiently and achieve a Pareto optimal outcome.[20] A belief in free markets, therefore, has nothing to contribute to questions of distributive justice.

Endowments in the sense used here include not just private property which a person might inherit and hence enter the market already possessing. Endowments also include personal characteristics with market value such as intelligence, strength, skills, or ambition. Since as a matter of fact these are never equally distributed among human beings, free markets will never result in equal distribution of property unless resource endowments are intentionally distributed to compensate for personal characteristics.[21] This is the point behind Robert Nozick's famous example of Wilt Chamberlain: in a free market, someone with Wilt Chamberlain's skills will inevitably acquire more property than those without such spectacular endowments. In Nozick's view, if the process of free exchange is morally acceptable, then the resulting inequality is morally acceptable. Free markets do not distribute property equally, but it can be argued that this is a morally acceptable form of inequality.

Even if one grants the moral acceptability of unequal property distribution, the extremes of distribution in actual capitalist systems raise some serious moral issues. These issues centre around the super-rich and the very poor.

The first question about the super-rich is how they got to own so much property; people often find it hard to believe that one person can contribute so much in a free market that he or she can honestly earn billions of dollars. And indeed, no moral justification of free markets justifies organized crime, drug lords, or large-scale fraud. But huge fortunes can also be obtained honestly, such as by inheritance, inventiveness, or entrepreneurial skill. Since allowing inheritance determines some original endowments, the moral justification or denial of inheritance lies outside of the moral assessment of markets.[22] But the fact remains that some huge fortunes are acquired by inventiveness, entrepreneurial skills, business acumen, or simple luck. Are such fortunes morally justified? It would seem so, if free markets are justified.

There is one limit on huge fortunes, even ones honestly acquired in the marketplace, that a defender of free markets might think morally required. Free markets depend on no one being able to manipulate or corner the market; if one person or a small group of people are so rich that they can control the market, then the free market ceases to exist. A moral commitment to free markets would imply a moral commitment to breaking up fortunes that are so large they disrupt free markets. How large would a fortune have to be to violate such a limit? In global markets, large indeed; perhaps the failure of the billionaire Hunt brothers to corner the world's silver market is instructive. On the other hand, much lesser sums are needed for greenmail, stock market or currency manipulation, or other ways of profiting by causing market failures.

Ethical issues arise at the other end of the scale because huge numbers of people bring to the market no endowments and so cannot enter into consensual exchanges. As a result, a free market leaves them in abject poverty, which most people find morally objectionable. Everyone lacks the ability to enter the market when they are infants and children. Obviously, a moral obligation to care for children must exist somewhere in any society, and this must be outside the free market in the sense that babies and children cannot bargain on their own behalf for the care they need. Elderly people may also need care, but their case is different from children in that they have had many years to prepare for these needs and may own substantial property with which to bargain on the market. But they may not. Or they may have resources but lack the ability to bargain. Also some disabled people and the very ill may not have anything they can bargain with for the care they need, or they may require substantially more care than they can afford.

Since the needs of people with nothing to offer the market cannot be met by capitalism, many argue that capitalism must be augmented by government-sponsored systems of welfare, social security, and subsidized education, health care, and housing. Others argue that the moral responsibility for the needy lies with individuals such as parents, family, and philanthropists. In either case, the responsibility must lie outside the market.

Amartya Sen has demonstrated that external factors can change relative prices in markets in ways that leave entire groups in such weak bargaining positions that they starve to death. He points out that this change in entitlements has even caused famines when the availability of food in an area has not declined. He writes, for example:

> ... many large famines – in which millions of people have perished from hunger and hunger-related diseases – have taken place (even in the recent past) without any overall decline in food availability at all, with no 'natural cause' making the famines inescapable. People have been deprived of food precisely because of sudden and violent shifts in 'entitlements,' resulting from the exercise of rights that people 'legitimately' have within the given legal system. Loss of employment and wage income have often led to starvation. Changes of relative prices have sometimes driven the losers to the wall.[23]

Sen's point can be generalized into a moral issue about capitalism as a socioeconomic system. With some distributions of endowments, entitlements for some groups of people in a free market may be less than what is necessary to sustain human life. This is true even without significant market failures. Sen argues that actual markets have resulted historically in mass starvation. We can add to Sen's examples the great Irish potato 'famine' of the 1840s. Throughout the famine, Ireland continued to export grain to England because the English gentry could afford to outbid Irish peasants for the grain. The result was well-fed horses for the pleasure of the gentry and mass starvation for those without entitlements. The reality of such results throws great moral doubt on the institution of free markets. Can the unequal distribution of property that results from the market be morally justified if it can and sometime does lead to mass starvation?

Alienation

Besides being criticized for creating inequality, capitalism has been morally criticized, especially by Karl Marx, for causing people to be alienated. Marx and others have argued that human beings have an inherent desire and propensity to work together in meaningful, creative, cooperative production. The structure of capitalism inherently turns work into competitive labour which is meaningless in itself and pursued only as a means of obtaining money for consumer satisfaction. Equal distribution would not solve this estrangement of people from their essential nature caused by the structure of capitalism.

People under capitalism are alienated both from other people and from the product of their labour. True relationships cannot develop between people because the nature of relationships is determined by the role of each person in the capitalist system of production. Wage and salary earners are alienated from the owners of resources because those who earn a living must not only rely on the 'boss' for employment but must curry favour with whoever controls the nature and context of their working life. Wage and salary earners are alienated from each other because they see each other as competition for jobs. Today most job competition is regional competition for investment, but this competition is divisive and bitter. Men and women are alienated from each other when their lives are dominated by the need for jobs – jobs which put them on different schedules, require them to work in different locations, and separate and alienate both from their children, who grow up in day care or are at home alone.

On the job, people are alienated from their own labour because they have little control over their work and work environment, and because they have no control over the goods and services they produce. The goods produced under capitalism are not the property of those who make them; they are the property of the owner of the resources, who sells them for profit. This allows the owner to accumulate capital, acquire more resources and hire more workers; thus the process of alienation continues and grows.

In actual capitalist systems, the feeling of estrangement that results from alienation on the job is particularly strong recently. There is perhaps no better expression of this than the shock of recognition so many corporate employees feel when reading *The Dilbert Principle*. People feel they are being treated as a means to an end which is foreign to them, and they themselves treat their jobs only as a means to getting money, not self-fulfilment. If it is true that people find self-determined, creative, and cooperative labour to be inherently desirable and meaningful, then the estrangement felt under capitalism is a serious moral objection.

It can be objected to this that there is nothing morally wrong with people choosing to do something distasteful, such as working at a meaningless job, as a means to more worthwhile ends.[24] This is true, but it misses the point that in contemporary capitalism this is a choice that very few people have. Many people have difficulty in finding jobs at all, and the opportunity for meaningful employment is very rare. Even professionals, who have the best opportunities for finding satisfaction and meaning in their jobs, often discover that the priority of profit (or cost cutting) can prevent them from performing their jobs in the way they choose. Furthermore, as Kymlicka points out, 'Under capitalism ... those with the best jobs also have the best consumption and leisure, while those with poor jobs get no compensating increase in leisure or consumption.'[25] This is hardly compatible with claims that people choose meaningless work as a means to achieve more consumption and leisure. Under capitalism, alienation is not chosen as a means to valuable ends; for most people there is no alternative to meaningless work.

Democracy and Capitalism

The freedom of choice provided by a free market might seem to be a natural match for the political freedom of democratic governments. But even in theory the question is more complicated. In their chapters, David Copp and Dan Usher argue opposite sides of this question, although their positions do not actually contradict each other. Usher argues that the free market is useful in supporting democracy, the rule of law, and good government. Copp argues that the unequal distribution of wealth under capitalism can be a threat to democracy if money can have a serious influence on votes.

In actual capitalisms there has been a long historical coincidence between societies that are democratic and societies that have free markets.[26] But there have been exceptions, such as the flourishing of German industry in the 1930s, and there may currently be an increasing number of exceptions among the tigers of Asia; Singapore, Hong Kong, Korea, and Taiwan have no or only limited democracy. China is currently developing capitalist markets in certain regions but shows no signs of moving towards democracy. And there are those who claim that the unequal distribution of wealth is corrupting democracy in the United States.[27] It has also been pointed out that global markets are developing outside all political control,[28] in which case the question of capitalism's compatibility with democracy may become irrelevant. Watching developments in capitalism's impact on governments is going to be fascinating.

Contradictions within Capitalism

The idea that there are contradictions within capitalism that may cause its demise derives from Hegel's and Marx's belief that history develops dialectically. For Hegel and Marx, all stages of history (at least so far) develop or contain contradictions, the resolution of which moves history on to its next stage. Is contemporary capitalism any different? Let us consider two moral contradictions that have been suggested for contemporary actual capitalism: the values of consumerism and capital accumulation, and the ethics of self-interest and trust.

Daniel Bell, in his book *The Cultural Contradictions of Capitalism*, argues that there are many deep contradictions between the values and lifestyles implied by capitalist modes of production, and the values and lifestyles of capitalist consumer culture.[29] In modern capitalist economies, most production is controlled by large hierarchial bureaucratic corporations in which workers, including managers, are assigned predetermined roles where they do what 'the boss' decides. They are expected to be disciplined, hard-working, restrained, and career oriented, and they must accept money rather than job satisfaction as their reward. When they leave their jobs at the end of a long day, however, these same people live in a consumer culture which uses advertising, magazines, television, and other means to preach self-exploration, self-definition, self-gratification, self-realization, and self-fulfilment. The lifestyle of consumption is centred on libidinal, impulsive, glamorous, gluttonous, and immediate hedonism. The contradictions between work and consumption extend to the underlying principles; work is organized on the principle of functional rationality dominated by calculation and economizing. Off the job, we live in a culture of emotional expressiveness dominated by image and debt-financed impulse.

In this situation ethical? Is it ethical, for example, to deluge young people with ads telling them to be any person they want, or even just 'to be,' and then expect these same young people to take jobs in fast food chains where their every step (literally and figuratively) is measured and determined, and where they must smile on cue and dress in identical uniforms? The complete suppression of individuality by the mode of production may by itself raise ethical issues; the intense confusion it can cause in a consumer culture is surely undesirable.

Free markets assume that all individuals pursue their own rational self-interest in economic transactions.[30] It is also true that all transactions within a free market depend on trust. Buyers and sellers have to trust that the goods and money (cheques, credit cards, and even cash) they exchange are what they seem, and we all prefer to do business with people and companies that we trust to fix problems if there are any. Of course, there are mechanisms of accountability such as guarantees, contracts, and ultimately lawyers and courts which assume that trust is not always justified, but these support trust, they do not replace it. They are also expensive, significantly increasing transaction costs. In the case of lawsuits, use of the mechanism generally prevents further normal business transactions between the parties. Business cannot be conducted through lawyers; they only provide the contracts that support trust, and they sort out the mess when trust collapses. In all cases, the need for lawyers increases transaction costs.

When all parties are motivated by self-interest and yet need to trust each other, pursuing self-interest by violating trust is a persistent destabilizing temptation. In theory, self-interest and trust may not conflict if the relationship between the parties is ongoing and both take a long-term view of self-interest. But in practice the multitude of steps businesses and consumers take to increase trust indicates that the temptation of short-term self-interest cannot always be resisted.

Since trust increases efficiency and decreases transaction costs, the general level of trust in a capitalist system can be viewed as an important asset of society – it is part of the 'social capital' that capitalism requires.[31] If the emphasis on self-interest that capitalism requires tends to undermine trust, then there is a contradiction in capitalism which would tend over time to erode social capital.

In capitalism, possibly the most important exchange which requires trust is the exchange of labour for wages or salaries. Employers cannot supervise every action of their employees, nor are employees paid on the completion of each task. Furthermore, employees have access to company resources and secrets, and frequently make commitments on their employer's behalf. Trust is essential, which means that the employee must suspend the direct pursuit of her own interests and pursue those of her employer while on the job. Yet capitalism, and most economists, assume that people pursue only their own interests. This discrepancy is known as the 'agency problem.' Fukuyama argues that it is precisely lack of trust in employees that prevents low-trust societies from forming the large business enterprises of advanced capitalism.

Is there an erosion of trust taking place in contemporary capitalist systems? Fukuyama's claim that there are high-trust and low-trust societies does not show that trust tends to decline – in fact, the high-trust societies he identifies (United States, Germany, and Japan) all tend to have been capitalist longer than the low-trust societies he identifies such as China. However, many people in North America suspect that trust is currently eroding, especially trust in the relationship between employers and employees.

Ethics and the Structure of Capitalism

Theoretical and actual capitalism can both be structured in different ways; there is no single form that capitalism must take.[32] Cultural differences can profoundly affect the kinds of behaviour people display within capitalism, which leads to differences between national capitalist systems. The structure of a capitalist system is also profoundly affected by the laws which govern its basic institutions; especially important are the laws which govern property rights, corporations, and the limits of the free market. Since these laws are passed by governments, they can be thought of as external factors which structure any capitalism from outside the system.

Cultural Structure of Capitalism

As Fukuyama's recent book makes clear, trust is one of the key cultural factors which determine the nature of a capitalist system. Trust of strangers, he argues, allows the creation of large corporations; cultures without such trust tend towards capitalist systems made up of smaller family-based businesses. Closely related to the issue of trust are systems of obligation. In most European and North American countries, economic obligations are largely created by consensual contracts, such as the contracts between employer and employee, or buyer and seller. For the most part, these obligations are written or well understood, and largely fulfilled. We have all experienced some failures to fulfil such obligations, serious or trivial, but the problems such failures create show how much our economic system depends on the normal observances of these obligations. As people doing business in the new global marketplace are finding out, obligations can work differently in other cultures. In some cultures, obligations can only exist within ongoing personal relationships which must be built slowly between specific individuals. These relationships often involve reciprocal gift-giving, a practice which some Western corporate employees feel creates conflicts of interest with their own obligations.[33] Many cultures recognize significant obligations that override the sorts of contractual and employment obligations Europeans and North Americans are used to.

Other cultural factors with significant impact on the nature of capitalism include attitudes and laws concerning the role of women, class or caste systems, and the treatment of immigrants. Basic economic factors such as the savings rate and attitudes towards risk can also vary greatly between cultures and have significant economic impact.

Variations in Property Rights

One of the most significant legal impacts on the structure of a capitalist system is the definition of property rights. Owning property confers not a single or absolute right, but a bundle of rights which can vary significantly. The rights to control, use, profit from, and exchange property are basic to free market systems, but there can be considerable variation within them. Consider, for example, land, which is often thought of as the most basic type of property. Zoning and planning laws, environmental regulations, historical preservation orders, agricultural policies, fire regulations, and a multitude of other laws define what rights an owner of land has. These vary greatly in different legal jurisdictions, as do laws concerning mineral rights, hunting rights, water rights, rights of way, and so on.

More abstract forms of property also show great variations. Consider differences in patents, copyrights, trademarks, and even the 'ownership' of images, genes, information, and ideas. In contemporary capitalist systems, these abstract forms of property are often far more important than land.

One of the most significant rights that laws may or may not allow property owners is the right to bequeath and inherit property. Inheritance taxes, especially when they are near 100 per cent, are a way of denying that inheritance is a property right. Rules on inheritance greatly affect the distribution and concentration of wealth, and this can be significant for the moral assessment of capitalism. Haslett, for example, in his book *Capitalism with Morality*, argues for capitalism without inheritance.

Corporations and the Structure of Capitalism

Most capitalisms allow the owners of resources to form corporations; in advanced capitalist countries, and in the new global economy, corporations are the most important institutions. They dominate many sectors of the economy and often rival governments in wealth and power. Corporations exist because governments pass laws that allow corporations to own property and engage in market transactions as though they were individuals, laws that limit the liability of the corporation's owners and regulate the creation and selling of shares, and laws that establish and enforce forms of corporate governance. Governments also establish and regulate stock markets and provide the legal framework necessary to limit the fraudulent and criminal abuse of corporate wealth. Without the creation of this legal framework, corporations could neither exist nor get investors to buy their stocks and bonds.

Are corporations an essential part of capitalism? The theoretical models of free markets often do not include them, or they label them simply as 'producers' of goods and services. Other models deal with monopolistic competition and oligopolies, which often occur when a few powerful corporations dominate an industry. There are also theoretical explanations that show corporations exist in free markets because they can reduce transaction costs, gain economies of scale, diversify risk, and/or externalize production costs. But these do not answer the question of whether governments are morally justified in passing the laws required for corporations to exist.

One way of thinking about this is to ask what a modern capitalist system would look like without corporations. Most likely, production would be in the hands of family and private businesses. These could be quite large, but family businesses tend to be more limited in size than corporations, and much more limited in how long they exist; family businesses seldom last more than a generation or two after the death of the founder.

The distribution of wealth and resources would be radically different without corporations. Since the unequal distribution of wealth under capitalism is a major moral concern, the existence of corporations substantially affects the moral assessment of capitalism. Whether there would be as much wealth and production without corporations, and what other effects might follow, is difficult to determine.

This uncertainty makes moral assessment of capitalism difficult. We have several existing examples that allow us to assess the effects of corporate capitalism, though these effects may be dramatically changing even as we make our assessment. We could separately assess whether corporations ought to be allowed, but such moral assessment is limited by lack of information on how an advanced non-corporate capitalism would function. To abolish corporations and see what happens seems like a leap in the dark.

Limits of the Market

The question of which human activities ought to fall outside free markets, and which inside, is complicated by the vast variety of activities people take part in, only some of which can be considered economic. Further, the reasons for limiting free markets are often not based on ethical concerns; there are often practical reasons for certain activities not being part of the market, and in some cases tradition or cultural habit may determine non-market arrangements. However, sometimes specifically moral reasons have been advanced for limiting or not limiting the scope of market activities.[34]

Government and private activities are best considered separately when discussing which kinds of activity ought to fall outside the market. Governments have long supplied both public and private goods and services; they have also carried on some activities, such as elections and parliaments, not designed to supply goods directly to people. In his chapter, David Copp considers why voting should be outside the market. Most people think politics should not be a market activity and most people, including most economists, reject the idea of sellable votes. Are there any general moral criteria for deciding which activities governments ought to perform?

In supplying private goods, governments have become heavily involved in many industries – air travel, railways, telecommunications, mines, mail delivery, and innumerable other things. Recently, governments have tended to get out of these various businesses, selling them to the private sector. The justification offered for most of this denationalization has been based on the non-moral grounds of efficiency;[35] private industry can usually supply these goods more effectively than governments. In many cases, technical changes have made competitive markets possible for industries once dominated by government-controlled monopolies. But there have also been moral reasons given for denationalizing industries. Since governments often claim monopolies for their corporations, such as the historical monopoly of most postal services, it is sometimes claimed that denationalization increases competition and hence people's freedom of choice, or at least consumer freedom. On the other hand, historically when governments were nationalizing, both moral reasons and reasons of efficiency were offered in justification. In some industries, such as mining in Great Britain, the worker safety record of private owners was thought to be unethically low, and in some industries, such as health care, making profits out of human suffering was thought to be immoral.[36] Overall, many people think these moral considerations both for and against nationalization seem minor compared with the huge efficiency issues involved in the nationalization–denationalization debate. Given the magnitude of the extra efficiency that is claimed for private competitive industry, perhaps society would be better off making other arrangements to deal with moral concerns about the effects of private ownership. Worker safety can be dealt with through liability laws, insurance, regulations, and unions. And profiting from suffering can be justified on utilitarian grounds if efficiency makes everyone, even the sufferer, better off. For industries that supply private goods, therefore, efficiency arguments often seen to overwhelm moral concerns.

The moral issues involved in government provision of public goods seem much more significant than with private goods, though there is still the non-moral question of whether the government is the most efficient supplier of any particular public good. Public goods are of two types. First, any good which does not diminish with use is a public good. For example, my enjoyment of the quiet and safety of my neighbourhood does not diminish the quiet and safety that my neighbours enjoy. It is problematic to expect free markets to provide such goods because, as Cobb and Daly point out, 'Whenever use by one person is at no cost to others, the marginal opportunity cost is zero and therefore the price should be zero ... There is no market incentive for any firm to supply costly goods for a zero price, and so they can never be supplied by the market alone.'[37]

The second type of public goods include those that, when not consumed, can cause harm to the non-consumer's neighbours. For example, an individual's failure to use proper sewage disposal methods can put not only that individual but whole communities at risk of cholera, diphtheria, and other epidemic diseases. Sewage disposal and the supply of clean water are among the most important public goods in urban areas, and they have for thousands of years been thought to be government responsibilities. Other possible candidates for public goods include national defence, crime prevention, the education and socialization of the next generation, environmental protection, cultural activities, public roads, and public parks.[38]

Efficiency arguments concerning government supply of public goods often concern the extent of government involvement. In some cases, the government can mandate a public good but leave the rest to the free market; requiring smoke detectors in hotel rooms might be an example. Enforcement might be by either inspection or liability. In other cases, the government might cover the cost of a public good through taxes or compulsory service charges, but contract out the supply. The integrity of infrastructures such as sewerage systems, water supply, and roads, for example, are most efficiently supplied in this way. Finally, the government can itself be the primary supplier, paying costs from taxes. National defence and policing are generally in this category. The issue with defence and policing is not so much efficiency, but the government monopoly on violence and military power.

The debate over government supply of public goods often centres not on efficiency but on some key ethical views. One side of the debate is often represented in business ethics textbooks by John Kenneth Galbraith who argued that the 'dependence effect' and advertising led capitalist societies to spend too little on public goods and too much on private goods.[39] Galbraith is here advancing a utilitarian moral argument that capitalism tends not to produce the greatest possible good. In his reply to Galbraith, Hayek argues that Galbraith's arguments in favour of government spending are a form of socialism, whose 'aim is ... progressively to increase the share of resources whose use is determined by political authority and the coercion of any dissenting minority.'[40] This is clearly an ethical argument based on the view that any taxation is a violation of people's rights to their income and property, and that government supply of public or any other goods necessarily involves coercion and the violation of rights. A free market based on consensual exchanges would not violate such rights.

Hayek's view that all democratic decisions about the public supply of public goods are unethical is perhaps a bit extreme (or meant rhetorically), but it demonstrates how arguments based on freedom and rights tend to oppose Galbraith's utilitarian position.

Clearly, the debate over whether public goods should be supplied outside the market has moral arguments on both sides. Those in favour of the government supplying public goods rest their case on utilitarian grounds. Those against deny that public goods are morally relevant goods, or they claim priority for individual rights and freedoms. Others argue that responsibility for at least some public goods does not rest on the government. These moral debates take place against a background of major disputes about economic efficiency.

Besides government activities, much of our private lives and welfare fall outside the market.[41] There is no moral significance to many of the cultural variations in which private activities fall inside and which outside the market; for example, business people in Canada usually eat lunch in a restaurant which makes food preparation a market activity, but business people in India often eat food prepared at home and so food preparation is outside the market. There is no inherent moral significance to this, but there are subsidiary moral issues such as whether work done outside the market is evenly divided between men and women. And there are questions about the effect on policy making of excluding from economic measurements all labour which happens to be outside the market. This is an issue discussed by Julie Nelson in her chapter.[42]

Many other human activities that are of great moral value also lie outside the market; examples include love, friendship, families, parenting, religion, artistic creativity, knowledge, and most self-fulfilment. These activities are outside the market because they do not involve conscious and consensual bargaining by self-interested maximizers. It has been argued that people in some of these activities behave *as though* they were acting in a market; for example, Gary Becker in *A Treatise on the Family* has supplied 'economic' explanations for behaviour within families. Such explanations have been criticized,[43] but however successful they are as explanations, this does not mean we should actually bargain in love, parenting, and so on.

The material goods supplied by free markets seem morally insignificant compared with these non-market goods, even though material goods are necessary for all human activity. Perhaps then the market is only a means to pursue morally good ends, most of which are outside the market. This would not be problematic if the market did not greatly impact these morally valuable ends, but does capitalism leave people with the time and energy for more morally worthwhile activities? Does the market tempt people into mere materialism? Does image advertising corrupt people's identities, preventing sincere relationships and self-fulfilment?[44] Does the competition of free markets prevent the formation of friendships and communities? In other words, should the free market be limited to a role as the material means to morally valuable ends, and if so, how should it be limited? Many moral critiques of the market are concerned with this issue.

Government Regulation of Capitalism

Types of Regulation

For many years there have been heated debates about the extent to which governments ought to regulate free markets. The proponents of deregulation see themselves as championing a great cause against the forces of interfering governments, incompetent politicians, bungling bureaucrats, and socialism. Those who favour regulation see themselves as protecting helpless victims from a harsh and amoral economic system. Ethical issues are often raised in this debate: regulations are said to violate people's freedom and their property rights; they are also said to protect innocent people from great harms.

One of the problems with this debate is that the issue is presented simply as *how much* regulation governments should impose rather than *what kind* of regulation. Government regulations are of various kinds; regulations can have the intent and effect of either supporting, structuring, limiting, or controlling free markets. Supporting regulations protect private property, enforce contracts, and prohibit non-consensual exchanges such as violence and fraud. Structuring regulations define private property rights, permit the formation of corporations, and supply services to the market such as creating the central bank and monetary system. Limiting regulations try to remove certain transactions or sectors from the market; examples include medicare, public education, rent controls, public housing, construction of highways, and so on (see the section entitled 'Limits of the Market'). Controlling regulations try to control the outcome of free markets; examples include corporate subsidies and development grants, duties and tariffs, taxes on specific goods and services, and direct regulation of certain industries such as airlines, telecommunications, or taxis. It is regulation in this final sense, of trying to control the outcome of the free market, that is considered in this section. Are there moral arguments for or against such government control?[45]

Moral Arguments in Favour of Regulation

The most powerful moral argument in favour of at least some government control of markets is that free markets offer no guarantee that everyone will be able to meet basic human needs for food, medical care, and shelter. Many people have nothing to contribute to the market (see the section on unequal distribution), but even those who can contribute labour have no guarantee that the value of their labour will be sufficient to feed and house themselves and their families.[46] In fact, in periods of high unemployment, their labour may have no exchange value at all. As we already established, the distribution of goods in a free market is entirely dependent on initial endowments, and this distribution may leave some people, even willing and able-bodied people, starving. Many view the failure of markets to meet some or many people's basic needs as morally objectionable.

A second reason governments ought to control some of the results of free markets is the problem of externalities and other market failures. In producing and exchanging goods in a free market, people not party to the exchange are often affected. Sometimes such effects can be to the outside party's benefit (a positive externality), but sometimes the effects can also harm them (a negative externality). Common examples of negative externalities include pollution, noise, nuisances, and unsightliness. Faced with negative externalities, governments have several options. They can pass laws which force the payment of compensations to outside parties who are negatively affected; this will internalize the cost of the harm to the process that causes it. However, in some cases, identifying the costs and the harmed parties is difficult; acid rain, for example, can affect people thousands of miles away and in other countries. Furthermore, internalization of costs is often resisted; David Korten argues that one of the primary functions of corporations is to externalize costs, especially risk.[47] A second option of governments is to physically separate businesses from people they might annoy or harm; this is the primary purpose behind zoning laws that, for example, prevent building factories and large stores in the middle of residential areas. A third option is for governments to simply ban the process that causes the harm. The bans on the use of DDT and other dangerous chemicals prevent harmful externalities.

The two key moral arguments in favour of government regulation to prevent negative externalities are, first, that it is unfair that innocent third parties should suffer annoyance or harm, and second, that externalities often interfere with an owner's free and quiet use of her property, and hence that they are an infringement of private property rights. There is also a theoretical argument which claims that externalities cause the misallocation of resources and hence prevent the invisible hand of the market from achieving the common good.

Governments often try to control specific products using such techniques as special taxes (in the case of alcohol and tobacco), banning or limiting sale and possession (e.g., guns and narcotics), banning or limiting advertising (e.g., alcohol and tobacco), registration (guns, cars), or by taking direct control of the distribution of the product (alcohol, gambling). The moral argument in favour of such controls is that they help prevent people from harming themselves, their families, or other people. The products subject to these special controls tend to be either addictive, very dangerous, or both.

In general, the ethical case for government control is based on the belief that governments have a moral responsibility to prevent significant harm to any of the people they govern. People can be harmed by free markets when they cannot earn the basic necessities of life, when they are affected by negative externalities, when they or those around them buy and use dangerous products, and when they do not have access to public goods. Part of the moral responsibility of democratic governments is to regulate capitalism so that these harms do not occur.

Moral Arguments against Regulation

One of the most important arguments against government regulation of markets is not directly a moral argument, but it tends to undermine some of the moral arguments in favour of regulation. This argument claims that governments should not try to control capitalism because

they cannot do so. More specifically, the claim is that the result of government controls on free markets is seldom the result that the government intended. For example, the intention of prohibiting the
production and sale of narcotics in the Unites States was to reduce
usage and addiction; the result has been increased usage, the targeting
of children and others by pushers, and the domination of the 'industry'
by fabulously wealthy and extremely vicious drug barons. There are
many other examples of attempts to control capitalism that have backfired; sometimes governments have had to remove the controls, as did
the Canadian government when smuggling forced it to reduce tobacco
taxes. Or, most famously, when the United States had to abandon the
prohibition of alcohol in 1933.

There seems to be a political 'mood' in the United States at the
moment which is sceptical of *all* attempts by government to 'interfere'
with capitalism in any way.[48] However, it should be pointed out that
examples of effective government controls can be cited, such as many
municipal sewage and water systems, some public education systems,
perhaps medicare in Canada, and some, but not all, attempts at pollution control. These government endeavours have reduced epidemics,
created general literacy, reduced infant mortality, increased life expect-
ancies, and reduced some forms of pollution. For example, the killer
smogs that London, England, used to experience until the 1960s have
ended because of government regulation. Perhaps in none of these cases
government control of or alternatives to capitalism is perfect, but it can
be argued that they have achieved many of the results that were
intended; they certainly have not backfired in the disastrous way nar-
cotic controls in the United States have. These examples do not by themselves show that governments ought to act – that was defended in the
previous section – but only that governments can act. The mood of anti-
government scepticism should not blind us to looking at actual results;
maybe we should conclude that governments ought to act with great
care when trying to control capitalism, not that they cannot act at all.

There are also direct moral arguments against government controls
on capitalism, most of which appeal either to the moral value of freedom or to property rights. Since free markets, by definition, consist of
property rights and consensual exchanges, any government control of
any part of the market must violate property rights and/or the freedom of people to enter into consensual exchanges. This, however, is
not necessarily morally objectionable unless the moral values of
economic freedom and property rights outweigh the moral value of

preventing harm, promoting the public good, and making the economy fairer. Those who believe that freedom and property rights are moral absolutes take precisely that view.

The most common argument for the moral priority of property rights and economic freedom is based on the distinction between positive and negative rights, and on the parallel distinction between positive and negative freedom.[49] A negative right, sometimes also known as a liberty right,[50] is a right not to be interfered with; it implies an obligation on all other people not to stop the right-holder from being, doing, or owning what she has a right to. A positive right is a right to be, do, or have something. Positive rights, have sometimes been called welfare rights, because the most common positive right advocated is the right to the basic necessities required for human welfare.[51] Those who claim priority for negative rights argue that recognizing positive rights, necessarily violates freedom and property rights, because if a person has a right to basic welfare, then other people must have an obligation to give (whether they want to or not) necessities to that person. The right to have even basic necessities requires that things be taken from their 'rightful' owners and given to the destitute. There is a further problem with positive rights in that it is not clear *who* has the obligation to fulfil them. This is not an issue with negative rights since *everyone* has an obligation not to interfere with a legitimate right-holder. For these reasons, some people conclude that negative rights take absolute moral priority, which effectively denies that there are any genuine positive rights. If negative rights are absolute, then any government interference with consensual exchanges and property rights – and hence any government attempt to control free markets – is morally objectionable. This is the line of reasoning that led Nozick to propose the concept of the ultra-minimal state.[52]

The debate over the ethics of government and control of capitalism thus resolves into a more fundamental debate about the priority of moral values. On the one side are the values of fairness, preventing harm, and caring for those in need; on the other side are the values of freedom and property rights. Solving this dilemma is beyond the scope of this survey.

Ethical Behaviour within Capitalism

The issues of ethics and individual human behaviour, and ethics and organizational policies, are directly relevant to the moral assessment of capitalism for two reasons. First, any economic system which discourages or does not permit morally responsible behaviour on the part of its participants is morally suspect as a socioeconomic system. It is essential to know whether or not capitalism has this fault. Second, a general level of moral behaviour within capitalism can lead to a very different type of capitalism than that which results from a high level of untrustworthy, criminal, or corrupt behaviour. A moral assessment of capitalism depends on which type of capitalism is being assessed.

Ethics and Corporate Behaviour

There are three basic theories of ethical corporate behaviour in the current literature on business ethics. The normative version of each of these theories provides a framework for choosing and morally assessing corporate actions and policies. The three theories are based on stockholder interests, stakeholder analysis, and the idea of a social contract.

The interests of stockholders have most famously been defended by Milton Friedman when he argued that corporate executives have a direct responsibility to their company's stockholders 'to conduct the business in accordance with their desires, which generally will be to make as much money as possible while conforming to the basic rules of the society, both those embodied in law and those embodied in ethical custom.'[53] Friedman bases the moral aspects of this claim on three different moral values: rights (especially property rights), freedom, and the utilitarian value of the greatest good. He argues that corporations are the private property of the stockholders, and that corporate executives are the agents of those owners. If executives use corporate resources in any way other than pursuing the interests of the owners, they are violating the right of shareholders to the use of their own property. Second, Friedman argues that any use of corporate resources for social purposes (instead of profit making) is a form of socialism and thus is 'undermining the basis of a free society.'[54] Finally, Friedman uses a version of the invisible hand argument when he argues that corporations should pursue only profits because the free market is the best way to 'determine the allocation of scarce resources to alternative uses.'[55]

Stakeholder theory, in its normative form, asserts that corporate actions and policies ought to balance the interests of all groups who have a stake in the firm because they are affected by it. Stakeholders would include stockholders, but the concept of a stakeholder would also include customers, suppliers, employees, communities, and possibly other groups. Edward Freeman in the classic statement of stakeholder theory, *Strategic Management: A Stakeholder Approach*, argued for stakeholder theory on prudential, not moral grounds. Freeman believed that it was in the long-run interests of the corporation to take into account the concerns of all groups affected by the firm; failure to do so could lead a stakeholder group to actions, such as refusing to do business with the firm, that would have a negative impact. Later advocates of stakeholder theory have advanced moral reasons in its favour. For example, R.A. Phillips argues that fairness requires a stakeholder approach.[56]

The third framework for ethically choosing and assessing corporate actions and policies is social contract theory. This is based on the idea that societies allow corporations to conduct business and to own resources as one half of an understood contract between society and business; the other half of the contract is that corporations are expected to act within the bounds of acceptable business norms for that society. Acceptable norms usually cover such issues as employment conditions, use of resources, competitive practices, paying taxes, and donating to charities. Social contract theory usually requires corporations to respect business norms on these issues in each country in which they have operations. However, there are exceptions; international corporations do not operate in just one host country, they operate internationally in the global economy. There are recognized international social norms, which Donaldson calls hyper-norms, such as the United Nations codes on Human Rights.[57] In the case of conflicts, Donaldson argues that corporate actions should conform to hyper-norms rather than local norms.

Social contract theory has had to contend with the existence of both actual business norms in actual societies and the philosophical tradition of hypothetical norms, a tradition which bases the social contract on what would be agreed to given human nature and a theoretical choice situation. These two perspectives on norms have been integrated in Donaldson's and Dunfee's Integrative Social Contract Theory (ISCT).[58] Donaldson and Dunfee propose that actual business norms, including ethical norms, should be respected, but only if they are authentic and legitimate. Norms are authentic if the people they concern could, if they desired, exercise the options of voice or exit. Norms are legitimate if they do not violate hyper-norms, which resemble closely traditional human rights. Donaldson and Dunfee argue that accepting a wide variety of actual business norms, providing they are authentic and legitimate, is consistent with a hypothetical contract between business and society – it is what we would agree to if we were rational and given a choice.

Current theory in business ethics, therefore, provides corporations with three different frameworks for making ethical business decisions: profit maximization, stakeholder analysis, and social contract theory. Whether these approaches are compatible or contradictory remains an open question.[59] This is unfortunate given the huge number of ethical issues that corporations face.

Ethics and Individual Behaviour within Capitalism

Ethics is concerned with individual behaviour as well as social structures, so besides assessing capitalism and the institutions within capitalism, we should also ask how individuals who find themselves living within actual capitalist systems ought to behave.

All moral systems recognize that people have a variety of moral obligations and a need to keep these in perspective; people living within a capitalist economy need to recognize that many of the most morally important spheres of our lives are spent outside of economic activities. Economic activities need to be balanced with our moral obligations to care for our children and other dependents, to participate in democratic political processes, and to lead rich, self-fulfilling lives. One of the most basic moral obligations for those within capitalism, therefore, is to keep economic activities in perspective; in other words, to resist the complete domination of our lives by jobs, careers, acquisitions, and the pursuit of consumer satisfaction.

Of course, this is not to deny that many of the goods and services we need to fulfil our non-economic obligations are only available to us by participating in capitalist markets; capitalism can be viewed as a means, and arguably the best means when functioning properly, of fulfilling some of our non-market moral obligations. Viewing the economy only as a means for achieving non-economic ends is to keep our moral perspective.[60] Free markets can be the arena for satisfying desires, and there is no reason why moral desires should not be satisfied there. A profit-oriented supermarket can be an excellent place to get the means to feed one's children. Yet the market does not satisfy all varieties of desires, only those for material goods and services. Just as it can be shown that my own welfare cannot be defined in terms of satisfaction of desires or utility,[61] there is no reason to think that a person's moral obligations can be defined in terms of economic utility. In fact, the obligations of love, friendship, community, and self-realization are inherently not reducible to economic activities. Given that capitalist markets are a means of fulfilling some but not all of our moral obligations, what are our moral obligations when acting economically within free markets?

If free markets are morally justified, it would seem to follow that we have a moral obligation to accept those rules and procedures required for free markets to function in the morally justified fashion. This leads to a 'market morality' incumbent on all defenders of capitalism's morality. The most basic principles of such a market morality would be (a) to respect private property, (b) to exchange goods and services only by consensual contract, (c) to respect and fulfil all consensual contracts, and (d) to maintain competitive markets. Rule (a) includes a prohibition against theft; rule (b) would prohibit violence, fraud, cheating, deception, and many other dishonest 'business' practices. Rule (c) is a requirement to be trustworthy and to endeavour to be effective in fulfilling contracts. Rule (d) would prohibit monopolies, unfair competitive practices, and lobbying governments for special advantages. It is obvious from these rules that anyone who believes in capitalism on moral grounds is undertaking quite substantial moral obligations as a participant in the market. In short, pursuing an honest profit and an honest wage is morally acceptable, but the requirement of 'honest' in this context is adherence to the extensive requirements of market morality.

For an application of market morality to a contentious issue, consider bribery, an issue extensively discussed by A.W. Cragg in his chapter. In the central case of business bribery,[62] money is paid to the bribee with the intention of encouraging the bribee to violate a contract which the bribee has already undertaken, often with his employer. Since free markets require that consensual contracts be fulfilled, the fact that this form of bribery undermines the contract between the bribee and the bribee's employer makes both offering and accepting the bribe a violation of the moral presuppositions of capitalism.

So far this section has argued that the role of free markets in our lives has limits, and that the moral defence of capitalism requires moral respect for private property and consensual exchange. This creates the potential for conflicts between market morality and the moral values we are committed to in the non-market areas of our lives. This potential for conflict is greatly limited by the fact that a contract to do something immoral is never morally binding; market morality cannot, for example, morally require a Mafia hit man to fulfil his contract to kill someone. However, consider the moral conflict faced by an employee trying to decide whether to blow the whistle on an employer violating environmental laws. Her moral obligation to fulfil the agreed requirements of her job could conflict with her obligations to prevent harm to her community.[63] There is no abstract answer to such conflicts; the moral defence of capitalism may inherently generate moral conflicts between market morality and the moral obligations that arise in our families, communities, and life.

Finally, defenders of capitalism may also be under a moral obligation to help establish free markets where they do not already exist, and to help structure and support markets where they do. But it has been argued that market participants are not good at creating and maintaining free markets; that job should perhaps be left to governments.[64]

The Impact of Capitalism

Capitalism's Impact on Non-market Societies

Capitalism is taking over the world. Or so it seems at the moment, although history should make us exceedingly sceptical of any attempt to predict even the near future. The past is clear on the issue: in the past two hundred years and more, actual capitalism has expanded throughout much of the globe. In doing so, it has encountered and influenced numerous other cultures and economic systems. The reactions of these other cultures to capitalism have been various. Some, such as Japan, developed capitalist economies themselves; others, such as India, were conquered and their economy forced into a colonial role within capitalism. Russia, after developing the beginnings of a capitalist economy in the nineteenth century, sought an economic alternative to capitalism, and the attempt was ultimately not a success.

The effects of capitalism on other cultures are continuing today; especially affected are surviving indigenous cultures. What choices do such cultures have? And what choices do people within those cultures have? This issue is addressed by David Newhouse, an Onondaga member of the Six Nations, in his chapter entitled 'Resistance Is Futile: Aboriginal Peoples Meet the Borg of Capitalism.' He argues that absorption by capitalism is inevitable, although he recognizes that this is not a universally held opinion.

Capitalism's Impact on the Environment

There is a huge literature on ethics and the environment,[65] some of which relates to capitalism in various ways. Capitalism is sometimes blamed for causing most or all environmental destruction, but it is sometimes proposed as the solution to environmental problems, and many positions in between have been advanced. Perhaps the best way to see some structure in these debates is to begin with a theoretical model of capitalism and the environment, and then to try to classify the kinds of moral critiques of the model about which various debates cluster.

A model of the capitalist view of the environment might look like this:[66] natural resources are either owned as private property, or they are part of the commons which all people can use. If resources are part of the commons, every individual will tend to maximize her use of the resources because it is in her interest to do so. No one will practise restraint because the result of individual restraint will not be the preservation of the resources, but only that someone else will get them. The result is 'the tragedy of the commons,' the depletion of resources as everyone scrambles to get as much as she can. The solution is to privatize the resources so that their use is determined by an owner who, because of the exchange value of the resources, has an interest in their preservation. Thus private property and free markets are the keys to the preservation of the environment.

There are many moral objections to this model of how capitalism relates to the environment, and it is possible to see much environmentalism, insofar as it relates to capitalism, as informed by such objections.

One objection is that the propensity of property owners to preserve the environment applies only to those aspects of the environment, called resources, which have market value. This not only defines the value of the environment in human terms, but in that subset of human terms which are exchangeable in the free market. Furthermore, the market value of the environment may only exist in the destruction of that environment; minerals and trees often do not have market value except if they can be mined or cut down. There is considerable discussion about values in the literature on ethics and the environment, much of which maintains that capitalism cannot preserve the natural environment because the values of the free market are not the values of the environment.

A second kind of criticism of the capitalist approach to the environment is that it is impractical. These criticisms point out that assigning property rights to some portions of the environment is often difficult or impossible. How could we establish 'ownership' of the oceans, the ozone layer, rain, and the atmosphere? In lieu of ownership of a resource, economists sometimes propose ownership of the right to use the resource, but this leaves preservation responsibility in the hands of the issuer of the rights, not in the hands of the property (that is, rights) owners who now have no interest in preservation. And who is to issue the rights? The environment is a global concern, so if national governments issue rights, a scramble between nations will repeat the tragedy of the commons.

This problem of practicality applies even to such basic forms of property as land. An owner may have market incentives to preserve her own land, but the environment knows no boundaries; birds migrate, animals wander, winds blow, and water runs down to the sea. No one owns enough land to preserve species, the atmosphere, or a watershed.

A third sort of criticism of the capitalist approach to the environment is that the time-scales are wrong. Business people have short-term horizons, often thinking only about this quarter's results. Long-term strategic planning is for five years, or perhaps ten in some industries. Nature knows not this haste. To take a single example, replacing an old growth, rain-forest tree could take up to three thousand years. Businesses cannot think in these time-scales because the procedures used for estimating market value produce absurd results. This is especially true for discounting cash flows, the basis for time value under capitalism.[67] Nature and markets function on radically different time-scales.

A further problem with the capitalist approach to the environment is that it is based on a false dichotomy – either private property or the tragedy of the commons. This framing of the issue prevents examination of alternative solutions to the tragedy. That there are other alternatives can be seen from the historical fact that some societies have managed to survive for many centuries without private ownership of resources, even land. This is not to deny that the tragedy of the commons has never happened; it happened dramatically on Easter Island, and human activity has often led to deforestation, desertification, and other disasters.[68] But some societies without private property have avoided it, perhaps through systems of group ownership,[69] or through socially enforced environmental responsibilities, such as the care ethics among the Native Peoples of Eastern North America prior to contact.[70] Whether alternatives to private property are practical needs discussion; the possibility should not be dismissed by theoretical fiat.

Finally, in actual capitalist systems resources are perhaps not even preserved according to their market value but are exploited based on the non-market power of corporations, such as their power in negotiations with governments and their power to oppose environmental groups. Actual treatment of the environment under existing capitalist systems is an empirical question. In general, there have been both successes and failures at environmental protection. Actual capitalisms may be better at environmental protection than other economic systems such as planned economies, but it is not clear whether this is the result of either free markets or private property, and it is not clear if this is only temporary. In the present collection, Lionel Rubinoff investigates with care specific instances of how capitalist corporations actually do approach environmental issues.

Thus it can be seen that capitalism's approach to the environment has many problems. It brings the wrong values to environmentalism, it is impractical, the time-scale of business is wrong, and it fails to consider other alternatives.

Conclusion

With the death of one of its terms, the debate between capitalism and socialism is over. It is time to start a much more interesting discussion: What form of capitalism is morally legitimate? This new question can be broken down into several subsidiary questions. Important concerns still remain about the overall moral justification of capitalism, and there are divergent views about how to approach such a justification. There are also some very important moral criticisms of capitalism, the most pressing of which is surely the continued presence of destitute people (including innocent destitute people such as children) in even the richest of capitalist societies.

Perhaps the most fundamental issues about capitalism are questions about the moral legitimacy of private property and free markets which are the basis of capitalism. What rights should be included in the rights of ownership? Are those rights overriding natural rights or are they morally justified on utilitarian grounds? This is a question that Dan Usher addresses in his chapter.

The moral legitimacy of capitalism is dependent on whether it can be limited in ways which allow non-economic values to flourish. Is capitalism compatible with the moral value we place on family, community, truth, beauty, democracy, and civic and personal virtue? This topic in its entirety is huge. David Copp discusses the compatibility of capitalism and democracy.

Any morally legitimate capitalism will be a regulated capitalism. At a minimum, private property and free markets require government support to exist. Unregulated markets can suffer from market failures which have morally devastating results. But markets require more than regulatory support from governments; they also require morally responsible and trustworthy behaviour by the people and institutions working within capitalism. Without a widespread acceptance of 'market morality,' capitalism can quickly descend into piracy and organized crime. One morally significant aspect of this problem in the global capitalism currently developing is the issue of corruption. Wes Cragg considers the nature and prevalence of business corruption, and to what extent the solution lies in external regulation or in an improvement in the behaviour of business practitioners.

Part of the difficulty in discussing the limits and regulation of capitalism is the suspicion that our understanding of capitalism may itself be biased. There is the huge question of whether the available economic models apply to the various actual existing economies usually thought of as capitalistic, but there is also the issue of whether the models themselves are biased and therefore misleading. Julie Nelson argues that they are.

We are discovering that capitalism as it actually exists has huge impacts beyond just free markets and the economy. Morally, the most significant of these impacts is on the natural environment of our entire planet, and on societies which have been and might (or might not) prefer to remain outside of capitalism. There is no question that the destruction of the world's natural environments is of immense moral concern to ourselves and to future generations. But it is not obvious whether this destruction is inherently part of capitalism, or whether capitalism structured in some new way might not be more protective of nature. Lionel Rubinoff argues that a lot of the problem is with corporations and their place within larger social and political structures.

Non-capitalist societies view capitalism with both fear and desire. They face the bittersweet choice of whether or not to adopt the ways of capitalism and accept the changes this will force on their traditional social structure and on their very view of the world. Or do they have this choice? Perhaps capitalism's adsorption of other socioeconomic systems is inevitable. David Newhouse argues that resistance to capitalism is futile.

These issues make one wonder what form of capitalism or mitigated capitalism would be morally legitimate. This question is addressed directly by Leo Groarke.

Notes

1 The works referred to in this paragraph are as follows: Adam Smith's main work on capitalism is *An Inquiry into the Nature and Cases of the Wealth of Nations* of 1776; his key work on ethics is *The Theory of Moral Sentiments* (1759). Karl Marx's ethical criticisms of capitalism are outlined most clearly in his pre-1848 writings available in *The Revolutions of 1848: Political Writings*, vol. 1, (London: Penguin, 1973). Weber discusses the moral prerequisites of capitalism in *The Protestant Ethic and the Spirit of Capitalism* (London: Allen and Unwin, 1930). Tawney's criticisms are in *The Acquisitive Society* (New York: Harcourt Brace, 1929), Galbraith's in *The Affluent Society* (London: Hamish Hamilton, 1958). Mandeville's provoking defence of consumer luxuries is *The Fable of the Bees: or Private Vices, Publick Benefits*, originally published in 1714. McLuhan examined consumer culture in *The Mechanical Bride: Folklore of Industrial Man* (New York: Vanguard, 1951). Of Sen's many works on ethics, seminal is *On Ethics and Economics* (Oxford: Basil Blackwell, 1987). For a guide to current thought, see D.M. Hausman and M.S. McPherson, *Economic Analysis and Moral Philosophy* (Cambridge: Cambridge University Press, 1996).

2 This has in fact been defended by subscribers to Hegelian ideas on property; see Jeremy Waldron, *The Right to Private Property* (Oxford: Clarendon Press, 1988), esp. chap. 10.

3 Huron trading practices at the time of contact with Europeans is described by Bruce G. Trigger in *The Huron: Farmers of the North* (Fort Worth: Holt, Rinehart and Winston, 2nd ed. 1990), 42–8.

4 In his book *Sour Grapes: Studies in the Subversion of Rationality* (Cambridge: Cambridge University Press, 1983), Jon Elster argues against standard theories of how individuals tend to make rational choices based on their preferences. Hausman and McPherson, *Economic Analysis*, discuss thoroughly the relationship between ethics and the economic concepts of choice, preference, utility, and economic rationality.

5 See R. Boadway and N. Bruce, *Welfare Economics* (Oxford: Basil Blackwell, 1984), esp. the introduction.

6 Good introductions are Hausman and McPherson, *Economic Analysis*; Sen, *On Ethics*. For a highly technical study of economic theory and theories of justice, see J.E. Roemer, *Theories of Distributed Justice* (Cambridge, MA: Harvard University Press, 1996). For a theory of value in economics, see E. Anderson, *Value in Ethics and Economics* (Cambridge, MA: Harvard University Press, 1993).

7 See Jan Narveson, *The Libertarian Idea* (Philadelphia: Temple University Press, 1988); also Robert Nozick, *Anarchy, State, and Utopia* (New York: Basic Books, 1974).

8 For example, see N. Lawson, 'Some Reflections on Morality and Capitalism,' in S. Brittan and A. Hamlin, *Market Capitalism and Moral Values* (Aldershot: Edward Elgar, 1995). To compare two analyses of the nature of existing capitalisms, see R.L. Heilbroner, *The Nature and Logic of Capitalism* (New York: W.W. Norton, 1985), and P. Berger, *The Capitalist Revolution: Fifty Propositions about Prosperity, Equality, and Liberty* (New York: Basic Books, 1986).

9 For a survey of currently existing capitalist systems, see L. Silk and M. Silk, *Making Capitalism Work* (New York: New York University Press, 1996).

10 Onora O'Neill discusses the distinction between idealization and abstraction and its application to economic concepts in *Towards Justice and Virtue: A Constructive Account of Practical Reasoning* (Cambridge: Cambridge University Press, 1996), esp. 100–13.

11 For a thorough survey of possible moral justifications of free markets, see A. Buchanan. *Ethics, Efficiency and the Market* (Totowa, NJ: Rowan and Allanhead, 1985).

12 For a good comparison of actual capitalist and socialist societies using several criteria, see P. Rutland, 'Capitalism and Socialism: How Can They Be Compared' in *Capitalism*, ed. by E.F. Paul, F.D. Miller, J. Paul, and J. Ahrens (Oxford: Basil Blackwell, 1989).

13 The full passage is:

> As every individual, therefore, endeavours as much as he can both to
> ·employ his capital in the support of domestic industry, and so to direct
> that industry that its produce may be of the greatest value, every indi-
> vidual necessarily labours to render the annual revenue of the society
> as great as he can. He generally, indeed, neither intends to promote the
> public interest, nor knows how much he is promoting it. By preferring
> the support of domestic to that of foreign industry, he intends only his
> own security; and by directing that industry in such a manner as its
> produce may be the greatest value, he intends only his own gain, and

> he is in this, as in many other cases, led by an invisible hand to pro-
> mote an end which was no part of his intention. (IV.ii.9)

For an extensive discussion of Smith's version of the invisible hand argument, see J.D. Bishop, 'Adam Smith's Invisible Hand Argument,' *Journal of
Business Ethics*, 14 (1995), 165–80.

14 For a discussion of capital mobility and comparative advantage, and other
reasons a global economy may not advance the common good, see D.C.
Korten, *When Corporations Rule the World* (West Hartford, CN: Kumarian
and Berrett-Koehler, 1995), esp. 78–80.

15 For arguments that the invisible hand does not work in the kind of global
economy we now have, see G. Teeple, *Globalization and the Decline of Social
Reform* (Toronto: Garamond, 1995); and Korten, *When Corporations Rule*.

16 A distribution of utility is Pareto optimal if no one in a society can be made
better off without someone else being made worse off. Pareto optimality is
consistent with unequal distribution of wealth, including destitution in rich
societies, if making the poor better off in any way reduces the utility of the
rich. For a fuller explanation of Pareto optimality and its connection (if any)
to ethics, see Sen, *On Ethics*, esp. chap. 2.

17 For example, Francis Hutcheson; see J.D. Bishop, 'Moral Motivation and
the Development of Francis Hutcheson's Philosophy,' *Journal of the History
of Ideas*, 57 (1997), 277–95.

18 The connection between welfare and preferences has been widely discussed; see, e.g., Amartya, Sen, 'The Moral Standing of the Market,' in E.F.
Paul, J. Paul, and F.D. Miller, *Ethics and Economics* (Oxford: Basil Blackwell,
1985) 1–19; L.W. Sumner, *Welfare, Happiness and Ethics* (Oxford: Clarendon,
1996), esp. 149–50; and Hausman and McPherson, *Economic Analysis*. Elster,
in *Sour Grapes*, addresses the issue of when it might be rational not to have
a preference rather than seek its satisfaction.

19 This is the second law of welfare economics. See Boadway and Bruce, *Welfare Economics*.

20 The issue of Pareto optimality and initial distribution is discussed in books
on welfare economics, such as Boadway and Bruce, ibid. It is discussed in
the context of ethics by Sen in *On Ethics*, 31–8, and Hausman and McPherson in *Economic Analysis*, chap. 7.

21 See W. Kymlicka, *Contemporary Political Philosophy: An Introduction* (Oxford:
Clarendon, 1990) and R. Dworkin, 'What is Equality? Part I: Equality of Welfare,' *Philosophy and Public Affairs*, 10 (1981), 185–246, and 'What is Equality?
Part II: Equality of Resources,' *Philosophy and Public Affairs*, 10 (1981), 283–
345, for guidance on whether there are moral grounds for doing this.

22 See the section entitled 'Variations in Property Rights' on which property rights are justified; also D.W. Haslett, *Capitalism with Morality* (Oxford: Clarendon, 1994), who justifies capitalism without inheritance.

23 Sen, 'The Moral Standing of the Market,' 5–6. See also Amartya Sen, *Poverty and Famines: An Essay on Entitlements and Deprivation* (Oxford: Basil Blackwell, 1981).

24 See Kymlicka, *Contemporary Political Philosophy*, 186–92.

25 Ibid., 192; 186–92 provide a good brief overview of the moral arguments about alienation.

26 See Daniel Bell, *The Cultural Contradictions of Capitalism* (New York: Basic Books, Twentieth Anniversary Edition, 1996), 14.

27 R. Dworkin, 'The Curse of American Politics,' *The New York Review of Books* (17 October 1996), 19–27.

28 See Korten, *When Corporations Rule*.

29 Bell, in *The Cultural Contradictions of Capitalism* also argues that both of these contradict the values of democracy, a topic considered by David Copp in his chapter in the present volume.

30 By self-interest is meant here the rational pursuit of the individual's utility through maximizing the satisfaction of her desires or preferences. Self-interest does not imply selfishness since one person's preferences may include the promotion of other people's utility, esp. the utility of one's own family members and friends.

31 On the idea that trust is a form of social capital, Francis Fukuyama, *Trust* (New York: Macmillan, 1995).

32 In his chapter, Copp points out that no actual capitalisms are 'pure.' But the point made in this section is that even without impurities, capitalism itself can be structured in different ways. In his concluding chapter, Leo Groarke argues that only a mitigated capitalism can be ethically legitimate.

33 See J. Fadiman, 'A Traveler's Guide to Gifts and Bribes,' *Harvard Business Review,* July–Aug. (1986), 122–36. For a discussion of obligations, ethics, and corruption, see A.W. Cragg's chapter herein.

34 For a sustained and thorough discussion of the limits of markets, both moral limits and otherwise, see R. Kuttner, *Everything for Sale: The Virtues and Limits of the Market* (New York: Knopf, 1997).

35 Although in itself efficiency is not a moral issue, it sometimes can be connected to ethics by utilitarian arguments. In this section, the distinction between efficiency and direct moral arguments is maintained.

36 French socialists are more extreme when they 'refuse to further privatize public services because they claim that education, health care, postal service and telecommunications, and public safety must not be turned into

"objects of profit."' S. Hoffman, 'Look Back in Anger,' *New York Review of Books*, 17 July (1997), 49.

37 Herman E. Daly and John B. Cobb, *For the Common Good: Redirecting the Economy Toward Community, the Environment, and a Sustainable Future* (Boston: Beacon Press, 1989), 51.

38 This list is not intended to be complete, but is meant to show the variety of things which have been proposed as public goods. Apparently, giraffes are also a public good; see Matt Ridley, *The Origins of Virtue: Human Instincts and the Evolution of Cooperation* (New York: Viking, 1997), 110–14.

39 Extracts are usually from John Kenneth Galbraith, *The Affluent Society* (London: Hamish Hamilton, 1958). For example, see W.M. Hoffman and R.E. Frederick, eds., *Business Ethics: Readings and Cases in Corporate Morality* (New York: McGraw-Hill, 3rd ed., 1995).

40 F.A. von Hayek, 'The *Non Sequitur* of the "Dependence Effect,"' reprinted in Hoffman and Frederick, *Business Ethics*, 412.

41 See L.W. Sumner, *Welfare, Happiness and Ethics* (Oxford: Clarendon, 1996), esp. 118–19, for a philosophical analysis of why welfare includes non-marketable goods not included in the economists' definition of utility.

42 See also Cobb and Daly, *For the Common Good*.

43 For example, see Julie A. Nelson, *Feminism, Objectivity and Economics* (London: Routledge, 1996).

44 For sustained arguments that advertising has negative effects on people's self-image, see C. Moog, *Are They Selling Her Lips? Advertising and Identity* (New York: William Morrow, 1990), and N. Wolf, *The Beauty Myth* (Toronto: Random House, 1990).

45 In his chapter, herein Copp draws a slightly different distinction between internal and external regulations.

46 This is theoretically true both at equilibrium and on the way to equilibrium.

47 Korten, *When Corporations Rule the World*, esp. 76–7.

48 See R.C. Leone's Foreword to Kuttner, *Everything for Sale*, and L. Menand, 'Inside the Billway,' *New York Review of Books* 14 August (1997), 4–7.

49 This distinction was originally made by Isaiah Berlin in 'Two Concepts of Liberty' published in *Four Essays on Liberty* (Oxford: Oxford University Press, 1969).

50 See O'Neill, *Towards Justice and Virtue*, esp. 129–35.

51 For discussions of positive rights and welfare, see Partha Dasgupta, *An Inquiry into Well-Being and Destitution* (Oxford: Clarendon, 1993), 40–6; also O'Neill, 130–6.

52 Nozick, *Anarchy, State and Utopia*, 26–8.
53 Milton Friedman, 'The Social Responsibility of Business Is to Increase Its Profits,' republished in Hoffman and Frederick, *Business Ethics* 138.
54 Ibid., 137.
55 Ibid., 139. N. Barry in 'What Moral Constraints for Business?' published in S. Brittan and A. Hamlin, *Market Capitalism and Moral Values* (Aldershot: Edward Elgar, 1995) discusses this invisible hand argument of Friedman's, 59. See T. Mulligan, 'A Critique of Milton Friedman's Essay "The Social Responsibility of Business Is to Increase Its Profits,"' *Journal of Business Ethics*, 5 (1986), 265–9, for a critique of Friedman's argument.
56 R.A. Phillips, 'Stakeholder Theory and a Principle of Fairness,' *Business Ethics Quarterly*, 7 (1997), 51–66. See also the October 1994 issue of *Business Ethics Quarterly*, which is dedicated to stakeholder theory with eight articles on the subject.
57 See T. Donaldson, *Corporations and Morality* (Englewood Cliffs, NJ: Prentice-Hall, 1982); and T. Donaldson, *The Ethics of International Business* (Oxford: Oxford University Press, 1989).
58 See T. Donaldson and T.W. Dunfee, 'Toward a Unified Conception of Business Ethics: Integrated Social Contracts Theory,' *Academy of Management Review*, 19 (1994), 252–84; and T. Donaldson and T.W. Dunfee, 'Integrative Social Contracts Theory: A Communitarian Conception of Economic Ethics,' *Economics and Philosophy*, 11 (1995), 85–112.
59 For a clear guide to current thinking on normative theories of business ethics, see J. Hasnas, 'The Normative Theories of Business Ethics: A Guide for the Perplexed,' *Business Ethics Quarterly*, 8 (1998).
60 This is argued by Bell, *The Cultural Contradictions*, xii.
61 I.M.D. Little, *A Critique of Welfare Economics* (Oxford: Oxford University Press, 1950); Sen, 'The Moral Standing of the Market'; Sumner, *Welfare, Happiness and Ethics*; section entitled 'Limits of the Market.
62 There are other forms of bribery in which the bribe is paid to encourage the bribee to violate other types of obligations, such as obligations to family, country, or a sport.
63 On the issues involved in whistleblowing, see the articles in Hoffman and Frederick, *Business Ethics*, chap. 7; and the different articles in R. Larmer, ed., *Ethnics in the Workplace* (Minneapolis: West, 1996), chap. 7.
64 This is argued by Jane Jacobs in *Systems of Survival: A Dialogue on the Moral Foundations of Commerce and Politics* (New York: Random House, 1992).
65 For comments on approaches to environmental ethics and a substantial

bibliography, see Alex Wellington, Allan Greenbaum, and Wes Cragg, *Canadian Issues in Environmental Ethics* (Peterborough, ON: Broadview Press, 1997).

66 Ridley, *The Origins of Virtue*, defends a version of this model, although he acknowledges group ownership as well as individual private property. For further comments on alternative property systems and care for the environment, esp. with respect to the Iroquoian peoples, see John Douglas Bishop, 'Locke's Theory of Original Appropriation and the Right of Settlement in Iroquois Territory,' *Canadian Journal of Philosophy*, 27 (1997), 311–37.

67 If an old growth tree is worth $500,000 in today's dollars, and takes 2000 years to grow, then (ignoring inflation and allowing a real discount rate of 5%) a newly planted tree is worth $0.00 according to a Texas Instruments BA.35 financial calculator. Reforestation would not be undertaken on such a basis.

That old growth trees can be one or more thousand years old is startling, but is not unusual for some species. Douglas firs, which are still often cut for lumber, can be over 1000 years old; see R.C. Hosie, *Native Trees of Canada* (Don Mills, Ont.: Fitzhenry and Whiteside, 1979), 82. For coastal redwoods, 'the maximum age count in annual rings is 2200'; in the case of giant sequoias, 'felled trees show annual rings indicating up to 3200 years of age'; and 'the oldest known dated living trees are Bristlecone Pines more than 4600 years old'; see E.L. Little, *The Audubon Society Field Guide to North American Trees: Western Region* (New York: Knopf, 1980), 270, 301, and 300.

68 See Clive Ponting, *A Green History of the World: The Environment and the Collapse of Great Civilizations* (New York: Penguin, 1993).

69 This is argued with respect to Iroquoian peoples in Bishop, 'Locke's Theory,' 311–37.

70 The extent to which Native peoples practised care of hunting grounds by restraint is greatly debated; see C. Notzke, *Aboriginal Peoples and Natural Resources in Canada* (Toronto: Captus, 1994), 145–9, for recent comments on and references to this debate.

2

The Justification of Private Property

DAN USHER

If property goes, everything goes.

The justification of private property is that we need it. Virtually every-thing we value in society – prosperity, progress, democracy, freedom to conduct our lives as we please, and even such equality as is attainable in this imperfect world – is dependent on the private ownership of the means of production. Life without private property would be dreadful. There is no serious notion of the common good such that the common good is not better served by an economy with private property than by an economy where the means of production are owned collectively through the intermediary of the state.

This, to say the least, uncompromising statement will have to be modified here and there, but I argue in this essay that it is substantially correct.[1]

By private property, I mean that a large share of the land, buildings, machinery, and other instruments of production in the economy is owned privately rather than collectively. The term is meant to encom-pass, but is not restricted to, contemporary capitalism where much of the world's work gets done by large widely held corporations and where property rights are protected by law. Not all property need be private for the virtues of private property to be realized. Indeed, there has never been and cannot be a society where all property is private. Roads are not private. The police station is not private. The courts are not private. The legislature is not private. Even property we call pri-vate, including ownership of our own labour, can be looked upon as partly public in that the revenue from such property is shared by the general public through the intermediary of taxation. I am not defending libertarianism.

That much private ownership is necessary for the preservation of what most of us see as a good society, does not imply that more private ownership is necessarily better. The virtues of private property emerge when 'enough' of the means of production are private, although the exact boundary between enough and not enough is hard to draw. I am being deliberately vague about the boundary to defend the proposition that a core of private ownership is a requirement for a good society. Nor do I argue here that property is a sufficient condition for what we see as a good society. The argument is that property is necessary rather than sufficient. A society with private property may turn out to be dreadful for a variety of reasons, but no society without private property can be anything but dreadful. Some essentially capitalist societies, such as Nazi Germany, have turned out very badly indeed, but all communist societies have turned out badly, notwithstanding a considerable idealism on the part of the their founders. It is my purpose here to explain why that is so.

A justification of private property must come to terms with three valid opposing arguments. The first is that property is theft. Ownership is the loot of a thief made secure by a conspiracy of thieves; that may not be the whole truth of the matter, but neither is it entirely wrong. North America was stolen by the Europeans from the Native people. Land occupied by tribes of Native people at the time of the European Conquest had been stolen by their ancestors from other tribes whose members rarely survived to claim their historic rights. The respectable landed fortunes of England originate in the banditry of William the Conqueror. Trace back the origins of almost any large fortune today, and you will find evidence of plunder or chicanery. The history of the founding of the Canadian Pacific Railway is perhaps not atypical of the dubious reciprocity between business and politics in Canada.

The second argument is that the aesthetics of capitalism can be, to put it mildly, unfortunate. The pollution of television by advertising may be a price worth paying for the diversity of programs that the medium provides, but the price is undeniably high. A significant portion of our lives is wasted passively accepting advertising messages. The electronic spectacle of obsequious bankers and their grateful clients, of grinning men and women talking up the virtues of products most us could very well do without, of children acquiring poor eating habits and of governments encouraging citizens to gamble, is surely a blight upon the land. Capitalism's defenders must remind themselves day after day that television can be regulated in the public interest, that the messages neutralize one another to some extent, and that television in the hands of a government with a monopoly of the means of production has to be very much more pernicious. Nor can one take much comfort in the reports in the financial section of one's daily newspaper of the comings and goings of the industrial plutocrats whose buying, selling, and bankrupting of corporations to augment their own wealth is not always in the public interest. Again one must remind oneself that a radically different industrial governance could be very much worse. Prudent legislation may improve this or that, but we may have to choose in the end between Disney and the Great Leap Forward.

The third, and most important, argument is that every society where the means of production are privately owned is characterized by an unequal distribution of income and property. Some people are born poor and others born rich. To be sure, capitalism has no monopoly on inequality, and it is certainly arguable that inequality under capitalism has on the whole been less extensive and less oppressive than under most other forms of industrial organization. But inequality is intrinsic to capitalism. Full and permanent equality of property and income would destroy the incentives to work and save on which a capitalist society depends. Inequality extends beyond the distribution of goods, for unequal ownership breeds unequal political power. The rich enjoy a disproportionate access to politicians and a disproportionate influence on political decision making that compounds their initial economic advantages. Although societies without private property have turned out badly in the past, there persists an ideal of equality which might conceivably be attained in some new form of economic organization in which the means of production are collectively owned.

These arguments against the institution of private property have some validity and a strong emotional appeal. The case for private property holds regardless. It holds despite the disreputable origin of the allocation of property to people, despite the dubious aesthetics of much of contemporary capitalism, and despite a distribution of income that is wider than most of us would like. It holds because property is an indispensable ingredient of the best approximation to what most of us see as a good society that is attainable in this imperfect world. Specifically, the argument in this chapter is that property is a requirement for prosperity, a source of civic virtue and an indispensable component of what, for the want of a better term, I call the liberal society. By a liberal society, I mean a society with four indispensable and interconnected institutions – property, voting, administration, and law – which together make possible a degree of individual freedom, some control by the citizen over the choice and the conduct of leaders, and protection from the worst excesses of predatory government. Property does not stand alone, but neither can the other institutions of the liberal society be maintained without it. The chapter ends with a dismissal of several other arguments for private property – among them the origin of property rights in labour, first possession, the social contract, and natural law – as either subordinate to the argument from need or simply mistaken.

Justification requires a criterion. The criterion for the justification of private property in this essay is broadly consequentialist and utilitarian. Private property is justified as promoting the common good, where the common good can be identified for our purposes by the 'veil of ignorance' test: Consider a public choice between alternative laws or ways of organizing the economy. The veil of ignorance test picks one of these alternatives as the more conducive to the common good if that is what *you* would choose, in your own interest, behind a veil of ignorance where you know a great deal about how society works and about the consequences for society of each alternative, but you know nothing about your place in society except that you have an equal chance of occupying the circumstances of each and every person when the veil is finally lifted. Your choice between alternatives in these circumstances is then said to reflect your sense of the common good.[2] The test is open to a number of objections, among them that people with different preferences may choose differently behind the veil of ignorance and that the test tends to confuse altruism with risk aversion. Regardless, the test is satisfactory for our purposes because it abstracts from the obvious conflict of interest between the rich and the poor, and because the justification of private property is sufficiently robust to bear a certain vagueness in the criterion.

As employed in this chapter, the utilitarian criterion evaluates alternative economic arrangements according to what people see, all things considered, as the good life. Utilitarianism is sometimes interpreted as identifying one's duties to society. Here it is just a criterion for public policy.[3] Utilitarianism is sometimes interpreted as an injunction to maximize the sum of the utilities of each person in society, where each person's utility is a concave function of his income. Here this interpretation of utilitarianism, although not wrong, is unnecessary because the justification of private property is valid for a wide range of specifications of the common good. Here, as elsewhere, utilitarianism is above all the refusal to invoke a God-given right to property or to anything else.

By itself, a criterion justifies nothing. To play its role in the justification of private property, our utilitarian criterion must be juxtaposed with technical or social constraints to public policy. Private property may well be inappropriate for a society of angels. The argument here is that the common good is better served by an economy with private property than by an economy without private property in a complex society of fallible people where good will is scarce and each person looks to his own, narrowly-defined self-interest most of the time. The emphasis in the argument is not on the objective, but on the constraints. The first principle of social science is that society is ornery and recalcitrant. We can design institutions as we please, but we cannot always make the institutions work as we would like. I can afford to be cavalier about the criterion because it is not decisive. The argument to be developed here is that there is in practice no tolerable substitute for private property. No other form of economic organization is so conducive to virtually anybody's understanding of the common good. Private property is warranted, almost regardless of how the good society is envisioned, because the alternatives to private property are so obviously undesirable.

Two Virtues of Private Property

Private property – the private ownership of a substantial portion of the means of production and the protection by the state of at least part of the return to property for its owners – can contribute to the well-being of the great majority of people in several ways, some unique to a democratic society, others independent of the form of government.

Protection of property rights is beneficial to all societies – democratic or otherwise – as a means to prosperity. Capitalist societies tend to be prosperous. Other societies are not. This is not to deny that extensive provision of social services – the old age pension, unemployment insurance, socialized medicine, and so on – is consistent with considerable prosperity in a society where the means of production are for the most part privately owned. What is not consistent with prosperity is the complete, or nearly complete, ownership of the means of production by the state. That, if nothing else, has been demonstrated by the sad fate of communism. Except at moments when order was established out of chaos and anarchy, there has, in the entire history of the world, been no instance of a country where income per head has grown significantly over many years without private ownership of the means of production, including, of course, one's own skill and labour power.

It is hardly surprising that this should be so. If there is any lesson to be learned from the discipline of economics, it is that, with certain qualifications, markets direct the usage of a multiplicity of resources to maximize the national income. Common greed is harnessed to the common good. Resources are directed where their product is greatest. Lure of profit draws forth innovation. The price mechanism coordinates widely dispersed and minutely specialized knowledge of markets and technology in a deployment of the world's resources that looks from a distance as though it has been planned by one all-knowing mind, but was not and could not be planned by any normally fallible human being or planning commission.[4] Government must enter the economy to protect property rights, supply public goods, correct for a million externalities in private markets (especially in the usage of the world's common heritage of land, forests, air, water, and biological diversity), break up extreme concentrations of economic power, provide basic research, and moderate the gross inequalities of income that luck, cunning, corruption, skill, and inventiveness tend to generate from time to time. Especially in a democratic society, people must not be allowed to starve and children must not be too poverty-stricken or too badly educated, regardless of how stupid, improvident, or unlucky their parents may be. But the fact remains that an economy with property rights is the foundation of prosperity and the only assurance that resources will be used well to maximize current income and to promote economic growth.

A second, although much more contentious and ambiguous, virtue of private property is its effect on the character and personality of the citizen. That one's character is moulded by the environment of the economy – by one's work and by one's relations of subordination, command, or equality at work – is an idea imbedded in our very language. Free men become liberal; bosses become bossy; slaves become servile. Aristotle justified private ownership as the source of the virtue of generosity. Marx reviled private ownership as the source of alienation of the worker, and he drew a distinction between structure and superstructure, between an amalgam of technology, economic organization, and social class, on the one hand, and the resulting self-images and false-consciousness that a class system necessarily entails.

One can, of course, accept the general proposition that work moulds thought, without at the same time supposing that there is any privileged vantage point from which one can see the truth or that the character of the citizen would be in any way improved in the society that Marx and his followers envisioned. Whether life as an anonymous cog in a machine would be less dehumanizing if the machine were owned by the people through the intermediary of the government than if the machine were owned by top-hatted, cigar-smoking capitalists, and whether the class system would be any less humiliating to the underclass if the entire means of production were linked to the means of violence and to a monopoly of information in the hands of the state, is, to say the least, doubtful.[5]

Thomas Jefferson[6] saw a society of small farmers as the social foundation of democracy, and he advocated measures to reduce disparities of income and wealth: 'legislators cannot invent too many devices for subdividing property ... The descent of property ... to all children ... is a politic measure and a practicable one. Another means of silently lessening the inequality of property is to exempt all from taxation below a certain point, and to tax the higher portions of property in geometrical progression ... it is not too soon to provide by every possible means that as few as possible shall be without a little portion of land.'

Disturbed as he was by the considerable inequality of wealth and status in nineteenth-century England, John Stuart Mill[7] could not bring himself to advocate a socialist society because of its deadening effect upon the character of the citizen:

> Even if the government could comprehend within itself, in each department, all the most eminent intellectual capacity and active talent of the nation, it would not be less desirable that the conduct of a large portion of the affairs of society should be left in the hands of persons immediately interested in them. The business of life is an essential part of the practical education of the people ... There cannot be a combination of circumstances more dangerous to human welfare, than that in which intelligence and talent are maintained at a high standard within a governing corporation, but are starved and discouraged outside the pale. Such a system, more completely than any other, embodies the idea of despotism, by arm-

ing with intellectual superiority as an additional weapon, those who already have the legal power ... The only security against political slavery, is the check maintained over the governors, by the diffusion of intelligence, activity and public spirit among the governed.

A democratic constitution, not supported by democratic institutions in detail, but confined to the central government, not only is not political freedom, but often creates a spirit precisely the reverse, carrying down to the lowest grade in society the desire and ambition of political domination. In some countries, the desire of the people is for not being tyrannized over, in others it is merely for an equal chance of tyrannizing ... In proportion as the people are accustomed to manage their affairs by their own active intervention, instead of leaving them to the government, their desires will turn to repelling tyranny rather than to tyrannizing; while in proportion as all real initiative direction resides in the government ... popular institutions develop in them not the desire of freedom, but an unmeasured appetite for place and power; diverting the intelligence and activity of the country from its principal business, to a wretched competition for the selfish prizes and the petty vanities of office.

Broadly speaking, those who see a line from the organization of the economy to the character of the citizen are inclined to believe that the discipline of the market is a better education for democracy than the discipline of the hierarchy, and that independence and self-reliance in the economy inculcate the civic virtues that a democratic society requires. Whether this is really so is hard to prove, although I, like most people today, am inclined to believe it is. This line of argument speaks against national planning, but it also speaks to a lesser extent against the concentration of industry in a few large firms, however much they may compete against one another. It speaks for the small farmer, the small businessman, and the small trader. It speaks for the experience of entrepreneurship on a small scale as the 'educative ladder' for commerce and for democracy. It also speaks for the freedom of the market, for the option, when one dislikes one's firm or one's immediate boss or one's customers, of bypassing particular people and trading in a wider economy at whatever prices one's skills or resources can command. Thus the protection of property rights is not just the protection of the incomes of property-holders. Coupled with policies to restrict the concentration of ownership, it is the protection of a certain type of person who, so it is believed, is uniquely fitted for participation in a democratic society.

The Liberal Society

The usefulness of private property extends beyond these virtues. Over and above the connections among private property, the prosperity of the economy and the character of the citizen is a technical link to the maintenance and stability of what most of us see as a good society. We want to conduct our lives as we see fit, to choose our occupations and our friends, to go where we please, to express our views even when others disagree, to be protected by the law from arbitrary arrest or imprisonment, to exert some influence on the composition and conduct of government, to live without fear of visitation by the secret police, and with reasonable assurance that millions of us will not die in poverty or in concentration camps at the whim of the great leader or as a by-product of competition among would-be rulers. We may not care about private property for its own sake, but private property is frequently, and in my opinion correctly, alleged to be indispensable if we are to live as free people in a free society.

In developing this argument, it is helpful to think of a 'liberal society' as four pillars: private property, voting, administration, and law. Together, these four interconnected institutions enable us to live our lives as nearly as possible, in this imperfect world, as we would wish. Together, they are our defence against anarchy on the one hand and despotism on the other. All four pillars are essential; remove one and the edifice is sooner or later destroyed.

What needs to be emphasized in this context is that the institution of private property is not self-contained, as an incautious study of microeconomics might lead one to suppose. The usual story in the chapter on general equilibrium begins with a given allocation among people of the different factors of production and proceeds to the identification of the nice properties of the competitive economy. What needs to be emphasized here is that the supposedly given allocation of property among people can only be sustained by institutions that are, strictly speaking, external to the market. Private property needs the protection of the state not just from the thief, but from its own inherent limitations. The state must prescribe the boundaries of property rights. It must specify what I may or may not do with my property, resolve disputes among property-holders, and establish a schedule of punishments for crimes. The terms and conditions for the establishment of corporations, the rights and obligations of shareholders, the governance of the stock market, the assignment of wave lengths for radio and television, the regulation of pollutants, and the apportionment among fishermen of the allowable catch to ensure the preservation of the stock of fish are among the many and diverse matters that must, one way or another, be resolved politically if the rights of property are to be well defined. Legislature, administration, and courts are all essential as technical and social infrastructure without which property rights are meaningless. Nor can we be sure that the inequalities of wealth and income in an unconstrained system of private property – in a society where the state protects property rights but lets the distribution of income develop as it may with no attempt to assist the poor or to redistribute property or income at all – will not grow to the point where private ownership of property becomes unacceptable to the great majority of citizens. Some degree of publicly sponsored redistribution is in the interest of the typical citizen and may be required to preserve support in the general population for the private ownership of the means of production. But relations among property, voting, administration, and the law are, as we shall see, reciprocal.

Quite apart from its links to the prosperity of the economy and the character of the citizen, private property is a technical requirement for government by majority-rule voting. Voting is society's only alternative to autocracy, but public decision making by voting is a fragile instrument that requires the support of private ownership of property, of an administrative structure, and of an independent judiciary. A standard objection to democracy (by which I mean no more than government by majority-rule voting) has for centuries been raised by democracy's enemies and has been recognized as correct, although not, of course, dispositive, by democracy's friends. Quite simply, the anti-democratic argument is that, by its very nature, voting is unstable and destined to self-destruct. Inevitably, some majority of voters – usually but not necessarily a majority of the poor – will employ the power of the vote to dispossess the minority mercilessly and completely. Drawn by the powers conferred upon the majority in a democratic society, factions coalesce around any nucleus – income, race, language, location, religion, or social class – to direct the lion's share of the national income to their members. Understanding the danger, the party in office and its supporters are irresistibly tempted to dispense with the elections whenever there is a risk of loss of office at the ballot box. Monarchy, dictatorship of the proletariat, religious oligarchy, or some other form of autocratic government would be established to preserve the authority and the economic privileges of the higher ranks of the people or to defend one's class, ethnic group, or religion from the exploitation by others.

The force of the anti-democratic argument – as a demonstration of the impossibility of democracy or as a sign of danger that can and must be averted – depends critically on technical, economic, and social conditions. In a community where all of the means of production are owned and administered by the state, the legislature *must* take upon itself the ultimate responsibility of allocating the entire national income among citizens, for there is no other institution to do so. The whole national income would be up for grabs in the deliberation of the legislature. Each man's prosperity and status would rest entirely on the outcome of the vote. The privileges of majority status and the perquisites of office would be too great to risk at the ballot box, especially as the party now in office would have little ground for trust in the willingness of its successor to step down in its turn. The temptation to rig or abolish elections would indeed be irresistible.

Who is to be the president of the corporation? Who is to be the janitor? Who is to be unemployed when workers are in surplus? Are doctors to be paid more than lawyers, and, if so, by how much? Which towns are to expand and which to contract? Without private property, all of these questions would have to be answered by the legislature, directly or through the intermediary of the civil service. Private property supplies answers and, in doing so, provides the legislature with the option of silence. This is not to deny or to belittle the influence of government on the economy through tariffs, the progressivity of taxation, the old age pension, and in a thousand other ways. It is, rather, to assert that there is a limit to public influence beyond which the powers of office become too large to risk at the ballot box. In a community where the means of production are privately owned and prices are set in the open market, the legislature acquires the option of not concerning itself with the allocation of the national income, or it may be content to influence allocation at the fringes, leaving the core of the market allocation untouched.

With an historically given apportionment of property among people, the market automatically generates prices that direct resources to their most productive uses and allocate the national income among people in accordance with the earnings of the resources they own. As long as property rights are secure, the assignment of goods to people is arranged without the intervention of the government to determine who gets what. It is this allocative role of property that upholds government by voting, and that compels democratic governments to protect property rights to some extent if democracy is to be maintained at all. The legislature respects existing property rights in the interest of self-preservation.[8]

Property upholds democracy in another respect as well. Democracy requires a viable opposition to the ruling party. It requires that the Liberals are not denied a livelihood while the Conservatives are in office. It requires that the powers of government are not so extensive that opponents of the ruling party can be impoverished. Without private ownership of the means of production, the economy must necessarily be administered by the state. Once the economy is administered by the state, the livelihood of each and every person is at the discretion of the ruling party, for a person denied a job by the government would have no alternative employment. In such an environment, opposition to the party in office can only be maintained at great personal sacrifice. Opposition becomes a desperate if not impossible enterprise, and it may be squelched altogether.

James Madison[9] recognized the force of these arguments when he wrote in the Tenth Federalist letter:

> A pure democracy, by which I mean a society consisting of a small number of citizens, who assemble and administer the government in person, can admit of no cure from the mischiefs of faction. A common passion or interest will, in almost every case, be felt by a majority of the whole; a communication and concert, results from the form of government itself; and there is nothing to check the inducements to sacrifice the weaker party, or an obnoxious individual. Hence it is, that such democracies have ever been spectacles of turbulence and contention; have ever been found incompatible with personal security, or the rights of property; and have, in general, been as short in their lives, as they have been violent in their deaths.

Madison wrote that as a defence not of property, but of a particular form of government. His concern was with the political bases of democracy, especially the division of the powers of government among legislature, executive, and judiciary, and the resulting checks and balance among the branches of government. He was writing in an age when private ownership of most of the means of production was taken for granted, when most people were engaged in subsistence agriculture, and when it was not feasible for the government to play as

large a role in the economy as is common today because the required
technology of information, transportation, and communication had yet
to be invented. Now, with the means at hand to restrict the scope of
property rights beyond anything Madison could have imagined, the
political reason for not doing so becomes especially compelling.

A distinction should be drawn between the redistribution and the
reallocation of income. A pure redistribution of income narrows the
gap between rich and poor, reducing the variance of the income distribution without at the same time changing the ordering of people on
the scale of rich and poor. A pure reallocation of income reorders people on the scale of rich and poor, so that some people who were poor
become rich and others who were rich become poor. It is a reassign-
ment of people to slots without affecting the histogram of the distribution of income. Typically, public policy involves both redistribution
and reallocation, but one or the other may predominate. The significance of the distinction is that the political task of private property – to
supply the economic foundation of government by majority-rule voting – is not significantly affected by a degree of redistribution of
income, but is hindered substantially when property can be arbitrarily
reassigned from one person to another.

There is here a natural division of labour between voting and property. Voting cannot allocate the national income without destroying
itself, but it can redistribute without too much difficulty. Property, on
the other hand, allocates income automatically, but may stand in need
of a substantial redistribution of income. Redistribution by voting,
while not quite innocuous, is rendered feasible because there is a natural limit beyond which the median voter – the voter half way along the
scale of rich and poor – will not wish to go. The crux of the matter is that
the pie shrinks as you share it. A rise in the progressivity of the income
tax narrows the gap between the net incomes of the rich and the poor
but, at the same time, reduces the national income by weakening the
incentive to work and save. In voting on each extra bit of redistribution,
one must balance his gain, if he is among the poor, as a recipient of
redistribution against his loss from the resulting shrinkage in the
national income. The better off one is, the sooner does the loss outweigh the gain. The stopping place for the decisive median voter lies
well short of a massive, and costly, transfer to the poor. Contentment of
the median voter with the extent of the redistribution of income signi-
fies an acceptance of the existing allocation of the ownership of property which might otherwise be lacking in a system of private property

untempered by political intervention.[10] Voting and property reinforce one another, each supporting the other where it is weak and each governing a domain of life from which the other must be excluded if the entire system is to be preserved.

The third pillar of the liberal society is administration. It is a brute fact of the technology of social interaction that many public decisions cannot be resolved by voting. This is partly a matter of time. The legislature can at best conduct a couple of dozen votes a year which must, necessarily, be directed to large political questions, leaving a million details to be sorted out by the civil service, the army, the courts, and the police. The day-to-day governance of society – the assessment and collection of tax, the conduct of elections, the maintenance of roads, bridges, and airports, the provision of schooling, the oversight of immigration and foreign travel, relations with other countries, and so on – involves an infinity of small tasks that only an hierarchically organized bureaucracy can perform, although these tasks must ultimately fall within the authority of the legislature. Modern society requires a vast administrative apparatus where every person in the chain of command takes orders from his superior and gives orders to his subordinates.

There is, in addition, a mismatch between the beneficiaries and the ultimate providers of the goods and services that the government supplies. Many public services convey benefits to a relatively small group of people, but must necessarily be financed from taxation upon the population at large. A direct consequence of this mismatch is that self-interested voting by legislators on projects or programs considered one at a time must necessarily yield unsatisfactory outcomes, a deficiency that can only be rectified by the establishment of broad principles for administrative decision making. Road-building is a good example. The legislature may well decide how much to spend on road-building in total, but some non-political procedure must be agreed upon for deciding which roads to build and which to reject. Roads cannot be chosen or rejected by the legislature, one by one. A rule must be supplied to the Ministry of Transport for choosing which roads to build, or not to build as the case may be.

To see why this is so – why voting about roads one at a time is politically infeasible – consider a country with three regions, A, B, and C, but where all public expenditure is financed by uniform taxation in the country as a whole. Suppose for simplicity that the populations of the three regions are the same and that public revenue is acquired by a head tax. The legistlature of the country is considering three new roads, one in each region. Each road costs $5 per person in the country as a whole, yields benefits of $10 per person in *its* region, and yields a benefit of $3 per person in each of the other two regions. A road in region A, for example, supplies a net gain of $5 to each person in region A (the difference between the benefit of use, $10, and the cost of taxation, $5), and imposes a net cost of $2 on each person in regions B and C (the difference between the cost of taxation, $5, and the benefit of use, $3). Voted on one by one, each road would be turned down by the legislature because two out of every three people are made worse off. Voted on altogether in a package, the three roads would be built because their combined benefit to each person ($16) exceeds their combined tax cost to each person ($15). The 'right' procedure in this example is for the legislature to pass a comprehensive road-building bill.

Whether self-interested legislators would adopt the 'right' procedure depends on what other proposals may be entertained. With a hard-and-fast rule that all public expenditure must be financed by a head tax, people in, for example, region A and region B might form a coalition to vote for roads in their regions only and to reject the road in region C. As compared with a policy of building all three roads, the dropping of the road in region C conveys a benefit of $2 to each member of the coalition ($5 − $3) at the expense of people in region C who each suffer a loss of $5 ($10 − $5).[11] The coalition raises the net benefit of each coalition member, in regions A and B, from $1 to $3, lowers the net benefit per head among the excluded minority, in region C, from $1 to −$4, and lowers the average net benefit to people in all three regions from $1 to 67¢. Voting only works well when such options are somehow off the agenda. The attempt by the legislature to choose roads, one by one (or to decide in detail which hospitals to build, which medical procedures to employ in a public hospital, which immigrants to admit to one's country, or how much tax each person must pay), can only result in chaos because majority-rule voting supplies any two parties with an incentive to exploit the third.

An equally serious impediment to decision making by majority-rule voting is concealed by the symmetry of this simple example. A comprehensive bill makes no sense at all without a rule for deciding which roads to build. Some roads ought to be built; others not. In practice, a comprehensive road-building bill must specify criteria for choosing among projects or must specify total expenditure on the understanding that criteria will be supplied by the Ministry of Transport. The legislature must content itself with the establishment of general rules,

entrusting a multitude of specifics to a necessarily hierarchical administration which must, in turn, appeal to rules for deciding what to do
and what to desist from doing if a modicum of order is to be maintained in public affairs. Rules for the conduct of the administration
may be actively imposed or passively recognized by the legislature.
They are not, typically, the subject of a vote in which each legislator
casts his ballot in accordance with his own immediate self-interest or
with the interests of his constituents. Legislators must accept the rules
for the good of the country as a whole.

Part of the work of the administration can be conducted under the
principle of equality. Any two welfare recipients, children in grade 3,
cancer patients, or victims of robbery are to be treated alike by the state,
at least to the extent that the same resources are devoted to each. Police
protection on the block where I live ought not to be significantly better
or significantly worse than on a block at the other end of town. One
need only state the principle of equality as a guide for the administration to recognize that it is applied, at best, imperfectly and that there are
circumstances where it cannot be applied at all. The principle cannot be
applied, for example, in allocating of resources between the education
of children in grade 3 and the alleviation of the suffering of cancer
patients when both must be financed from a limited budget, or for
deciding whether a new airport is to be located on the east side or the
west side of town. For such choices, the administration must have
recourse to a more or less precise cost-benefit rule. Values must somehow be placed on the different consequences of public decision making, so that projects or programs may be undertaken if and only if the
balance of costs and benefits is favourable. It is, of course, arguable that
a cost-benefit rule is itself a variant of the principle of equality because
one cannot predict *ex ante* whether the rule will in time be more beneficial to me or to my neighbour. In practice, the immediate winners and
losers from the principle that benefits be weighted equally 'to whomso-
ever they may accrue' know perfectly well who they are, and are
actively competing for influence within the legislature.

These two rules for the bureaucracy – 'treat everybody equally' and
'maximize the gap between benefit and cost' – are not entirely compatible. A benefit-cost rule may bias public policy towards the rich, especially if non-monetary benefits, like time-saving and life-saving, are
weighed at the recipient's valuation. An equality rule may benefit the
poor who naturally pay less tax per head. Sometimes it is obvious
which rule to apply. In a regime of socialized medicine, a benefit-cost

test governs the choice of services to provide, while an equal-treatment rule ensures that nobody is favoured *ex ante* when it is unknown which services he will require. (Canada's practice of treating top politicians and generals in a special hospital is an inexcusable violation of the equality rule.) Sometimes it is unclear which of these rules is applicable. It is not accidental that the locating of airports and the closing of military bases is politically contentious, for there is no simple formula in these cases to guide the bureaucracy in deciding what to do.

The greater the tasks of the bureaucracy, the less can it be guided by general rules of conduct. The range of discretion expands together with the authority of the bureaucracy over the economy. Discretion can never be eliminated altogether, and it varies from one ministry to the next. It is usually evident how the Ministry of National Revenue ought to behave. The Ministry of Health is probably less rule-bound. The Ministry of Industry very much less. And the less rule-bound the bureaucracy, the greater the influence of the legislature and the executive over its activity, and the more contentious does ordinary politics become.

Administration is never entirely rule-bound or entirely public-spirited.[12] To a greater or lesser degree, all bureaucracies are inefficient, corrupt, or predatory. Self-interest, which is normally presumed rampant in the private sector of the economy, cannot be expected to stop short at the door of the public sector. Powers over the economy will inevitably be misused to some extent, and have at times been altogether uncontainable. Hierarchy has throughout history been an instrument of oppression. To the old question, 'Who guards the guardians?' there has been a simple answer, 'Nobody.' Guardians would take what they please, constrained only by a fear of banditry if they are too acquisitive or by 'the Laffer curve for the Leviathan,' the realization, in Hobbes's words, that 'the greatest pressure of Sovereign Governours, proceedith not from any delight, or profit, they can expect in the damage, or weakening of their own Subjects, in whose vigor, consisteth their own strength and glory.'[13] That an organized few can dominate an unorganized many is reason enough for the absence of any semblance of popular government (except in tribes and city-states) throughout most of recorded history.

What needs to be explained is not the dominance of the hierarchy in the many times and places where the hierarchy has been dominant, but its subordination to the legislature in many countries today. I have no complete explanation, but something of an explanation may be found in private property and in the law. Property tempers the bureaucracy by reducing the size of the administrative apparatus that society requires and by supplying a refuge for people the bureaucracy does not employ. While it is true that the organized few can often dominate the unorganized many, it is also true that a large organization is likely to be more dangerous than a small one and that an organization encompassing the entire economy – as the bureaucracy must do in the absence of private ownership of the means of production – would be virtually uncontainable.

Size fosters obedience. In a capitalist economy, a civil servant who comes to believe that the actions of his ministry are mistaken or who is asked to do the unconscionable can quit in the knowledge that he can probably find a job in the private sector. Resignation does not lead to ostracism or impoverishment, as it surely would if there were no private sector where one could be employed. The private sector is the matrix of opposition to the bureaucracy as well as to the party in office. Thus private property constrains the administration in two respects: by restricting its authority to a domain within which there are fairly well-recognized rules of conduct, and by providing an escape from the vengeance of the bureaucracy for those who challenge its authority.

Necessary as it is for taming the administration, private ownership of the means of production is almost certainly not sufficient. Equally necessary is 'the rule of law,' our fourth pillar of the liberal society. Broadly speaking, the rule of law is a splitting off from the administration and the granting of considerable independence to a judiciary whose business it becomes to apply the law to individuals, so that the administration cannot punish those who displease it on the pretext that the law of the land has been broken. 'Courts of law are established for the expressed purpose of limiting public authority in its conduct toward individuals.'[14] There is, of course, a sense in which the judiciary is a part of the administration. Judges are often appointed by the executive or by the legislature. The rule of law is maintained nevertheless by the convention that, once appointed, judges cannot be summarily dismissed. The convention is strong enough that violation by the government of the day would trigger massive civil disobedience among the political elite. Judicial independence is maintained by tenure with guaranteed salary until the age of retirement, except where judges are deemed by Parliament to have broken the law. In its classic formulation by Dicey, the rule of law is juxtaposed with the supremacy of Parliament, in a division of labour where Parliament has ultimate responsibility for the content of laws and the judiciary ensures that the laws are uniformly applied.[15] Property and the rule of law are mutually reinforcing as defences of the citizen from the administration. Even together, these defences are not always sufficient, but they would both appear to be necessary if the freedoms of the individual – not the least of which is the assurance that one will not be whisked away to a concentration camp because one has offended the party in office – are to be preserved.

As with any neat schema in the social sciences, the dichotomy between rule of law and sovereignty of Parliament fits the facts imperfectly.[16] Dicey's boundary between the domains of Parliament and the courts is violated in both directions. Legislatures sometimes reach beyond the establishment of general laws to convey harms or benefits on particular people. Judges sometimes reach beyond the application and enforcement of law to the making of law. Both violations may be dangerous. Although there is no bright line for the legislature between the establishment of general laws and the provision of harms or benefits to particular people or groups of people, some actions by the legislature would be recognized as beyond its conventional mandate. *Ad hominem* taxation of one's political opponents – a special tax imposed by a Liberal government on the ex-cabinet members of the preceding Conservative government – is clearly out, and would, one hopes, be effectively blocked by the Canadian courts. But subsidies for groups of producers who happen to vote for the party in office – schemes to raise the price of milk and tobacco, or investment subsidies offered for the flimsiest of reasons and administered without public scrutiny by officials who can expect, on retirement, to be hired by the recipients – would seem to be acceptable. There appears to be a convention that the conduct of civil and criminal justice is strictly out of bounds to the legislature, that people or groups cannot be singled out for special mistreatment, but that a degree of favouritism is acceptable. Taxation is also out of bounds, but public expenditure is not. Governments may give *ad hominem* to a far greater extent than they may take. That may be as close as we can get to the rule of law, and it is clearly better than nothing.

The line between the rule of law and the sovereignty of Parliament is also crossed in the other direction. There is a large body of 'judge-made' law that may be in cooperation with the legislature or in opposition to the legislature. Judge-made law is in cooperation with the legislature when litigation must inevitably be interpreted in the light of the case at hand, or when new situations conform badly to old pre-scriptions so that – with little guidance from Parliament on how to pro-ceed – the courts must seek rules in commercial custom or in their interpretation of natural justice. Much of the common law, including most of the law of torts and contract, is said to be judge-made in this sense.[17] Judge-made law in cooperation with the legislature, filling gaps in the law when the legislature is silent, would seem supportive on balance of the rule of law and of the individual against the bureau-cracy. Ambiguity in the law is an opening for extortion and victimiza-tion. Arbitrary behaviour on the part of the administration is best contained within a framework where the requirements of the law are known.

Judge-made law in opposition to the legislature is more problematic. Judges must oppose the legislature when the rule of law itself is in jeopardy. This is explicit in the U.S. Constitution, which empowers the Supreme Court to strike down legislation that causes a person to be 'deprived of life, liberty, or property, without due process of law' or 'to abridge the privileges and immunities of citizens.' There is an implicit equivalent in every democratic country. Control of the citizen by the government would be unlimited, and the prospects for democratic government would be dim indeed, if the legislature could routinely get away with *ad hominem* legislation. The government could simply tax away the means of support of the opposition. The logic of the argu-ment extends to discrimination against groups of people identified by language, race, or social origin.[18]

Necessary as it is in some circumstances, judge-made law in opposition to the legislature carries a serious risk of excess. Take nine old and successful men or women, dress them in black robes, venerate them, empower them with authority to nullify acts of Parliament on the basis of a document as ambiguous as the Canadian Charter of Rights and Freedoms, and, human nature being what it is, they will from time to time employ their powers to replace acts of Parliament with the law as they, personally, would like it to be.[19] Courts may choose to respect decisions of the legislature except where individuals or groups are victimized, denied the vote, or excluded from public ser-vices that others enjoy. Or the courts may choose to be active, interpret-ing the rights in the constitution so broadly as to encroach on ordinary public policy.

Among the dangers in judicial activism are that the judges are wrong in their evaluation of public policy,[20] that politics will be redirected from the election of legislators to the appointment of judges and that courts will lose the moral authority required to uphold the rule of law. Let the courts restrict themselves to the adjudication of civil disputes, to the determination of guilt or innocence of people accused of specific crimes, and to an oversight of the legislature extending no farther than is necessary to block victimization or discrimination quite narrowly defined, and the elected officials whose task it is to appoint judges will be content to base their selections on the judges' learning in the law, for we all realize how much is at stake in the maintenance of the rule of law. Let the courts adjudicate cases in accordance with the law as they believe it should be, and the temptation to appoint judges who see matters 'correctly' becomes irresistible.[21]

Once again, the protection of private property by other institutions is reciprocated. An independent judiciary is a defence of property rights, but a viable private sector is a defence of the independence of the judiciary. An independent judiciary protects property from appropriation not just by thieves and other predators in the private sector, but by the government of the day. It would be all too easy for the party in power to slant the law against its opponents if the judiciary were a part of the ordinary administrative apparatus. The stakes of office would rise and the inhibitions of the majority faction in the legislature would diminish accordingly. At the same time, property protects the independence of the judiciary by providing the environment for an active legal profession outside the administrative apparatus. Judges can resist political pressure, not just because they have tenure, although tenure is surely important, but because most judges were successful and independent lawyers in the private sector before they became judges. Unschooled in obedience to authority, they are less likely than ordinary civil servants to be swayed by the prospects of promotion, and they could, in extreme circumstances, become lawyers again.

Taking Rights Casually

The justification of private property in this essay is, quite simply, that for a variety of strong reasons we would rather live in a society with property rights than in a society without property rights. There is no more to it than that. There is on the other hand a long and very different tradition in political philosophy, a tradition that may be called rights-based as distinct from needs-based because property rights are seen as derivative from prior rights of a different kind or from something in the cosmos that establishes private property as good or noble in itself almost regardless of the consequences. Maintain private property though the heavens fall rather than because, as is argued here, the heavens will fall if you do not.

Fundamentalists might be content to justify property as the will of God. One need look no further than the Seventh Commandment, 'Thou shall not steal!' The injunction against stealing is, almost by definition, an assertion that private property in land and things is acceptable and just. Punishment of the thief and protection of private rights by the state are two sides of the same coin. The Bible is full of examples of divine sanction for private property. Scholastics in the Middle Ages were especially fond of citing God's condemnation of King Ahab for stealing the orchard of Naboth.[22]

The secular equivalent of divine sanction is the doctrine of natural rights.[23] God may not command the protection of property rights directly, but something in the cosmos or in the nature of man requires us to do what God, in an age of faith, used to command and to respect rights that He would have us respect. Thus Robert Nozick,[24] a modern exponent of the doctrine, asserts: 'Individuals have rights, and there are things no person or group may do to them (without violating their rights). So strong and far-reaching are these rights that they raise the question of what, if anything, the state and its officials may do.' Nozick goes on to say that 'a minimal state, limited to the narrow functions of protection against force, theft, fraud, enforcement of contracts, and so on, is justified; that any more extensive state will violate persons' rights not to be forced to do certain things, and is unjustified.'

Satisfactory as they may be as myth or pedagogy, the theological or rights-based justifications for the protection of private property are open to several objections: First, it is by no means obvious what God commands. As a guide for public policy, Holy Writ requires a definitive interpretation by an authoritarian priesthood, buttressed in practice, by the Inquisition, the stake, the Gulag and the NKVD. Nor is the content of rights self-evident. Is progressive income taxation a violation of property rights as some authors maintain?[25] Is entitlement to an old age pension a part of my property rights that no legislature may diminish?[26] It is hard to see how these questions can be answered within the confines of theology or natural law. Considerations beyond rights would have to be invoked to explain why rights are what they are. Second, the inequality argument against private property is especially telling in a theological context. If God ordained property rights,

He must have ordained the inequalities they necessarily entail. He must approve of the plutocrat in his mansion and the bum begging on the street. That divine authority stands behind the great disparities of wealth we observe around us is a proposition which may be congenial to the wealthy but is somewhat difficult for the rest of us to swallow. Third, a theological or rights-based justification of private property can be too easily dismissed with the statement that 'I'm sorry, but I simply do not believe.' I do not believe in a God who said, 'Thou shall not steal.' I do not believe that you have thus-and-such rights. I do not believe that the Party is the vanguard of the proletariat. If I do not believe and if you are not prepared to argue beyond God's command-ments or beyond natural rights to some human good that the com-mandments or rights are deemed to foster, there is nothing you can say to convince me. But if you are prepared to ground God's command-ments or natural rights in some human objective, then you have demoted God's commandments or natural rights to mere links in the chain from the ultimate justification of property rights to specific laws or customs.

Justification by 'first occupation' is similar in some respects to the doctrine of natural rights, but with a curious pseudo-historical flavour. The standard example of first occupation is the finding of a pebble on the beach. I pick up the pebble, and it is mine. Or I discover ore in the ground. Or I catch fish from the sea. Or I occupy unowned and unculti-vated land. In each case, what was owned by nobody is discovered, occupied, and thereby acquired as property. As first occupant, I acquire a right which ought to be protected by the state.

The doctrine of first occupation contains an important lesson about the nature of property rights, a lesson encapsulated in the phrase, 'pos-session as the root of title.'[27] The lesson is that there is no mileage in attempting to explain or justify the actual distribution of property among people, no ethically grounded reason why A is rich and B is poor. That today's property rights originate in conquest, inheritance, ancient fraud, or acquisition in accordance with rules now seen as rad-ically unjust has little or no bearing on the validity of those rights. What matters is possession as recognized by the law. We need some allocation of property to people, and the existing allocation is in a sense part of the social capital of a good society. Turning a blind eye to ancient wrongs, we accept the present allocation as we find it, not because it is *per se* better than a different allocation, but because it is there, and because a new allocation is difficult, costly, and disruptive to create. To make this case is not to deny that huge disparities of income or wealth may be dangerous or that a degree of redistribution need not kill the goose that lays the golden eggs. How much and what kind of redistribution can be undertaken without destroying the basis of liberal society is one of the more difficult questions in social science.

Nevertheless, as a justification of private property, the doctrine of first occupation is open to several objections: Well-established property rights may not have been acquired by first occupation. First occupation may not convey property rights at all. Some principle beyond first occupation is required to establish the content and limits of property rights.

First occupation is neither necessary nor sufficient to secure property rights. It is not necessary because title to property may be secure, even though the property itself was acquired by the ancestors of present owners through conquest, fraud, or violence. Land claims, if valid at all, rest upon present occupation or upon the willingness of the law to cut history short, recognizing first occupation as of some date in the past. William the Conqueror did not find England, but land titles originating in the distribution of spoils among his henchmen are no less valid on that account. If property rights can be traced to a first occupation, then there must be a well-established body of property law to determine which of the many occupations of each plot of land is first.

First occupation is not sufficient to secure property rights because the occupation itself must be in conformity with the laws and customs of one's society. First occupation conveys title only insofar as the laws allow. The pebble discovered on the beach is not really mine unless the law determines it to be so. It is usually mine if it is just a pretty stone. It may not be mine if it contains a rare fossil; its discovery may even impose upon me the duty to hand over the fossil to the proper authorities. The distinction between base and noble metals harks back to a time when newly discovered base metals – lead, copper, iron, and so on – belonged to the discoverer, while newly discovered noble metals – gold and silver – belonged to the king. Like the granting of patent rights to an inventor, the assignment of property rights to the first occupier is expedient in some contexts as an incentive to discovery and as a way of avoiding conflict over who owns what, but first occupation is not a self-contained principle.

That first occupation provides no guidance about the content of property rights becomes evident when one considers that property 'is a relation not between an owner and a thing, but between the owner and other individuals in reference to things.'[28] The value to me of a pile of stones may depend on whether I am allowed to build a wall around my property, and that in turn may depend on whether the wall would be in conformity with the rules and by-laws of the town where I live. Nor is a right of inheritance implicit in a right of first occupation. It might be claimed that, once the pebble is mine, I can dispose of it as I please, when I please, and to whomoever I please. The claim is far from self-evident and not always persuasive. A case can be made that a right to bequeath property is expedient and in the long-run interest of the community as a whole, but that is a different matter altogether. Even ordinary rights to use one's property for this or that purpose may be expanded or abridged over time, as, for instance, when a long-established right to dump sewage in a river is abolished in response to new occupation of sites downstream.

My main objection to the doctrine of 'first occupation' as a justification for private property is that it is upside down. The validity of the rule, to the extent that it is valid, is derived from the usefulness of the institution of private property. Private property justifies first occupation, not the other way round. The doctrine of first occupation involves a kind of political synecdoche in which the roles of the whole and the part are interchanged. Private property can be looked upon as a complex institution with an elaborate set of rules, among which are the rules specifying how property may be acquired and how to resolve disputes among rival claimants to the same thing. The right of first occupation is a useful, possibly essential, ingredient in the large set of rules we call property rights, and, as such inherits a value to society from its status as a part of the whole. The correct syllogism is: We need private property. First occupation is an essential ingredient of private property. Therefore first occupation is a desirable rule. As a matter of simple logic, the doctrine of first occupation is not, and cannot be, a justification of private property.

Similar objections may be raised against the doctrine that private property rights are acquired by the application of labour. In the words of Locke,[29] with whom this doctrine is primarily identified:

> Though the earth and all inferior creatures be common to all men, yet every man has a property in his own person: this nobody has any right to but himself. The labour of his body and the work of his hands, we may say, are properly his. Whatsoever then he removes out of the state that nature hath provided and left it in, he hath mixed his labour with, and

joined to it something that is his own, and thereby makes it his property. It being by him removed from the common state nature hath placed it in, it hath by this labour something annexed to it that excludes the common right of other men. For this labour being the unquestionable property of the labourer, no man can have a right to what that is once joined to, at least where there is enough and as good left in common for others.

Of all of the justifications for the protection of property rights, this strikes me as the least persuasive. Robert Nozick dismissed the argument with the observation that if I own a can of tomato juice and if I pour the tomato juice into the ocean, I cannot by that act be said to acquire the ocean, even if nobody has ever poured tomato juice into the ocean before. Furthermore, if one begins with premises about acquisition of ownership by mixing labour, it is hard to see why the first instance of mixing takes precedence over any subsequent mixing. If one begins with premises about mixing labour, then Karl Marx would seem to have a more persuasive case than John Locke. Present labour would seem to have a better claim to the national income than past labour.

Once again, the rights-based argument is backwards. That I am entitled to the produce of my labour (as reflected in the wage my labour can command) is part of the complex web of rules we call property rights. Entitlement to the produce of one's labour is a good rule if and insofar as it produces good consequences in the context where it is employed. A rule assigning my labour to somebody else would not be a good rule because I would prefer not to be a slave and because, for a variety of reasons, the common good as I see it is better served by a society without slavery than by a society where slavery is permitted. But there is nothing *per se* unjust about a rule forbidding people from clearing unowned land without permission from the government. Compensation for clearing land may take some form other than ownership of the land, or the clearing of public land may be disallowed altogether. Right to the produce of one's labour is derivative of property rights in general.

Finally, private property may be justified by an appeal to a real or imaginary social contract. Think of a state of nature with no government to protect property rights, where people produce what they can and take what they can, and where life is 'solitary, poor, nasty, brutish, and short.' One day people, who the day before were fighting and pillaging one another, come together peacefully in a constitutional assembly where they agree to establish a civil government to protect property rights. Everybody signs the contract and is, from then on, bound by the contract to protect property rights collectively through the intermediary of the government.

Attractive as it may be as a myth for the reinforcement of this or that virtue of a democratic society, the social contract story is unlikely to persuade anybody of the desirability of private property unless one is already inclined to be persuaded for other reasons. The story of the social contract is encapsulated, or stylized, history, quite distinct from actual events at particular times and places. As such, the story may inculcate a sense of obligation towards the rules of one's society, but it cannot serve as a defence or justification for any specific set of rules. Nothing in the story explains why the laws are what they are. Nothing in the story explains why property is owned privately rather than collectively, except on the entirely gratuitous assumption that property was already allocated among people at the time when the contract was signed. The story of the social contract is about why we should desist from stealing when property rights are, in fact, protected. It is not about why private ownership of the means of production is worthy to be protected at all.

Nor can one infer from the story which institutions are to be preserved or which reforms might be warranted. Consider the government and institutions of Canada. Did the contract establish the government of Canada as it was in 1867 when Canada became independent, or in 1900, or last year? Is the contract synonymous with the present Constitution, or will the contract only be completed once my pet reforms are enacted into law? Did the contract protect property rights at all, or are property rights a perversion of the contract for the benefit of the few at the expense of the many?

Justification of property rights by their origin – in the word of God, in natural law, in first occupation, in the mixing of labour with land, or in a social contract – was decisively, and in my opinion, correctly rejected long ago by David Hume[30] in an argument that was directed explicitly at justification by social contract but is equally applicable to any rights-based justification of private property rights.

What necessity, therefore, is there to found the duty of allegiance or obedience to magistrates on that of fidelity or a regard to promises, and to suppose, that it is the consent of each individual which subjects him to government, when it appears that both allegiance and fidelity stand precisely on the same foundation, and are both submitted to by mankind, on account of the apparent interests and necessities of human society? We are bound to obey our sovereign, it is said, because we have given a tacit promise to that purpose. But why are we bound to observe our promise? It must here be asserted, that the commerce and intercourse of mankind, which are of such mighty advantage, can have no security where men pay no regard to their engagements. In like manner, may it be said that men could not live at all in society, at least in a civilized society, without laws, and magistrates, and judges, to prevent the encroachments of the strong upon the weak, of the violent upon the just and equitable. The obligation to allegiance being of like force and authority with the obligation to fidelity, we gain nothing by resolving the one into the other. The general interests or necessities of society are sufficient to establish both.

The Core and the Margin

The justification for the protection of private property in this essay is not a maximalist stance. It does not require the full and complete protection of each and every right that the most extreme libertarians have claimed. It is not a case against the 'taking' from the rich for the benefit of the poor in the progressive income tax. It is not a decisive argument against measures, such as antitrust policy, to reduce the concentration of power in the economy. It provides no neat demarcation of the appropriate boundary in a democratic society between the equal rights of people as voters and the unequal rights of people as property-holders. It is not a condemnation of public provision of education or medical care. It does not automatically determine the proper place of money in the courts, in hiring lawyers, and in fitting (or not fitting) penalties to the wealth of the convicted. It does point to a core of private ownership without which the free society cannot be maintained.

We uphold private property not because it is just, not because it is sanctified by some ethical principle in the sky, not in deference to some ancient agreement, and in spite of its dubious origin in plunder and chicanery. We uphold private property because we need it. We uphold private property because it is a requirement for what we all see as a good society and to keep autocracy at bay. There is a technical connection – social technology, but technology all the same – among property, voting, administration, and law. These four pillars of the liberal society stand or fall together. Property is the foundation of prosperity, a source of civic virtue, a requirement for majority-rule voting, a necessary constraint on the administration, and a prerequisite for the rule of law. But the connections are reciprocal. Property is as dependent upon the other pillars as they are dependent upon it.

Notes

1 For an analytical summary and critique of arguments for and against private property, see L.C. Becker, *Property Rights: Philosophic Foundation* (London: Routledge and Kegan Pual, 1977). For an instructive discussion of the views about property of Locke, Rousseau, Kant, Bentham, Hegel, Mill, and Marx, see A. Ryan, *Property and Political Theory* (Oxford: Blackwell, 1984). For a more comprehensive survey from the ancient Greeks to the present day, see R. Schlatter, *Private Property: The History of an Idea* (London: George Allen & Unwin, 1951). A useful selection of excerpts from the classics on property rights is contained in C.B. Macpherson, ed., *Property: Mainstream and Critical Positions* (Toronto: University of Toronto Press, 1978).

2 The veil of ignorance test was proposed by John Harsanyi as a justification of utilitarianism. John Rawls, who introduced the term 'veil of ignorance,' adopted the same test as a justification for what he calls the 'two principles of justice.' Harsanyi's argument makes sense in my opinion. Rawls's does not. See J. Harsanyi, 'Cardinal Welfare, Individualistic Ethics, and Interpersonal Comparisons of Utility,' *Journal of Political Economy* (1955), 309–21; J. Rawls, *A Theory of Justice* (London: Oxford University Press, 1971); and D. Usher, 'Rawls, Rules and Objectives: A Critique of the Two Principles of Justice,' *Constitutional Political Economy* (1996), 103–26.

3 I think the variant of utilitarianism adopted in this chapter is what Goodin calls 'government house utilitarianism.' See R.E. Goodin, *Utilitarianism as a Public Philosophy* (New York: Cambridge University Press, 1995), chap. 4.

4 F. Hayek, 'The Use of Knowledge in Society,' *American Economic Review* (1945), 519–30. See also Hayek's *The Road to Serfdom* (Chicago: University of Chicago Press, 1944).

5 See M. Djilas, *The New Class* (New York: Praeger, 1957).

6 Quoted in Schlatter, *Private Property*, 196–7.

7 John Stuart Mill, *Principles of Political Economy* (Boston: Charles C. Little and James Brown, 1848), vol. 2, 522–4.

8 I developed this theme at length in *The Economic Prerequisite to Democracy* (Oxford: Blackwell, 1981).

9 James Madison, 'The Federalist Papers: Number 10,' in *The Federalist Papers*, ed. A. Hacker (New York: Washington Square Press, 1964).

10 The *locus classicus* of this argument is A.B. Atkinson, 'How Progressive Should the Income Tax Be?' in E. Phelps, ed., *Economic Justice* (London: Penguin, 1973), 386–408.

11 This is a classic paradox of voting in an unusual context.

12 On the contrast between free markets and rule-bound bureaucracy, see Max Weber, 'Bureaucracy,' in *From Max Weber*, ed. H.H. Girth and C.W. Mills (New York: Oxford University Press, 1946), 196–244.

13 Thomas Hobbes of Malmesbury, *Leviathan or, the Matter, Form and Power of a Common-Wealth Ecclesiastical and Civil* (London: Andrew Cooke, 1651), 238.

14 Sir James Steven quoted in J. Dickenson, *Administrative Justice and the Supremacy of the Law in the United States* (Cambridge, MA: Harvard University Press, 1927), 93.

15 'The law of the constitution ... is ... the result of two guiding principles ... worked out by the more or less conscious efforts of generations of English statesmen and lawyers ... The first of these principles is the Sovereignty of Parliament ... [which] ... has preserved intact and undiminished the supreme authority of the State ... The second is ... the rule of law, which means at bottom the right of the Courts to punish any illegal act by whomever committed [and] is the very essence of English institutions.' A.V. Dicey, *Introduction to the Study of the Law of the Constitution*, 8th ed., (London: Macmillan, 1915, reprinted by Indianapolis: Liberty Press, 1982), 313–4.

16 Better precise concepts that do not quite fit the world (they never do) than imprecise concepts which appear to do so. We need concepts to think at all, but the world is too various and interesting a place to conform precisely to our conceptions of it.

17 See 'Judicial Legislation' (Lecture XI) and 'Judge-made Law' (Note IV) of A.V. Dicey, *Lectures on the Relation between Law and Public Opinion in England in the Nineteenth Century*, 2nd ed. (1914, reprinted by New Brunswick, NJ: Transaction Books, 1981), 361–98 and 483–94. For a defence of judicial activism in the name of efficiency, see R.A. Posner, 'Utilitarianism, Economics and Legal Theory,' *Journal of Legal Studies* (1979), 103–40. However, in upholding efficiency as a criterion for the law, Posner may be speaking to the legislature as much as to the courts, and it in unclear to me how far he is prepared to see the courts pursue efficiency in opposition to the legislature.

18 *Brown* v. *Board of Education of Topeka* (1954, 1955) is the best-known case of this type.

19 Nothing in the U.S. Constitution limits the authority of the state legislatures to determine the law on abortion, legalizing it or banning it as they see fit, but, in *Roe* v. *Wade*, the U.S. Supreme Court chose to read a right to abort

into the U.S. Constitution, redirecting the politics of abortion from the legislature to the courts. The story is told in R. Bork, *The Tempting of America*
(New York: Free Press, 1990). In *RJR-MacDonald Inc* v. *Canada (Attorney General)*, [1995] 3 S.C.R 199, the Canadian Supreme Court struck down a federal
law banning cigarette advertising as a violation of the right to 'commercial
free speech' read into the Canadian Charter of Rights and because the
Court was unprepared to accept the judgment of Parliament that cigarette
advertising induces young people to smoke. I happen to believe that, as
public policy, abortion should be permitted on demand and that cigarette
advertising should be banned, but that is not the question at issue here. The
question is whether public policy in each case should be determined by the
legislature or by the courts.

20 To justify private property in general – to argue that a substantial core of
property rights is an indispensable component of a good society – is not at
the same time to favour each and every enlargement of the scope of property rights or to see virtue in every instance of judicial activism to extend
the boundaries of property rights. It is now widely believed that the U.S.
Supreme Court was wrong to strike down the regulation of hours of work
for bakers (and, by inference, for other trades or groups of people) in *Loch-
ner* v. *New York* (1905). Under pressure from the Roosevelt government in
'the switch in time that saved nine,' the Court reversed itself in *West Coast
Hotel Co.* v. *Parrish* (1937). In *Dred Scott* v. *Sandford* (1857), the U.S. Supreme
Court professed to see a constitutionally mandated right of property broad
enough to protect slave-holding in any state of the Union, a decision commonly seen as one of the causes of the U.S. Civil War.

21 That is the real moral of the Clarence Thomas–Anita Hill fiasco.

22 See Schlatter, 'Early Christian Theories of Property,' in chap. 3 of *Private
Property.*

23 See A.P. D'Entreves, 'A Theory of Natural Rights,' chap. 3 of *Natural Law:
An Introduction to Legal Philosophy.* (London: Hutchinson's Universal
Library, 1951).

24 R. Nozick, *Anarchy, State and Utopia* (New York: Basic Books, 1974), ix.

25 R.A. Epstein, *Takings: Private Property and the Power of Eminent Domain*
(Cambridge, MA: Harvard University Press, 1985).

26 C. Reich, 'The New Property,' *Yale Law Journal* (1961), 733–87.

27 R. Epstein, 'Possession as the Root of Title,' *Georgia Law Review* (1979),
121–43. The converse is equally true. See also D. Lueck, 'The Rule of First
Possession and the Design of Law,' *Journal of Law and Economics* (1995),
393–436. Lueck discusses a variety of circumstances where property rights
are assigned by the state to first possessors as a *reward* for socially desirable

activities, patents, copyrights, and mineral discoveries being the principal examples. There is a world of difference between being first in a context where the race is socially advantageous and where there is no better way to reward the participants, and just being first. If being first were all that mattered, then patents would not be restricted to inventions, and discoveries in pure science would be patentable too.

28 M.R. Cohen, 'Property and Sovereignty,' in *Property: Mainstream and Critical Positions*, C.B. Macpherson, ed. (Toronto: University of Toronto Press, 1978), 159. (Originally published in the *Cornell Law Quarterly*, 1927.)

29 John Locke, *The Second Treatise of Civil Government* (1690), chap. 5, par. 27, in Thomas I Cook, ed. *Two Treatises of Government* (New York: Hafner Press, 1947), 134.

30 David Hume, 'Of the Original Contract,' in *Social Contract*, E. Barker ed. (London: Oxford University Press, 1947), 228.

3

Capitalism versus Democracy: The Marketing of Votes and the Marketing of Political Power

DAVID COPP

It is widely thought that democracy and capitalism are natural allies. Democracy places political power in the hands of the citizenry, and capitalism places economic power in the hands of consumers. In each case, there is a decentralization of power to the people most directly concerned, those most directly concerned with the products of the polity in the one case and with the products of the economy in the other case.

The idea that democracy and capitalism are strongly linked figures in today's political rhetoric as the thought that capitalism must be encouraged in Eastern Europe in order to strengthen democracy there. There is some plausibility to this thought. But there is, of course, no guarantee that democracy and capitalism will go hand in hand, as the examples of Hong Kong and Sweden make clear. Sweden is a democracy that has a history of welfarist intervention in the marketplace. Hong Kong has been one of the most successful capitalistic economies in the world, but it has never been governed democratically, even though there was a rush to introduce some of the familiar civil liberties into the law of the colony in the run-up to July 1997. Nor was there evidence of widespread dissatisfaction among Hong Kong capitalists with the colonial political situation.

My topic in this essay is a kind of *systemic* conflict between capitalism and democracy. It is a banal fact that democratic majorities might support certain measures that compromise capitalism, and even if it is true that the most purely capitalistic societies are not democracies, this is not of interest to me in itself. I am interested in certain ways in which an *unmitigated* capitalism would undermine the *root values* of democracy, even if it might leave the surface institutions intact. The issue is not merely academic, for, as I said before, it is common to argue that by strengthening capitalism one strengthens democracy. Milton Friedman argued that capitalism 'separates economic power from political power.'[1] I will be arguing to the contrary that there are deep reasons why an unmitigated capitalism is incompatible with the essence of democracy. Capitalism spawns inequalities in economic power, and inequalities in economic power produce inequalities in political power of a kind that is undemocratic.

The Nature of Capitalism

In capitalism, supply and demand determine the prices of commodities through the operation of free markets, and all commodities are produced by privately owned rather than by socially owned concerns. In order to be an example of pure capitalism, then, nothing that is bought or sold in the economy can be produced by a state-owned concern. There cannot be a state-owned bus company, for example. Moreover, all prices must be determined by the forces of supply and demand. A purely capitalistic economy would leave all production in private hands and would let all markets be self-regulating, except insofar as regulation might be required to facilitate the operation of markets.

Capitalism is compatible with regulations that are intended merely to facilitate the operation of markets. I will call regulations of this kind 'internal' because their motivation is the same as the motivation for capitalism itself. Included among internal regulations are those that are intended to cause the internalization of 'spillover' costs.[2] Laws of this kind contribute to the efficiency of markets by forcing agents to pay the full cost of their activities. For example, environmental regulations can be designed to force corporations to pay the cost of cleaning up pollution they cause, thereby forcing them to take this cost into account in their decision making, something they might otherwise have no motivation to do. Regulations that are intended to prevent the formation of monopolies are also internal in my sense for they are intended to ensure the competitiveness of markets. Even criminal prohibitions on theft can be viewed as preventing market failure since a criminal can be viewed as establishing his own price for the good he wants, the 'zero price.'[3] Criminal prohibitions on force and fraud and provisions for the enforcement of contracts can also be motivated by the goal of facilitating markets, so they can also be described as internal regulations.

Of course, regulations and laws of many other kinds are intended to achieve other goals than the facilitation of markets. I will call regulations of this kind 'external.' They include health and safety regulations, such as the prohibition of leaded gasoline, the requirement that automobiles be built with headlights that are set to light up whenever the automobile is driven, and the like. Other external regulations affect or limit property rights and include building code rules motivated by aesthetic considerations. Still other regulations prevent certain kinds of goods and services from being freely marketed. For example, criminal law may be used to prevent the marketing of sexual services in the prostitution trade. Many countries control or prohibit a variety of actual or potential enterprises, including the marketing of votes, of human beings, of human bodies and body parts, of babies, and of the work of children.[4] All regulations and laws of these kinds affect prices and result in a situation in which prices are not determined by supply and demand. Such regulations therefore affect economic behaviour in ways that compromise capitalism. Every society I know of engages in some external regulation of markets – regulation that is not meant merely to facilitate markets – so I am inclined to think that there are no purely capitalistic economies in the real world.

Leaving aside internal and external regulations of these kinds, there is the matter of income redistribution. Most tax systems are at least somewhat redistributive, and of course, the welfare state was constructed to achieve some of the effects of redistributing income. The typical measures of the welfare state shield workers from the effects of supply and demand in labour, thereby inhibiting the effect of supply and demand on the price of labour, that is, wages, and also inhibiting the effect of the price of labour on its supply. The result is to compromise capitalism, for in a capitalistic labour market, the cost of labour is determined by supply and demand, not by government policy. Income redistribution therefore compromises capitalism because it affects the cost of labour.

Once these ideas are understood, we can see that there is hardly a society today that is a pure example of capitalism, and we can see why. In Canada, for example, the Wheat Board, the Employment Insurance scheme, minimum wage laws, the medical insurance scheme, regulation of airline routes, and so on, all involve interference with markets. And Canada famously is in business. It owns or has owned businesses involved in everything from aircraft and steel manufacturing to petroleum retailing and the generating of electricity.

Capitalism is not an all-or-nothing affair, however. There are various degrees to which economies are capitalistic. For my purposes in what follows, I will count an economy as capitalist even if some markets are regulated to a significant degree, provided that the degree of regulation does not exceed what is required to prevent market failures or otherwise to facilitate the operation of markets. Rules or regulations designed to prevent or restrict the marketing of certain goods or services on moral grounds make an economy less purely capitalistic, however. The more economically significant the markets interfered with, the more significant the departure from pure capitalism. For example, if parents mainly do not want their small children to work and would not permit them to work, then laws prohibiting child labour may not significantly affect the degree to which a society is capitalistic. But given the large proportion of the gross domestic product that is accounted for by health care, the Canadian health insurance scheme obviously marks a significant departure from capitalism.

The Nature of Democracy

To properly understand political arrangements, we need the concept of authority as well as the concept of power. *Power* is the *de facto* ability to influence events. *Authority* is a normative matter; authority is the right to influence events by performing the duties or by acting within the area of competence of a role that is defined by the rules of a (legitimate) institution. Governments have authority, but they also have power, and in a democracy, the people have both authority and power.

The citizens of a democracy occupy the role of voter, and, in this role, they are able to influence both the choice of government and also, directly or indirectly, the choice of government policy. In a democracy, moreover, each voter has authority *equal* to that of every other voter. No one's votes are weighted more heavily than the votes of others. We can imagine a system in which votes are assigned to people in proportion to their wealth. This is not a democracy because the system's voters are not given equal authority.

In a democracy, the composition of the government is fully determined by the votes of the voters, by the rules governing voting, and by the actions of those elected under the rules. We can imagine a state in which every citizen has a vote, and voting determines the composition of part of the government, but some citizens have authority in government as a result of their wealth, or as a birthright. These citizens might belong to a House of Lords, and one of them might be a king or a queen. This state would not be a democracy if these unelected members of government had more than merely nominal authority. It would be a plutocracy or an aristocracy or a monarchy. Hence, to the extent that the Queen or the Lords in Great Britain still have genuine authority over government policy, Great Britain falls short of being a democracy.

It matters who counts as a citizen in a society that purports to be a democracy. During the period of slavery in the United States, for example, slaves were not counted as 'citizens' and they were denied the vote. Of course, women were also denied the vote, but the fact that the slaves were not permitted to vote is enough to show that the United States was not a genuine democracy during that period. Because of this, I will replace the word 'citizen' in my account with the word 'member,' and I will stipulate that anyone is a 'member' of a state in the relevant sense who either was born there or intends and reasonably expects to live her life there. Many legal immigrants are 'members' in this sense, of course, and they may not actually be voters, yet they have the right to become voters by taking out citizenship. Young children are denied the right to vote despite being 'members,' but in a democracy they have the right to register as voters when they reach maturity. I will therefore say that, in a democracy, each 'member' in the technical sense I explained occupies the role of *voter*, or has the *right* to take up this role (on reaching maturity), and everyone in this role has equal authority with every other voter over the choice of government and also, directly or indirectly, over the choice of government policy.[5]

The equal authority of all voters is not enough to give us democracy, however, as we can see if we consider a case in which authority was equal but power was not. In the southern United States, during the era of Jim Crow, African Americans were prevented from voting even though, as citizens, they had the same right to vote as was possessed by whites. They had political authority, or potentially had it, but lacked corresponding power, because people with power over them either forcibly prevented them from voting or else used voter registration rules selectively to prevent them from registering to vote.

The example shows that there are ways in which political power can be unequal that compromise democracy. It nevertheless would be misleading to say, without qualification, that democracy requires that the members of the state have equal political power. Elections result in some individuals being elected to offices that give them authority and effective power that is lacked by others. Moreover, it is inevitable that some individuals will be more persuasive than others and be able, because of this, to exercise more power than others over political outcomes. These kinds of inequality of power do not compromise democracy because the point of democratic voting in elections of the kind at issue here is precisely to elect governments. That is, the point is to give rise to a situation in which some individuals occupy offices carrying extra authority and power. Moreover, a person who is persuaded to vote one way rather than another is still voting for her own reasons. There is no compromise of her autonomy as a voter. Furthermore, there is a sense in which strictly speaking she still has the same power over the outcome of the voting as every other voter. The situation is analogous to one in which several people cooperate to lift a heavy object under someone else's direction. There is a sense in which the director has the power to lift the object, but there is another sense in which he does not, for although he influences the actions of the others, each of them acts autonomously in doing his part in the lifting. The persuasive person has the ability to influence people's votes, so she has power in this respect. But assuming she exercises it subject to the concurrence of those whose votes she influences, she does not have power over them, and there is a sense in which each of them has as much power as anyone else.

These considerations suggest the importance of the citizens of a democracy being able to act autonomously in carrying out their role as voters, and of their being able to do so without being under the power of others or subject to their authority to interfere. Democracy does not require equalizing the power to influence outcomes of the political process, for the reasons I have given. It *does*, however, require that no voter have greater power to influence the outcomes of political decision making than any other voter unless either her extra power is the result of her occupying an office in accord with prior political decisions *or* her extra power stems simply from the fact that other voters have autonomously come to agree with her views.

Civil liberties guarantee that no one has authority to interfere with our voting. They also underwrite our autonomy in deciding how to vote by permitting free discussion of political matters under the protection of freedom of speech and assembly. Hence, one explanation of the importance of civil liberties in a democracy is that they help to ensure the relevant kind of equality of power and authority. Civil liberties do, however, place moral and – in some countries – legal constraints on the exercise of power by democratic majorities. There presumably are other limits on the exercise of democratic power. For example, a liberal democracy would guarantee freedom of religion. As we will see, one question that my argument brings to centre-stage is the question whether there are property rights that limit the rightful exercise of power by democratic majorities.

Political Power and the Marketing of Votes

Imagine a political system in which votes can be bought and sold, accumulated, and exercised in bulk. In this system, citizens are not assigned the role of voters, rather each is given ownership of the right to vote, which is treated as an ordinary kind of property. We would view this system as undemocratic, but it clearly is capitalistic. The prohibition on selling one's right to vote obviously is not justified as necessary to facilitate markets; rather it prevents the establishment of a market in votes. The example therefore illustrates the systemic conflict between democracy and capitalism. A brief discussion of it will help us better to understand democracy and the conflict between it and capitalism.

To begin with, it is not obvious what is wrong with the marketing of votes, and it is not obvious why we view it as undemocratic. The right to vote is valued more by some people than by others. Some people would rather have money than to have the vote, and other people would be willing to pay them for their right to vote. A market in votes would permit the transfer of money from the latter to the former in exchange for the transfer of the right to vote from the former to the latter, with the result that both are better off by their own lights. What would be wrong with the arrangement?

The system that permits the marketing of votes is similar to the system we imagined before in which people are assigned a number of votes proportional to their wealth, for it permits people to accumulate and exercise votes in proportion to their wealth. Yet unlike that other imaginary system, it assigns to each voter the same political authority *ab initio*, and each voter is free to decide what to do with her vote. She may exercise her vote herself, sell it to the highest bidder, sell it to the political party whose policies she supports, or simply waste it. If citizens are able to make this decision autonomously, and if the state prevents coercion and fraud in the market for votes, it may seem unobjectionable. And since citizens begin with the same political authority, the system may even seem compatible with democracy.

Of course, although the system that permits marketing votes initially gives all members equal authority over the political outcome, it does not ensure that all of them retain this authority, and it permits some people to accumulate more authority than others. But we now have to face the question why democracy requires that people retain equal political authority and not merely that they begin with equal authority. The system permits wealthy individuals to acquire more power over political outcomes than others have, but, arguably, their extra power arises through individuals' exercising autonomous choices. And we agreed before that in a democracy voters are able to decide autonomously what to do with their votes, not being under the power of others or subject to their authority to interfere. Why then should we prohibit people from selling their right to vote?

The problem is quite deep. I believe that a system of marketing votes is both unjust and undemocratic, but it is not obvious why this is so. I believe that democracy rules out the direct exchange of political power and authority for economic resources. In this sense, democracy insulates political power and authority from economic power. It therefore prohibits a market in votes. This is why democracy requires that people *retain* equal political authority and not merely that they begin with equal authority that they are then free to sell. Why is it, then, that democracy requires insulating political power and authority from the market in this way?

One might think that the reason is that democracy aims to equalize political power and authority and that in a society where there is economic inequality, a market in votes would defeat the aim to equalize political power. There is of course truth in this, but it does not get to the bottom of the issue. There are two problems. First, although the market in votes may lead to inequality in power, this is also true of elections, which result in inequality of political power once people are elected to offices. The proposal does not explain why it is not sufficient to allocate everyone equal political power *ab initio* and to permit the market to determine the final distribution. Second, and more important, I think we would object to the marketing of votes even in the absence of economic inequality. There is something democratically objectionable about a market for votes, it seems to me, quite independent of whether the buyers and sellers begin with equal economic power. This needs to be explained.

Democracy and Equality of Political Power

Power is the actual ability to influence events, and political power is the ability to influence political decisions. The point of democracy is to equalize political power. Democratic institutions assign political authority to the members of a society in a way that is intended to equalize political power. Democracy is a matter of degree, but a set of political institutions can be justified as democratic only to the degree that they tend to achieve an approximate equalization of political power. Any justification of democracy would have to be a justification for this idea that a state ought to be organized in a way that equalizes political power – in a way that equalizes the ability of the members to influence political decisions.

In my view, the reason to favour equalizing political power among the members of a society is essentially as follows: Each of us has the same basic stake in our society. We have no option but to belong to some society. And our society organizes the most basic aspects of our lives, which affect our life prospects in a fundamental way. This is the respect in which we each have the same stake, and a centrally important stake, in decisions that affect the future of our society. Moreover, the society is the property of no one and of no group other than itself, and it consists simply of all of its members. The state organizes society, and it is similarly the property of no one. If the state is legitimate, moreover, it serves the needs of the society that it organizes. And the state has power to control every aspect of our lives together that can be subjected to control. Given all of this – given that we must and need to belong to a society, given that a society needs to be organized into a state in order that control can be exercised over the controllable aspects of our collective life that it is permissible to control, given that the society is the property of no one and of no group other than itself, and given that its members all have the same stake and an important stake in its future – the society ought in fairness to be organized in a way that enables its members to have equal power over decisions as to how and whether to exercise state control over the controllable aspects of their lives that it is permissible to control.

This is the 'equal stakes argument.' It is my proposal as to why it is that society ought to be organized in a way that equalizes the political power of its members. The idea that we all have an equal stake in society is vague, and I would need to give it more attention in a fuller discussion. But for present purposes, the more important idea is that of equalizing political power. I argued before that democracy basically requires equalizing political power and authority. What I am now saying is that the equalizing of political power is the deeper goal.[6]

I said before that democracy does not require equalizing political power without qualification. What it requires is that no one have greater political power than anyone else unless her extra power stems from her occupying an office in accord with prior political decisions, or from the fact that other voters have autonomously come to agree with her views. The equal stakes argument explains these qualifications. In the first place, efficiency in carrying out political decisions and administering the state may require that some people have more power than others. Our equal stake in society implies an equal stake in society being well run. Hence, the state may permit us to make political decisions that result in some people having extra power without thereby failing to acknowledge our equal stake. Our equal stake in society is still properly acknowledged, provided that the power to elect people to positions carrying extra power is allocated equally among all of us, and provided that the people so elected only possess the extra power for limited periods of time. More obviously, in the second place, if everyone initially has equal political power, there is no failure to acknowledge our equal stake in society merely because some people may end up having more power than others if enough others come autonomously to agree with them and to vote accordingly.

Now, it should be plain that a market in votes would undermine the ideal of equalizing political power, so understood. It would permit some people to acquire greater political power than others by permitting them to buy and exercise more votes than they are initially assigned by the system. Any resulting inequalities in political power would be the result of uncoordinated individual decisions to buy and sell, not of political decisions that every member of society had an equal ability to influence. And the inequality would not be a result of people coming autonomously to agree as to how their votes ought to be exercised. It would be the result of some people deciding to sell to someone else the right to determine how to exercise the votes that initially belonged to them. Accordingly, a market in votes upsets the goal of assigning political power to people in a way that recognizes their equal stake in the society. The equal initial assignment of the right to vote in a system that permits the marketing of votes does not equalize political power. This is the reason that democracy prohibits the system that allows marketing votes.[7]

The familiar institutions of democracy – institutions that assign the right to vote to each citizen and that guarantee civil liberties – can be justified on the basis that they lead to at least an approximate equalization of political power. But the essence of democracy is the institutionalization of people's equal stake in society. Hence, if there are circumstances in which the familiar democratic institutions are insufficient to equalize political power in a way that recognizes people's equal stake in society, democracy might require more than, or something different from, the typical institutions. This idea will be important in what follows. I will argue that democracy argues against permitting economic inequality of the kind that is produced by capitalism to affect politics. The reason for this is the same as the reason that democracy forbids the marketing of votes.

Capitalism and Political Inequality

Capitalism tends to produce significant inequality in income and wealth. It is not for me as a philosopher to attempt to explain why capitalism leads to such inequality. The important thing is that inequality is unavoidable in capitalistic economies given the facts of human nature.

People would have to be quite different from the way they actually are in order for capitalism *not* to lead to inequality. First, people would have to have perfectly interchangeable talents. Otherwise someone could have a talent that was much in demand, and by properly exercising it, that person could do much better economically than people with talents that are less in demand. Second, people would have to desire above all else to maximize their economic benefits. Otherwise, a person who could do quite well economically in a certain occupation – say, being a neurosurgeon – might decide to do something else instead – say, go surfing – with the result that she does less well than someone else who takes up neurosurgery. Third, people would have to have complete information about the economy. Otherwise, people might lack information about how to maximize their benefit. Some might do better simply because they have information that others lack. It is easy enough to see that differences in people's knowledge and understanding, differences in the marketability of talents, and differences in the degree to which people desire to do well economically, all contribute to economic inequality in a capitalistic economy.[8]

There are of course other factors that contribute to inequality, includ-

ing racial and gender discrimination, differences in educational opportunity, and the like. I am stressing the obviously unchangeable factors
because I want it to be understood that the fact that capitalism leads to
inequality results from facts about capitalism and about ourselves that
cannot be changed. We are not going to come to be fully informed
about the economy, or to have perfectly interchangeable talents, or to
care about nothing but our economic success. Inequality in economic
benefit is the outcome of market interaction in the real world, and it
will always be thus.

The relevance of this to democracy is that money can be used to purchase political power. Because of this, the wealthy have more power
over political outcomes than is possessed by others. The three most
important sources of this extra power appear to be the following.[9]

First is the cost of political campaigning in large complex societies.
In the United States, for example, the *New York Times* estimated that the
1996 presidential campaign cost between $600 million and $1 billion
and that a successful campaign for a seat in the Senate cost at least $5
million and went as high as $30 million in some states. Even a cam-
paign for a seat in the House of Representatives can cost $2 million.[10]
Given this, a wealthy person obviously has immediate advantages
over less wealthy people who might be interested in running for office.
If she is sufficiently wealthy, she can simply attempt a campaign without being dependent on contributions from sources other than her own
bank account, and if she does this, she will not be forced to modify her
platform in order to gain financial backing for her campaign. Ross
Perot's wealth enabled him to catapult to the forefront of attention in
the 1992 U.S. presidential campaign. He was able to some degree to
change the focus of debate in the election because of the stress he chose
to place on the deficit. Another example is Michael Huffington's failed
campaign in 1994 for a U.S. Senate seat from California. Although he
was initially unknown, and 'apparently inept,' he very nearly won,
after spending $28 million of his own money.[11] These failed campaigns
are not counter-examples to what I am arguing, for it is not part of my
argument that the rich always succeed. All I am arguing is that the
wealthy have more than their fair share of political power. And this is
the case despite the existence of restrictions on contributions to elec-
toral campaigns.

Given the cost of campaigning for office, moreover, every candidate
who is not personally wealthy is dependent in part on wealthy people
and capitalist business to finance his campaign. According to a private

research group, 'business' was the largest source of campaign contributions in the 1996 federal elections in the United States, contributing an estimated $242 million. As for contributions of $200 or more from individuals, the research group estimated that $13.3 million was raised in the Upper East Side of Manhattan alone, and the top ten zip code areas ranked in order of the amount contributed by their residents included five areas in Manhattan's upper east and west sides, Beverley Hills's famous zip code, 90210, two of Washington's most tony areas, as well as Century City in Los Angeles, and Palm Beach, Florida. Organized labour contributed about $35 million to the campaign.[12] But this is not really an example of a way that ordinary people can influence politics under capitalism, since, for one thing, it is not clear that labour organizations would be permitted under a pure form of capitalism, and, for another thing, the rank and file does not really control the budgets of organized labour.

That politicians cannot be elected in most cases without support from wealthy contributors or businesses means that they need to ensure that their platforms will attract support. They need to argue for positions that are agreeable to the beneficiaries of capitalism, and once in office, they need to support government policies that are favourable to business. These are generalizations, of course, for some of the wealthy do have social consciences and some are even socialists. The claim is simply that wealth enables one to exercise an extra measure of influence beyond one's fair share. In other words, not only do the wealthy have more influence over who wins elections, but because of that fact, they have far greater influence over what ideas come to be on the political agenda.[13]

Second, those who control the productive apparatus of a capitalist economy have an extra measure of power, for they can use covert threats and promises in attempts to achieve political results that are favourable to them. In some cases they can use explicit threats and promises. If political outcomes are contrary to their interests, they can often move their assets to another jurisdiction, and often be welcomed there for the jobs and tax dollars they bring with them. For example, an entrepreneur can threaten to close a factory that is a major employer of the voters in a particular community, and such threats obviously can affect people's votes or the policy of the government. Since government in a capitalist economy has no direct control over industry, it may need to offer incentives to industry, so-called corporate welfare, such as special tax breaks for industries that remain in regions where there is high unemployment. New Brunswick has been criticized by other provinces for offering incentives to industries that will locate there. The other side of the coin is that industries can exact corporate welfare by indicating that without it they might want or need to move, or to close shop. Canadian Airlines recently attempted to gain special treatment from governments in order to remain in business. Of course, such special treatments themselves would be departures from a pure form of capitalism. An unmitigated capitalism is not necessarily in the interest of the wealthy or of the captains of industry.

An interesting example from recent Canadian history is the movement of corporate head offices out of Montreal because of concerns about the economic effects if Quebec decides to secede from Canada. Montreal has lost a net total of 384 head offices since 1977. During the 1995 referendum campaign, Laurent Beaudoin, the federalist chairman of Bombardier Corporation, first said that Bombardier could move out of Quebec in the event of a 'Yes' vote, and then withdrew his remark in the face of criticism.[14] It may well be that secession would be bad for business in Quebec, and it may well be that corporations are rational to move for this reason and that voters are rational to take this into account in deciding whether to favour secession. My argument does not require that there be an intention on the part of corporations to influence the outcome of elections in Quebec by moving or threatening to move their offices. I am merely saying that the economic power of the wealthy and of those who control corporations in a capitalist economy gives them an ability to affect political decisions that is out of proportion to their numbers. This is true whether or not they intend to use their ability.

Third, the wealthy can affect the political process by buying special access to or control of the mass media, such as television stations and networks and newspapers, and by creating, or controlling through contributions, other institutions that shape political opinion, such as the 'think tanks.' An example is Ross Perot's purchase of half-hour time slots on the major television networks in the United States, which he used to argue for his point of view on the presidential election. A better example is Conrad Black's 1998 creation of the *National Post*, a newspaper that is circulated nationally in Canada. Black had acquired Southam Press in 1996, which already gave him control of 43 per cent of Canada's newspaper circulation, including the major papers in the largest cities in the country except Toronto.[15] In 1998, Southam acquired the *Financial Post*, Canada's major financial newspaper, which gave Black a national subscription base on which to build the *National Post*. After three months of publication, Southam announced that the *National Post* had the third largest readership among Canadian newspapers.[16] According to coverage in the Toronto *Globe and Mail*, editorial policies of Southam papers began changing soon after Black's purchase of the chain. In 1996, Black said that the editorial views of Southam papers were 'soft, left, bland, envious, mediocre pap.' In 1997, in the words of the *Globe and Mail*, the membership of the new editorial board at the *Ottawa Citizen*, for example, 'reads like a conservative think-tank,' and the views expressed in its editorials 'now often reflect Black's staunchly pro-business, anti-government opinions.'[17] It is arguable that Black's policies will improve the quality of Southam papers. It is also arguable that Canada will benefit from having a strong new national newspaper. I do not want to claim otherwise. I am merely claiming that wealthy individuals like Perot and Black have more than their fair share of political power because they can purchase special access to or control of institutions that shape political opinion, such as mass circulation newspapers.

Capitalism and Democracy

I said before that democracy is compatible with *certain* differences in political power – differences that arise from voting, since political offices carry special powers, and differences that stem simply from the varying abilities of individuals to influence the autonomous voting of others. It may seem that the inequalities of political power that I have been illustrating are simply examples of the second kind of inequality, inequality in ability of people to influence the autonomous decisions of voters.

This view is most plausible in cases where wealthy persons purchase access to or control of the mass media. The extra power acquired by wealthy persons in these cases is the power to express their opinions in a widely available medium and to control what other opinions are expressed in the medium. Yet voters remain free to evaluate these opinions and to make up their own minds about what weight to give them in deciding how to vote. Conrad Black might claim, for instance, that the influence he exerts over the voters as a result of owning so many newspapers in Canada is no different in kind from the influence exerted by a man standing on a soapbox at the corner. According to *Maclean's* magazine's coverage of the matter, Black actually claims in effect that he exerts *less* influence than the man on the soapbox, for he says that he never interferes with editorial policy at any paper he owns. Ironically, he said this in an article that he ordered all of his 58 newspapers to print.[18]

Although we need to recognize the intelligence of voters and their ability to evaluate the opinions to which they are exposed, we must not be naive. If a person has the power to control the range of opinions and issues that are given serious coverage in the major newspapers in most of the country, then even if readers respond intelligently in evaluating those opinions, the person with this power still is controlling the political agenda to some large degree, and power over the agenda is already political power. (It is known, for example, that the order in which issues are voted on can determine the outcome in cases where voters' aggregated preferences have a cyclical pattern.) If certain opinions are not discussed seriously in the major media, they may not be taken seriously by most voters who, because they have limited time to research political matters, accept the implicit verdict of the media as to what range of ideas is worth serious attention. In practice, this may mean that other ideas simply are not taken seriously, which means in effect that they are not political contenders even before voting begins. When a person's control over the media is extensive enough to enable him to set the agenda of serious discussion in widespread regions of the country, he already is exerting control over the range of possible political outcomes. He clearly, then, has the ability to influence political outcomes to a degree that exceeds the ability of others.

Milton Friedman would disagree. He argues that 'inequality of wealth' helps to preserve political freedom because wealthy patrons might support campaigns for unpopular political views that would otherwise not be taken seriously. Patrons aside, a 'competitive publisher ... cannot afford to publish only writing with which he personally agrees.' He must publish writing that will yield a satisfactory return on his investment.[19] Friedman is correct in outline, but note that his argument depends on acknowledging that the wealthy have more political power than others have, for only a wealthy person can become a patron of unpopular political ideas. Also, although a publisher must sell his newspapers or books, a publisher like Conrad Black can publish ideas that might not otherwise be published, or refuse to publish ideas that would otherwise be published, without running a significant risk of losing sales and advertising revenue because he controls the large papers that have the sports, business, and cultural coverage that people

want. Of course, he can subsidize the publication of arguments in support of the capitalist *status quo* but my argument does not depend on
what kind of ideas he chooses to subsidize. My point is that the ability
of the wealthy to subsidize publication – to become patrons, for example – gives them political power not possessed by others.

In some cases, there is plausibility to the idea that the 'promises' and
'threats' that can be used by the wealthy or by corporations to influence voting are unobjectionable because they are merely attempts to
influence the autonomous decisions of voters by giving them reasons
to vote one way rather than another. It may be said that the so-called
threats and promises are merely reports of the expected consequences
of various possible outcomes of voting. Suppose that a corporation will
go out of business if its taxes are not reduced, and suppose that an
executive brings this to the attention of voters. This might be called a
'threat.' But it might be said that the resulting vote about the tax break
is no more controlled by the corporation than a vote is controlled in
any other case where people's votes are affected by their understanding of what is likely to result from a decision.

The underlying issue raised here is the quite difficult one of distinguishing between coerced and uncoerced decisions. When a bandit
says, 'Your money or your life,' the rational person gives over his
money. But the decision is not autonomous, for it is coerced. In a full
discussion of the issue raised here, then, I would need to discuss
whether the kinds of threats and promises that are made by corporations in an effort to affect voting are coercive.[20] Threats and promises
that are coercive interfere with the autonomy of voters, and they are
illicit exercises of power. Those that are not coercive, however, can be
viewed simply as announcements of the consequences to be expected
from options faced by the government. Although I cannot go into
detail, I think it is clear that, at least in some cases, corporations are not
merely announcing consequences that will come about whatever they
decide to do, but they are announcing their choice to take a certain
action if governments or voters make certain decisions. At least in
some cases, corporations are acting coercively.

The most straightforward way in which wealth gives a person the
ability to purchase more than her fair share of political influence is
related to the cost of election campaigning. The very wealthy have the
ability to finance their own campaigns, and the wealthy have the ability
to gain favour with politicians who are not themselves wealthy by contributing to their campaign funds. Because of this, the wealthy have a

greater ability than the less well-off do to be elected or to have an impact on who gets elected. And because of this, as I said before, they also have a greater influence over the content of the political agenda.

I argued before that democracy aims at root to equalize political power. Each member of society has the same fundamental stake in the society and therefore should have the same power to influence decisions about its future. Capitalism, however, gives rise to economic inequality, and wealth enables a person to purchase extra influence over political decisions. The effect of marrying democracy with capitalism, then, is a system in which the distribution of political power reflects to a large extent people's varying economic success rather than their equal stake in the society. This is a fundamental conflict between capitalism and democracy.

Conclusion

I have suggested that democracies aim to equalize political power by creating institutions that equalize political authority and guarantee civil liberties. The equalization of political power is a requirement of fairness because people have an equal stake in society. I have argued that if the point of democracy is in this way to acknowledge fairly our equal stake in society, then the economic inequality that arises in capitalism undermines democracy. It gives the wealthy greater political power than is had by most others despite the fact that all have an equal stake in the future of society.

There remains the need for more analysis of some of the questions I have raised. I have not attempted to provide a metric of political power. Also, I have not attempted to explain fully the difference between objectionable forms of influence on people's political decisions and unobjectionable forms. I have relied on unanalysed notions of autonomy and coercion.

There also remains a need to say what ought to be done in face of this conflict between capitalism and democracy. On the one hand, *if* there are property rights with enough weight to make it unjust to interfere with the distribution of income and wealth brought about by capitalistic markets, then democracy must in justice give way to capitalism. We must accept that political power cannot rightfully be equalized, or at least that there are significant moral constraints on equalizing it. However, I do not believe anyone has established the existence of property rights of this nature. If, on the other hand, property rights are no barrier to redistribution designed to equalize political power, then, to the extent that we aim to achieve the underlying goal of democracy, we must either reduce the economic inequality that undermines democracy or somehow insulate the political system from that inequality. In an attempt to insulate the political system, we might try to reform election campaign finance laws and to regulate newspaper ownership.[21] I think we need to take actions of both kinds. But we also have reasons, including independent reasons, to favour efforts to reduce economic inequality, and we know that it will be difficult to make effective democratizing reforms to the political system as long as there continues to be significant economic inequality.

The reason we have election campaign finance laws, imperfect though they are, is surely because we want to try to equalize political power. But we need to go further, and we need to do so for the very reason that we would oppose allowing people to buy and sell the right to vote.

We have seen that capitalism is a matter of degree; it is not an all-or-nothing affair. It has attractive features, such as its efficient use of markets to adjust supply to demand. But we may be able to accept these features without accepting the less attractive features of capitalism, such as extreme economic inequality. Democracy is also a matter of degree in that the institutional arrangements of society can do better or worse at guaranteeing equality of political power. We need to realize that if we combine a relatively untamed form of capitalism with the mere institutional clothing of democracy, we may fail to achieve the essence of democracy, which is a political system that is fair, given our equal stake in our shared society. It may not be realistic to hope to achieve this goal fully, given the tension between it and our economic aspirations of prosperity, full employment, and the banishment of need. Yet it would be a mistake to ignore this tension, and we must not be too quick to conclude that an untamed capitalism is required in order to achieve these economic goals.

Notes

This chapter was written with the assistance of a fellowship from the Centre for Applied Ethics, University of British Columbia. I am grateful to Harry Brighouse and Jan Narveson for helpful comments on an earlier draft.

1 Milton Friedman (with the assistance of Rose Friedman), *Capitalism and Freedom* (Chicago: University of Chicago Press, 1962), 9.

2 Spillover costs are usually called 'external costs.' This notion is explained in standard introductory texts in economics.

3 'Market failure' is another notion that is explained in standard introductory texts in economics.

4 Government intervention may not be necessary to enforce regulations of all of the kinds at issue here. Perhaps some could be enforced by voluntary organizations.

5 'Guest' workers in Germany, and certain other countries, unlike immigrants in Canada and the United States, lack the right to become citizens. Yet, depending on the exact nature of the laws governing the status of guest worker, many guest workers will be 'members' in the relevant sense. If so, Germany does not qualify as a genuine democracy.

6 Thomas Christiano argues that democracy is justified because justice requires equalizing political power. See his *The Rule of Many: Fundamental Issues in Democratic Theory* (Boulder, CO: Westview, 1996). Harry Brighouse argues for a principle he calls, 'the principle of equality of political influence,' in 'Egalitarianism and Equal Availability of Political Influence,' *Journal of Political Philosophy*, 4/2 (1996), 118–41. Brighouse discusses the idea of buying and selling votes in his 'Political Equality and the Funding of Political Speech,' *Social Theory and Practice*, 21 (1995), 473–500.

7 Suppose the people vote autonomously to create a market in votes. Why would the resulting system be any less justified than a system that permits the voters to elect certain people to office? In both cases political inequalities result from a democratic political decision. But the same question could be raised about a case in which the people voted democratically to replace democracy with a dictatorship. It is a mistake to think that any decision that is reached by a democratic method can be justified as in accord with the underlying rationale of democracy. People who are elected to office can be removed at the next election, so the inequality remains in the control of the voters. In a system that permits the wealthy to purchase extra votes, however, the voters have no control over inequalities that may result.

8 Introductory economics texts contain discussions of these points.

9 I was helped with the thoughts in the following paragraphs by an unpublished essay by Harry Brighouse.

10 Max Frankel, 'TV Remedy for a TV Malady,' *New York Times Magazine*, 8 September (1996), 36–8. Quoted in Ronald Dworkin, 'The Curse of American Politics,' *New York Review of Books*, 17 Oct. (1996), 19.

11 Leslie Wayne, 'Hunting Cash, Candidates Follow the Bright Lights,' *New York Times*, 20 Oct. (1996), 5.

12 Ronald Dworkin, 'The Curse of American Politics,' *New York Review of Books*, 17 Oct. (1996), 19–24.

13 Harry Brighouse helped me with this sentence.

14 Konrad Yakabuski, 'Quebec Unshaken by Exodus,' *Globe and Mail*, 17 March (1997), B1 and B4.

15 Allan Fotheringham, 'One day, Conrad Will Buy Me – and Fire Me,' *Maclean's*, 25 November (1996), 132, and Jennifer Wells, 'He Styles Himself as the Saviour of Papers, but Critics Label Conrad Black as an Editorial Storm Trooper,' and 'Winds of Change,' *Maclean's*, 11 Nov. (1996), 56–62.

16 The announcement is found in a Southam press release dated 25 Jan. 1999. The text of the press release was found at www.southam.com.

17 Douglas Saunders, 'Black's Citizen,' *Globe and Mail*, 1 March (1997), C1, C3.

18 See the articles in *Maclean's* by Fotheringham and Wells that are cited above.

19 Milton Friedman, *Capitalism and Freedom*, 17.

20 See David Zimmerman, 'Coercive Wage Offers,' *Philosophy and Public Affairs*, 10 (1981), 121–45.

21 For a discussion of more imaginative ideas for reforms that to some extent would insulate politics from economic inequality, see Harry Brighouse, 'Political Equality and the Funding of Political Speech.'

4

Gender and the 'Separative Self' in Economics, Ethics, and Management

JULIE A. NELSON

The contemporary discipline of economics is often perceived as 'hard,' objective, and analytical, as compared to 'soft' areas of study such as those concerned with ethics, interpersonal skills, or communication. Moral arguments concerning capitalism often take one side or another of a similar dualism. On the one side are arguments about freedom and property rights belonging to the presumed autonomous individual, and discussions of environmental degradation in terms of discount rates and efficiency. Such arguments are often couched in terms of fundamentals and 'hard' analytical reasoning. On the other side are arguments for care and concern for the weak or less fortunate, and for harmony with the natural environment. These are often perceived as less fundamental, or 'soft' in their rationale.

This chapter argues that neither the high value given to certain kinds of models and methods within the discipline of economics, nor the ethical arguments for an individualist, extractive capitalism, rest on as firm bases as is commonly believed. Feminist research on the history of science, and on cultural associations between perceived value and perceived gender, helps to explain why some arguments are, without basis, considered more valuable than others. Feminist theory suggests new ways of looking at the acquisition of economic knowledge and at the functioning of economic systems.

The next several sections develop the argument in regard to how knowledge and skills are valued within the academic discipline of economics, and especially as this in turn affects the field of administrative studies. Once the bias of contemporary economics towards a notion of a radically autonomous agent – what I will call a 'separative self' – is understood, the implications of this bias for discussions of the ethical basis of capitalism will be, more briefly, explored.

Valuation of Knowledge and Skills

The Trent approach ... encourages students to develop those skills in communication, group work, and creative problem solving which are proving to be a key to competitiveness and career opportunities ... A distinctly human focus is indeed what especially makes the Trent approach stand out.

['Administrative Studies: The Trent Approach' (Peterborough: Trent University, n.d.)]

In a brochure promoting its Administrative Studies Program, Trent University claims that its approach to educating students is distinctive. I would like to raise the question, however, of why a 'human approach' is considered 'distinctive.' Perhaps it is that the norm in many areas of academia, business, and government might be more like the following exchange penned by the famous business analyst, Scott Adams (creator of the Dilbert cartoon strip):

Manager: Alice, I'd like you to meet the newest member of my management team. Keith is highly qualified. He has a master's in Business Administration.

Alice: Very impressive. They must have taught you a lot about motivating employees.

Keith: No, not really.

Alice: Well ... you probably learned how to identify and hire good people, right?

Keith: That might have been optional reading.

Alice: Did you learn negotiation skills?

Keith: No.

Alice: Strategic thinking?

Keith: No.

Alice: Business writing?

Keith: No. It was mostly finance and accounting. And economics.

Alice: So, you're a highly qualified leader because ... you're good at math?

Keith: (Aside to Manager) What should I do here?

Manager: (Aside to Keith) In these situations I like to use swearing.

[Dilbert comic strip, 27 October 1996]

Academics and administrators alike often tend to hold analytical, technical, or mathematical skills in a certain awe. Meanwhile, interpersonal skills, skills in creative thinking, and writing and speaking skills (and, one may add, thoughtfulness about ethical considerations), are sometimes looked upon as 'soft' qualifications – presumably less rigorous, and less difficult to obtain, than 'hard' skills in economic planning or finance. Anyone considering a career in administration should already be aware that, when comparing different kinds of managerial positions, these values are still quite evident. Personnel management, for example, is often thought to require more qualitative, human-centred, and relational skills. Financial or purchasing management are seen as requiring more quantitative, detached, or abstract analysis. While the rewards to these skills may be changing over time, personnel managers' salaries are on average still lower than financial and purchasing managers' salaries, in current U.S. data.[1] Personnel managers and public relations managers were also historically less well placed for movement up to top management than managers of production or finance, perhaps because the jobs were considered to involve more interpersonal, and less policy-making, skills.[2]

To buck this tendency towards valuing impersonal and technical skills over personal and relational skills, then, *is* to be distinctive. Why is this so? Perhaps this valuation is justified by real productivity advantages in the workplace, when managers with different skills are compared either across or within various types of managerial positions. Perhaps knowing how to choose and motivate employees is just *not* as important as understanding marginal cost curves or present value.

An alternative explanation, however, is that this ranking has more to do with deeply ingrained perceptions, habits of thought, and cultural beliefs than with any real differences in quality or productivity. My argument will be that these valuations are not primarily based on effectiveness, but on exactly such subjective biases. These biases, I will argue, have to do with cultural understandings of gender. One may note, for example, in the context of management positions, that the fields of personnel and public relations management, mentioned above, besides being relatively low paid, also tend to be disproportionately female.[3]

I would like to explore the ties among gender, value, and different kinds of knowledge and skills from within the context of my own discipline, economics. Since economists are on the 'hard,' analytical side of the stereotypic divide I have described, it may seem odd that *I* am doing this questioning. I have a creditable publishing record in quantitative economics, and teach subjects like statistics and econometrics. I would not inflict these subjects on my students if I did not think they had some value. My point is not that economics as currently taught has no value, but only that its claim to *centrality* is suspect, and that the content of courses in economic theory leaves much to be desired. I do not think that current mainstream economics is too rigorous; I think it is not rigorous enough. Various value-laden and partial – and masculine-gendered – perspectives have heretofore been mistakenly perceived as value-free and impartial. Traditionally male-associated activities have taken centre-stage as the subject matter of study and training, while models and techniques have reflected a historical and psychological tendency to value masculine-associated characteristics and ideals over those that are feminine-associated. In answer to the question 'Is economics gender-biased?' we can say that *economics, as currently practised, is masculine-biased.*

Let me lay out the argument, step by step, beginning by examining the relationship of gender to thinking about what it is that is valuable to know.[4]

Gender and Knowledge

The analysis of links between modern Western social beliefs about gender and about types of knowledge was the accomplishment of groundbreaking works by feminist scholars starting in the 1980s, such as the book *Reflections on Gender and Science* by physicist Evelyn Fox Keller[5] and *The Science Question in Feminism* by philosopher Sandra Harding.[6] Objectivity, separation, logical consistency, individual accomplishment, mathematics, abstraction, lack of emotion, and science itself have long been culturally associated with rigor, hardness – and masculinity. At the same time, subjectivity, connection, 'intuitive' understanding, cooperation, qualitative analysis, concreteness, emotion, and nature have often been associated with weakness, softness – and femininity. Sandra Harding argued:

> Mind vs nature and the body, reason vs emotion and social commitment, subject vs object and objectivity vs subjectivity, the abstract and the general vs the concrete and particular – in each case we are told that the former must dominate the latter lest human life be overwhelmed by irrational and alien forces, forces symbolized in science as the feminine. All these dichotomies play important roles in the intellectual structures of science, and all appear to be associated both historically and in contemporary psyches with distinctively masculine sexual and gender identity projects.[7]

That is, scientific knowledge has been socially constructed to conform to a particular image of masculinity.

Such associations were sometimes explicit in the language used by the early scientists to define their endeavour. Henry Oldenburg, an early secretary of the British Royal Society, stated that the intent of the society was to 'raise a masculine Philosophy ... whereby the Mind of Man may be ennobled with the knowledge of Solid Truths.'[8] The relation of masculine science to feminine nature is often expressed in terms of domination, as in Francis Bacon's words, 'I am come in very truth leading to you Nature with all her children to bind her to your service and make her your slave.'[9]

The Gender of Contemporary Economics

The way in which these gender associations are played out in contemporary economics may be laid out in a picture such as in Table 4.1. Economic training teaches one that the subjects, characteristics of methods, and assumptions laid out in the left-hand column are, if not 'right' in some metaphysical sense, at least 'more important than' or 'more rigorous than' the corresponding terms in the right-hand column. The gender association of the left-hand column tends to be, at least in modern Western and English-speaking societies, distinctly that of masculinity.[11] Rather than economics being concerned with provisioning, or how people organize themselves to provide for their lives, in general, the discipline of economics has come to be *defined* by the left-hand-side terms. For some, it is the study of markets. For others, mathematical rational choice models define the field.

If one believes that the current definitions and methods of economics come from outside of human communities – perhaps mandated by divine intervention – then of course the idea that such gender association constitutes a harmful *bias* will seem nonsensical. But if we allow that economic practice is human practice, developed and refined within human communities, then the possibility must be admitted that human limitations, interests, and perceptual biases will have effects on the culture of economics.

How, then, might gender influence economics? While women were historically excluded from the community of scholars, I think we need to use considerable caution in moving from the observation of women's exclusion to conclusions about the mechanisms by which gender biases take root. Feminist scholars make a subtle but important

Table 4.1. The Contemporary Definition of Economics[10]

Core	Margin
Domain	
Public (market and government)	Private (family)
Individual agents	Society, institutions
Efficiency	Equity
Methods	
Rigorous	Intuitive
Precise	Vague
Objective	Subjective
Scientific	Non-scientific
Detached	Committed
Mathematical	Verbal
Formal	Informal
Abstract	Concrete
Key assumptions	
Individual	Social
Self-interested	Other-interested
Autonomous	Dependent
Rational	Emotional
Acts by choice	Acts by nature
Gender/sex associations	
Masculine	Feminine
Men	Women

distinction between *sex* and *gender*. *Sex*, as the term is generally used in feminist scholarship, refers to biological differences between males and females. *Gender*, on the other hand, refers to the associations, stereotypes, and social patterns that a culture constructs on the basis of actual or perceived differences between men and women.

Masculine bias in the academic disciplines is primarily an issue of gender, not of sex. While the entrance of more women into economics and administration may contribute to the transformation of these fields, this is *not* primarily because women 'bring something different' to the field by virtue of femaleness. Most female economists I know do pretty much the same kind of work as male economists. Similarly, while there is some discussion of differences in management styles between men and women, many studies suggest that much of the difference in behaviour by sex, to the extent difference is observed at all, may be more a result of differences in occupational experiences and job status than in biology or even in socialization.[12] Even scholars associated with the notion that 'women think differently,' such as Carol Gilligan (author of the landmark book, *In A Different Voice*),[13] on closer inspection can often be recognized to see gendered behaviour as overlapping between the sexes, and dynamic over the life cycle and changes in circumstances, instead of as fixed traits. Rather than 'women bringing something different,' then, the causality as I see it is that illumination of gender biases at the level of the social structure makes gender biases at other levels – levels of belief and culture – more visible as well. To say that 'contemporary economics is masculine,' then, is to say that it reflects social beliefs about masculinity, not that it reflects the maleness of its traditional practitioners. This takes the emphasis away from differences between men and women and puts it on the common achievements that might be made by both men and women if sexism, that is, the systematic devaluation of women and things associated with women, were to be overcome.

Towards a More Adequate Analysis

Simple recognition that the characteristics most highly valued in economics have particularly masculine gender associations does not, however, suggest a unique response for scholars concerned with the quality of economic research and teaching. One response might be to endorse this association so that we can go on doing as we have always done. If this is masculine, so be it. The only alternative to masculine economics, our usual way of thinking about gender tells us, would be emasculated and impotent.

Another response might be to turn the tables, and seek to replace hard, objective, active androcentric (or 'male-centred') practices with soft, subjective, passive practices, perhaps identified as gynocentric (or 'women-centred'). One might focus on cooperation, for example, instead of competition, and eschew all quantitative methods in favour of qualitative ones. While such outcomes might be appealing to some, such a response merely trades one set of biases for another.

A third approach is the one I adopt.[14] It does not require endorsing one side or the other of the masculine/feminine dualism. The key to this approach lies in an unlinking of our judgments about value – that is, about what is meritorious or less meritorious in our practices – from our perceptions of gender.

The notion that masculine economics is 'good' economics (and that, in turn, management is best centred around the masculine discipline of economics) depends on a general cultural association of masculinity with superiority and femininity with inferiority, or, in other words, a mental linking of value (superior/inferior) and gender (masculine/feminine) dualisms:

Masculine (+)   Feminine (−)

Anyone who might question the asymmetry of this linking, preferring, perhaps, to think of gender differences in terms of a more benign complementarity, should ponder some of the more obvious manifestations of asymmetry in the social domain. Rough 'tomboy' girls are socially acceptable and even praised, but woe to the gentle-natured boy who is labelled a 'sissy'; a woman may wear pants, but a man may not wear a skirt. The sexist association of femininity with lesser worth implicit in such judgments, it should be noted, is not a matter of isolated personal beliefs but rather a matter of cultural and even cognitive habit.

Consider the different interpretations we can make if we think of gender and value, instead of as marking out the same space, as operating in distinct dimensions. Then we can think of there being both valuable and harmful aspects to qualities culturally associated with masculinity, as well as both valuable and harmful aspects to traits associated with femininity (see Figure 1).

Figure 1.

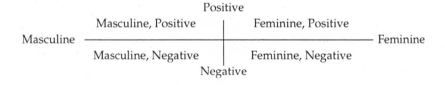

Consider, for example, the idea that a 'hard' economics is clearly preferable to a 'soft' economics. This judgment relies on an association of hardness with valuable, masculine-associated *strength*, and softness with inferior, feminine-associated *weakness*. However, hardness may also mean *rigidity*, just as softness may also imply *flexibility* (see Figure 2).

Figure 2.

M+	F+
Strong–hard	Flexible–soft
M−	F−
Rigid–hard	Weak–soft

A pursuit of masculine hardness that spurns all association with femininity (and hence with flexibility) can lead to rigidity, just as surely as a pursuit of feminine softness (without corresponding strength) leads to weakness. There is no benefit to 'specialization' on the side of one gender: neither rigidity nor weakness, the two extremes of hardness and softness, are desirable. Together, in fact, they define 'brittleness.' There is benefit, however, from exploiting the positive complementarity. Strength tempered with flexibility would yield a balanced and resilient economics.

The way in which the English language constrains anglophones' thinking about feminine-associated strengths and masculine-associated weaknesses, in a general sense, can be seen by thinking about the word 'virility,' which means 'manly vigour.' This is clearly an M+ term, and the F− term denoting its lack is 'emasculation.' Both these terms are in common use. Yet what about womanly vigour? Few native English-speakers have even heard of the term 'muliebrity,' defined in some dictionaries as the feminine 'correlative of virility.' A term for the lack of womanly vigour does not seem to exist. (See Figure 3.) By parallel to 'emasculation,' one would expect this to be 'effemination,' but 'effeminate' means an overabundance of (denigrated) feminine traits, not a lack of womanly vigour.

Economic Models

Consider the core economic model, which forms the basis of all mainstream economics courses. At the centre of this model is the character of the rational, autonomous, self-interested agent, successfully making optimizing choices subject to exogenously imposed constraints. In microeconomics classes, complex, multi-person organizations such as households and firms are commonly characterized only in terms of this unitary 'agent.' In macroeconomics and international economics

Figure 3.

M+ Virility	F+ Muliebrity
M− ?	F− Emasculation

classes, whole national economies are often subsumed into 'representative consumers,' agents with identifiable indifference curves.

This is not to say that all practising economists believe that humans are no more than *homo economicus*, and that complex organizations are no more than the immanent incarnations of *homo economicus*'s transcendent rationality (although there are a few true believers). Nevertheless, this model of behaviour is perceived as being the most useful and most rigorously objective starting point for analysis. Consider, however, the gendered biases implicit in taking this image as representative of what is important about economic behaviour.

In adopting this conception, economists have carried out the suggestion of Thomas Hobbes,[15] who wrote, 'Let us consider men ... as if but even now sprung out of the earth, and suddenly, like mushrooms, come to full maturity, without all kind of engagement to each other.' Economic man springs up fully formed, with preferences fully developed, and is fully active and self-contained. The economic agent has no childhood or old age, no dependence on anyone, and no responsibility for anyone but himself. The environment has no effect on him but rather is merely the passive material over which his rationality has play. Any interpersonal relations our agent may have are carefully hidden by the assumption that our agents are 'heads' of households, or that firms can be represented by the decisions of a single manager.

Yet if we think about it, humans do not simply spring out of the earth. Humans are born of women, nurtured and cared for as dependent children and when aged or ill, socialized into family and community groups, and are perpetually dependent on nourishment and a home to sustain life. These aspects of human life, whose neglect is often justified by the argument that they are unimportant, or intellectually uninteresting, or merely natural, are, not just coincidentally, the areas of life thought of as 'women's work.' For example, in labour economics classes where the concept of 'human capital' is discussed, a

Figure 4.

M+ Individuated	F+ Connected
M− Isolated	F− Engulfed

common approach is to focus on the college-choice decision of the presumably autonomous young adult.[16] Somehow, the contributions of nutrition, socialization, and informal and formal education of children within families and schools to future productivity, is deemed too unimportant to mention. Even when some amount of interpersonal interaction or interdependence is acknowledged, the realms more closely associated with women often seem to disappear. Consider this discussion from an introductory textbook: 'The unit of analysis in economics is the individual ... [although] individuals group together to form collective organizations such as corporations, labour unions, and governments.'[17] Families are, apparently, too unimportant to mention.

Homo economicus is not a good description of either women or men. The myth of the totally autonomous man can be believed only if the traditional work of women in supporting him is blotted out of our minds, just as the myth of the totally dependent woman can only have cultural resonance if women's intelligence and decision-making capacities are systematically denied. Both the autonomous, rational, detached, masculine projection and the dependent, emotional, connected, feminine one are equally mythical and distorting. What is needed is a conception of identity that does not confuse gender with judgments about value, nor confuse constructions of gender with biological destiny. What is needed is a conception of *human* identity that can encompass both autonomy and dependence, individuation and relation, reason and emotion, as they are manifested in individuals of either sex, and worked out in complex social organizations. Such an identity could be described in as in Figure 4. The M−, isolated, mythical agent is the Hobbesian agent, unaffected by community, emotion, or bodily needs – what we might call a 'separative self.'[18] The F-, engulfed, mythical person could be thought of as, for example, the wife in the old 'husband as head' models of families, or the female secretary image in the old models of the business organization in which the male boss was presumed to call the shots. Such a secretary had identity only through her boss (e.g., 'Jim's girl'), and was invisible on any official diagrams of flows of authority. These masculine and feminine images are equally mythical, and equally unhealthy as ideals. Without the ceaseless networking and 'smoothing over' of the stereotypical female assistant, for example, the stereotypical male 'work' would never have been able to go on. It is time for the perceptual biases that divided tasks into male/instrumental and female/expressive to be replaced with a perception of both males and females doing tasks that combine process and product orientation in complex ways. I call this notion of persons who are both individuated and connected, a notion of 'persons-in-relation.'

In addition, human motivations include emotional motivations, related to such things as self-perception, prestige, envy, concern, and loyalty. Since emotions, as well, are in the traditionally feminine realm, neglect of their consideration in mainstream models of worker or manager behaviour is not surprising. Yet one need not reinvent the wheel while looking for ways of building more satisfactory models that do not rely on the image of the isolated self. Consider the standard theory, taught in intermediate microeconomics, that says that wages are determined by marginal products. In contrast stands George Akerlof's and Janet Yellen's theory of efficiency wages as based on fairness.[19] In their model, agents are not hyperrational, isolated monads, but rather human beings capable of 'emotions such as "concern for fairness,"' or jealousy[20] and very concerned with their sphere of personal connections. Feminist analysis suggests that the current general neglect of social and emotional dimensions of human behaviour in economics should be considered a serious limitation, rather than a sign of rigor.

Economic Methods

While models of individual rational choice could conceivably be expressed and analyzed in a purely verbal manner, it seems almost a tautology to say that in the economics discipline quality *in method* is identified primarily with mathematical rigor. Strict adherence to rules of logic and mathematics, formalization in the presentation of assumptions and models, sophistication in the application of econometric techniques – these are the factors, in many people's minds, that set economics apart from 'softer' fields like sociology or political science. Use of formal and mathematical techniques is also often presumed to

Figure 5.

M+ Precise	F+ Rich
M− Thin	F− Vague

assure the objectivity of economic results. Within academic research, abstract and highly formalized analysis is often valued over concrete and detailed empirical work, and, while good writing and verbal analysis do not go entirely unrewarded, they are usually considered to be largely auxiliary to the real analysis. The result, for undergraduate and master's level classes, is an emphasis on graphs, algebra, and statistical theory, and a de-emphasis on institutions, writing skills, and data gathering.

The earlier-mentioned scholarship about the relation of gender and science suggests that such narrow views of knowledge and rationality are holdovers from a crisis about masculinity during the early years of the development of modern science, particularly manifested in the ascendancy of Cartesian philosophy. Far from protecting economics against biases, such a concentration on toughness and detachment hog-ties economists' methods of analysis. Emphasis on being hard, logical, scientific, and precise has served a valuable purpose, it is true, in guarding against analysis that is weak, illogical, unscientific, and vague. But if these are the *only* virtues we value in our practice, we are easy prey to other vices.

Emphasis on masculine hardness without flexibility can, as discussed above, turn into rigidity. Emphasis on logic, without sufficient attention to grasping the big picture, can lead to empty, out-of-touch exercises in pointless deduction. Scientific progress without attention to human values can serve inhuman ends. Arguments that have given up all richness for the sake of precision end up being very thin. For example, the emphasis on mathematics as the key to 'rigorous' understanding in economics, and the downplaying of language as having any importance to the business of knowledge seeking, can be understood using Figure 5. The left side highlights aspects of mathematical language and the right side aspects of common language. The advantage of the use of mathematics is the precision it supplies, as opposed to the vagueness or ambiguity that may be associated with words in all their diverse meanings. On the other hand, pure mathematics is precisely content-free; the application of mathematics to problems of human behaviour can come only through the use of mathematical formulae as metaphors for some real world phenomenon, and this drawing of analogies involves the use of words. In the process, meanings beyond that immediately present in the mathematical analogy will also be suggested. Mathematics can certainly be helpful in overcoming the failings of imprecise words, but, if concentration is put on maintaining the gender boundary rather than on recognizing the value boundary, the failure of thin, empty mathematics may sneak in unobserved. Including both masculine- and feminine-identified positive qualities, on the other hand, makes possible a practice that is flexible, attentive to context, humanistic, and rich as well as strong, logical, scientific, and precise.

The point is not that formalization and mathematics are wrong. The point is just that economists as a group tend to be prone to confusing formalization with knowledge, instead of seeing it as just one among many tools that might be instrumental in gaining knowledge. On the level of theory, for example, the problem is that economists are too often content with formalization per se and with a single model, and never move on to the next steps required for a science. For a formal model to actually contribute to knowledge it should aid our understanding (in ways significantly beyond what we could get from verbal reasoning alone), and explain the phenomena being studied better than alternative models when all are put up against the full range of the data. Should economists take more seriously this last challenge, we might find we need new types of data, and we may find that the formal models of rational individual choice (including, e.g., models of unitary firms and perfect competition) are less helpful than we expected, especially in their most sophisticated forms. Meanwhile, we might find that less precisely stated but richer models should not be dismissed because of a gender-biased misconception about the nature of knowledge, but that they rather may hold ideas which deserve exploration.

On the level of empirical work, economists have also tended to value masculine-identified formality, precision, and abstraction over feminine-identified less formal, less clear-cut, and more concrete issues. Economists tend to be highly skilled in mathematical and statistical theory, with an emphasis on formal testing of specific hypotheses.

However, we generally demonstrate far less skill in other aspects of scientific empirical work like the seeking out of new data sources, the improvement of data collection, responsible data cleaning and quality evaluation, replication, sensitivity testing, proper distinction between statistical and substantive significance, data archiving, and the search for overall patterns. We neither spend much time learning how to do these things right, nor do we teach our students how to do these things in any systematic way. The feminist critique suggests there may be much to be gained by decreased use of the technique of detached 'musing'[21] and increased use of the technique of 'hobnobbing with one's data.'[22]

Value judgments attached to 'hard' versus 'soft' data also deserve re-examination. Economists who overcome their prejudice in this area may be surprised at the sophistication in technique and the attention given to issues of validity and replicability demonstrated by other social scientists trained in such 'soft' and qualitative methods as oral histories or case studies. Personal experience should also not be discounted among ways in which we – consciously or not – gather data. It has been a matter of some ironic comment among feminist economists, for example, how what often really seems to matter in convincing a male colleague of the existence of sex discrimination is not studies with 10,000 'objective' observations, but rather a particular single direct observation: the experience of his own daughter.

The idea that one's personal, 'subjective,' position and opinions could influence the outcome of one's scientific work is, of course, anathema to those who believe that objectivity in scientific pursuits can be attained only by the cool detachment of the researcher from the subject of study, or that objectivity is assured by an individual's strict adherence to particular methods of inquiry. Such a notion of objectivity is considered in the feminist analysis (as well as in much contemporary philosophy of science) to be one more outgrowth of the Cartesian illusion.[23] Part of the practice of striving for objectivity, in fact, should be an examination of how the things that one believes from one's own experience may influence one's research. Sandra Harding (1995) calls the sort of objectivity in which one recognizes one's standpoint 'strong objectivity,' as contrasted to 'weak objectivity' in which the issue of perspective is kept under wraps. Within economics, Amartya Sen has similarly argued that objectivity begins with 'knowledge based on positional observation.'[24] The movement from subjective views to (strong) objectivity comes not through a sharp separation of the researcher from the object of study, but rather through a connection of the researcher to a larger critical community. According to feminist philosopher Helen Longino, 'The objectivity of individuals ... consists in their participation in the collective give-and-take of critical discussion and not in some special relation (of detachment, hard-headedness) they may bear to their observations.'[25] While concern with the reliability of results is still of prime importance, the criteria that guide research are internal to the community of researchers, not external. Formalization, then, rather than reflecting the height of objectivity, is simply seen as one tool in the toolbox. In the words of turn-of-the-century economist Knut Wicksell, the role of logic and abstraction is 'to facilitate the argument, clarify the results, and so guard against possible faults of reasoning – that is all.'[26]

Capitalism and the 'Separative Self'

An evaluation of the education of those who will make business decisions and governmental economic policy will reveal biases in the direction of 'separative self' models, to the extent that these educations are based on mainstream economic models. Such an education encourages a basic misunderstanding of people, and hence basic misunderstandings about the nature and limits of the capitalist form of economic organization. Decision makers are encouraged to ignore social life, emotional motivations, and questions of ethics. How can business decisions and government regulatory behaviour be correct, if the models on which they are based are fundamentally flawed?

Our hypothetical notion of a paradigmatic Market (spelled with a capital M to denote its status as an ideal) of autonomous, self-interested agents gets in the way of our understanding of real markets (lower-case m, denoting actual and experiential) made by socially embedded and physically embodied human beings. Our tendency to organize the world in Market/Non-Market terms leads to distorted understandings of the limits of capitalism.[27] I argue elsewhere that the common contrast of presumably materialistic and self-interested Market behaviour (like working 'for pay') with presumably non-materialistic and altruistic Non-Market caring behaviour (like care of one's own children, or talking with a friend), radically and needlessly confuses discussions about the nature of caring services provided on *real* markets.[28] The usual contrast seems to imply that phenomena like paid child-care by non-relatives, or talking with a therapist, are somehow contaminated by self-interest, greed, and pecuniary motives. Only if one gets beyond a notion of 'separative selves,' and into a discussion of persons who (having bodies) need to support themselves, who (having found identity in familial and social ties) take responsibility for others, and who (having complex emotions) have multiple motivations, can one better understand such activities and real markets in general.

Similarly, a rereading of much of the literature on the ethical bases of capitalism, in light of the insights from feminist theory, reveals how much of it is also implicitly based on the notion of a radically autonomous, 'separative self.'

The ideas that the moral values of freedom and/or property rights should be paramount, and that therefore state 'interference' in capitalism should be minimal, presupposes the existence – not to mention the pre-eminence – of the autonomous, independent individual. But, as already discussed, humans in fact spend significant periods of their life (in childhood, sickness, and old age) dependent on others, and usually much of their life enmeshed in various personal, familial, and social interdependencies. The autonomous agent of that theory is, if not a complete chimera, at least the exception rather than the rule. There is a fundamental contradiction, for example, in the labour theory of property appropriation. Given the amount of work that women traditionally (and necessarily) put into bearing and raising children, the labour theory of the appropriation of property as defended by Locke (and perhaps Nozick) seems to imply that every person should be the 'property' of his or her mother! But this contradicts the concept of the self-owning agent without which the theory falls apart.

If there are not autonomous individuals, and freely operating capitalist systems, that are fundamentally prior to social life and political organization, then the focus of ethical argument shifts dramatically. In discussions of good economic systems, freedom and property rights can, then, no longer be considered more fundamental than care and concern for dependants and attention to the quality of familial, social, and political life. The notion of 'persons-in-relation' weighs *both* individuality and connection; *both* freedom and mutual influence. Neither is prior to the other.

The 'separative self' is also separated from its natural environment. One can note that women and nature share similar treatment in Western thought. They are, variously, invisible; pushed into the background; treated as a 'resource' for the satisfaction of male or human needs; considered to be part of a realm that 'takes care of itself';

thought of as self-regenerating (or reproductive, as opposed to productive); conceived of as passive; and/or considered to be subject to male or human authority.[29] As put by Val Plumwood, 'What is involved in the backgrounding of nature is the denial of dependence on biospheric processes, and a view of humans as apart, outside of nature, which is treated as a limitless provider without needs of its own. Dominant western culture has systematically inferiorized, backgrounded and denied dependency on the whole sphere of reproduction and subsistence.'[30]

The images of women as natural, and of nature as female, play an important symbolic role in the construction and philosophical justification of extractive, environmentally insensitive economic systems. 'A transformative feminism,' writes Karen Warren, 'would involve a psychological restructuring of our attitudes and beliefs about ourselves and "our world" (including the nonhuman world), and a philosophical rethinking of the notion of the self such that we see ourselves as both co-members of an ecological community and yet different from other members of it.'[31] Such a transformation, extended to the analysis and construction of economic systems, would recognize that our human lives are intimately connected to our environment, in ways that the 'separative self' models, based entirely on notions of autonomy and ratiocination, deny.

Conclusion

I do not think that, in creating a 'distinctly human focus' in an administrative studies program, one could leave economics courses as they are and simply give more emphasis to the teachings of psychologists and other organization specialists. Economics itself needs to be challenged for distorted assumptions and fragile methods. Skills such as getting people to work together are not just 'frosting on the cake,' to be learned after one receives a drilling in received economic doctrine. The way in which real human beings work together – or fail to work together – must itself be a part of any explanation of how our economic world functions. Similarly, ethical arguments about capitalism must include consideration of real interconnections and interdependencies, of humans with each other and with the natural environment. The current economic and philosophical practice of basing theories on 'separative selves' is not a sign of rigor, but a sign of biases arising from cultural understandings of gender and value.

Notes

This chapter is based on a paper prepared for presentation at Trent University, Peterborough, Ontario, Canada, 23 January 1997, sponsored by the Bank of Montreal Distinguished Visitor Program. It was revised and retitled, September 1998.

1 U.S. Department of Labor, Bureau of Labor Statistics. *Employment and Earnings*, 43/1 (1996), Table 39.
2 Katharine M. Donato, 'Keepers of the Corporate Image: Women in Public Relations,' in *Job Queues, Gender Queues*, Barbara J. Reskin and Patricia A. Roos, eds. (Philadelphia: Temple University Press, 1990), 129–43. The reader might object that the lower salaries could be the result of occupational crowding. However, crowding would not explain the lowered career expectations for these occupations.
3 U.S. Department of Labor, Table 171; Donato, 'Keepers of the Corporate Image,' 129–30.
4 Much of the following draws directly from Julie A. Nelson, 'Gender, Metaphor and the Definition of Economics,' *Economics and Philosophy*, 8/1 (1992), 103–25; and *Feminism, Objectivity and Economics* (London: Routledge, 1996).
5 Evelyn Fox Keller, *Reflections on Gender and Science* (New Haven: Yale University Press, 1985).
6 Sandra Harding, *The Science Question in Feminism* (Ithaca: Cornell University Press, 1986).
7 Ibid., 125.
8 Keller, *Reflections*, 52.
9 Ibid., 39.
10 Thinking about administration, one might add in the left column such items and stereotypes as 'financial planning, economic analysis, instrumental roles, hard-driving decision maker,' and in the right column, 'human resources, public relations, expressive roles, assistant who "smooths things over."'
11 The cross-cultural variability of such associations can be seen as evidence of the usefulness of distinguishing between 'gender' and 'sex,' as discussed below.
12 See citations in Hetty van Emmerik, 'Gender, Paradigms, and Metaphors, and Some Implications for Research in Business Administration' (paper presented at the FENN seminar 'Theoretical Concerns in Mainstream Economics,' The Hague, December 1995).
13 Carol Gilligan, *In a Different Voice: Psychological Theory and Women's Development* (Cambridge, MA: Harvard University Press, 1982, 1993).

14 Nelson, 'Gender, Metaphor, and the Definition of Economics'; *Feminism, Objectivity and Economics.*

15 As cited in Seyla Benhabib, 'The Generalized and Concrete Other: The Kohlberg Gilligan Controversy and Moral Theory,' in *Women and Moral Theory,* D. Meyers and E.F. Kittay, eds. (Totowa, NJ: Rowman and Littlefield, 1987).

16 Ronald G. Ehrenberg and Robert S. Smith, *Modern Labour Economics* (New York: Harper Collins, 1994).

17 James D. Gwartney, Richard Stroup, and J.R. Clark, *Essentials of Economics* (New York: Academic Press, 1985).

18 Paula England, 'The Separative Self: Androcentric Bias in Neoclassical Assumptions,' in *Beyond Economic Man: Feminist Theory and Economics,* M. Ferber and J. Nelson, eds. (Chicago: University of Chicago Press, 1993).

19 George Akerlof and Janet A. Yellen, 'Fairness and Unemployment,' *American Economic Review,* 78/2 (1988), 44–9.

20 Ibid., 45.

21 Barbara R. Bergmann, '"Measurement," or Finding Things Out in Economics,' *Journal of Economic Education,* 18/2 (1987), 191–203.

22 Myra Stober, 'The Scope of Microeconomies: Implications for Economics Education,' *Journal of Economic Education,* 18 (1987), 135–49.

23 Nelson, *Feminism, Objectivity and Economics.*

24 Amartya Sen, *Objectivity and Position,* Lidley Lecture, University of Kansas, 1992.

25 Helen Longino, *Science as Social Knowledge: Values and Objectivity in Science Enquiry* (Princeton: Princeton University Press, 1990).

26 Quoted in Nicholas Georgescu-Roegen, *The Entropy Law and the Economic Process* (Cambridge, MA: Harvard University Press, 1971), 341.

27 John Bishop, in the Introduction to this volume, for example, sets up a contrast between bargaining 'in the market' and the activities of 'love, friendship, families, parenting, religion, artistic creativity, knowledge, and most self-fulfilment.' While the issues he is getting at are important, this formulation is an example of what I find unhelpful.

28 Julie A. Nelson, 'For Love or Money – or Both.' Paper presented at the conference 'Out of the Margin,' Amsterdam, 2–5 June 1998.

29 Val Plumwood, *Feminism and the Mastery of Nature* (London: Routledge, 1992); Julie A, Nelson, 'Feminism, Ecology, and the Philosophy of Economics,' *Ecological Economics,* 20 (1997), 155–62.

30 Plumwood, *Feminism and the Mastery of Nature,* 21.

31 Karen J. Warren, 'Feminism and Ecology: Marking Connections,' *Environmental Ethics,* 9/1 (1987), 3–20.

5

Business, Globalization, and the Logic and Ethics of Corruption

A.W. CRAGG

There can be few topics at this juncture of the development of human civilization that are more in need of careful exploration than 'Ethics and Capitalism.' It is now the virtually unanimous view of leaders in both the industrialized and the developing world that capitalism, or, as some put it, a free market economy, is the only viable model for organizing efficient and productive economies. This view, emerging as it has from the dramatic, non-violent, world-wide collapse of communism,[1] is no longer remarkable. What is striking, however, is the way in which the emergence of this global consensus has been paralleled by the emergence of 'a global marketplace.'

The phenomenon of globalization is significant because of the way in which, increasingly, free and global markets appear to have undermined both the willingness and the capacity of governments to exercise their traditional responsibilities for coordinating economic with social development. The result is a global market whose operation appears often to be quite divorced from any recognition that development or increasing economic wealth is of value not for its own sake but only insofar as it leads to improvements in the quality of life of the people and the communities that make it possible.

This sense of political impotence on the part of individuals and governments is disturbing enough in its own right. The accompanying unease is magnified, however, by the realization that many individuals and corporations doing business in the global marketplace have no clear sense of their responsibilities to the societies, cultures, and individuals that they encounter in the course of their international ventures. This is a cause for alarm, since the activities, of corporations operating multinationally can have devastating as well as beneficial impacts on individuals, communities and even nation states.

My purpose in what follows is to examine a phenomenon that has accompanied globalization, namely, corruption. It is clearly not the only challenge posed by globalization. It is, however, an important one. Further, although it is not often acknowledged, the long-term viability of free markets is very much tied to the capacity of those in a position to provide leadership to respond to this and a number of other ethical challenges to which globalization has given rise.

Is Corruption a Serious Problem?

Corruption is now widely thought to be thoroughly entrenched in the global marketplace. George Moody Stuart, the chairman of the British chapter of Transparency International, an international anti-corruption coalition headquartered in Berlin, Germany, suggests in a paper entitled 'A Good Business Guide to Bribery'[2] that while there were pockets of corruption thirty years ago, the great majority of countries in the developing world at that time were 'clean.' By the mid-1970s, Stuart contends, there was 'a growing awareness of the rapid spread of grand corruption in Africa' aided and abetted by European contractors who were 'all too willing to cooperate.'[3] Nevertheless, he suggests, it was still possible for experienced business people to do business internationally without encountering corruption in a serious form.

Over the past ten years, however, there has been serious deterioration, with grand corruption now the general rule rather than the exception in major government connected contracts in the developing world. Stuart concludes that in the 1990s, 'nobody in the business world pretends any more that it is not one of the most important and damaging factors in third world development.'[4]

There is much to confirm these observations both here and abroad. Media descriptions of the machinations of Canadian gold-mining companies in Indonesia, in response to the discovery of what was thought for a time to be one of the largest gold deposits in the world, reveal graphically both the problems that corruption can pose for multinational companies as well as the market and non-market solutions to which those companies turn to resolve it.[5] Neither are the problems of corruption restricted to third world business transactions. Whatever else is to be learned from Canada's own airbus scandal, for example, what emerges clearly from this unsettling incident in recent Canadian

history is the widespread belief in both government and corporate circles that bribery is widely used in the high technology sectors of the
economies of the industrialized world to win contracts in the north
and the south.[6]

There is a final clear signal that corruption is a serious problem.
Informal discussion and classroom debate show unmistakably that the
case against bribery and corruption as a business strategy is not at all
obvious to many business and government leaders nor to many students in business and management studies programs in Canada and
abroad.

Some examples will serve to point to the magnitude of the problem.
As recently as 1998, bribes were accepted as a legitimate, tax-deduct-
ible, business expense throughout much of Europe. The result was that
while it was illegal for a German company to bribe a German official, a
bribe directed to a French or Canadian or any non-German government official for the purpose of winning a contract, for example, was
legal. Indeed, many European countries did not even require that payments identified as bribes be documented with receipts or invoices.
What is more, until very recently most European and other western
governments have resisted any suggestion for change in tax law or regulations in this regard.[7]

In Canada companies have been blocked from treating bribes as a
legitimate business expense only since 1991. Furthermore, until
recently, the Canadian government has quietly resisted any effort to
vigorously discourage bribery because of a fear of damaging the competitive position of Canadian companies. Neither, it would seem, has
the Canadian government attempted to discourage Crown corporations from using bribery where that appeared to be necessary for the
procurement of foreign contracts. An example is the Canadian nuclear
energy industry, whose foreign sales are widely thought to have been
procured in at least some cases with the assistance of substantial bribes
to key decision makers of foreign countries in the market for nuclear
generators.

Among the countries of the world prior to 1998, only the United
States had a foreign corrupt practices act aimed at curbing the corruption of foreign government officials in the pursuit of business contracts. Until recently all other member governments of the Organization for Economic Cooperation and Development (OECD) have
resisted following suit on the grounds that to do so would put their
business community at a competitive disadvantage.[8]

The Paradox of Corruption

For many in the business community, the phenomenon of corruption has been treated in the past as no more than just another factor to be taken into account by those wishing to compete in the global marketplace. For those concerned about the defensibility of market economics, however, the willingness of the industrialized world to accept and adapt to corruption poses a genuine paradox. The reason should be readily apparent to any critical observer.

Corruption in the form of bribery, for example, is clearly a two-way street. There must be a briber as well as a bribee. Hence, if corruption is widespread, first world multinational companies must be cooperating. This is paradoxical for many reasons. It is virtually universally accepted on the part of the corporate community in the industrialized world that accepting bribes is grounds for immediate dismissal for both private and public sector employees at all levels. Consistent with this ethic is the fact that preventing corruption is widely regarded as one of the central tasks of modern governments. Exposing corruption is thought by the media in democratic countries to be one of their central obligations. Indeed, one of the basic justifications of a free press is the need for an unfettered watchdog that can expose corruption without fear or favour.

It is worth noting, in this regard, that there are no pockets of popular or academic resistance to the legitimacy of these perspectives. No economists have suggested that the market economies of the developed world would work more efficiently were corruption to be encouraged. No corporate leaders have argued publicly for softening corporate or legal anti-corruption strictures.

Why, then, is it so widely thought throughout the western world that corporations are justified in using corrupt practices to secure contracts in foreign countries? This question, I suggest, deserves serious consideration. No doubt, a complete answer would include a review of the various vices to which human nature seems prone. I want to suggest, however, that at least part of the reason lies in the conjunction of two clusters of theories. One of those clusters takes management as its focus. The other emerges from moral theory. Let us look at the influence of each in turn.

The first is a cluster of theories whose purpose is to describe and explain the role of management in the modern corporation. It draws on the language and explanatory models of economics. Its focus is individual self-interest and profit maximization. It is a cluster of theories in which the language of ethics is given little if any place. Neil Shankman describes it as lying at the root of many popular management theories or programs. He goes on to say that it is 'perhaps the dominant metaphor underlying much of what is written in the popular financial press.'[9] Two management theories illustrate the basic thrust of this cluster. The first, which I shall describe as the shareholder model of the firm, argues that a corporation's sole obligation is wealth maximization for the benefit of owners or shareholders. Popularized by the economist Milton Friedman, this theory builds on the assumption that people who invest in corporations want 'to make as much money as possible while conforming to the basic rules of society, both those embodied in law and those embodied in ethical custom.'[10] In defending this view, Friedman argues: 'Few trends could so thoroughly undermine the very foundations of our free society as the acceptance by corporate officials of a social responsibility other than to make as much money for their stockholders as possible.'[11]

The second version of this view is captured by the agency theory of management.[12] On this theory, managers are agents whose sole obligation is to pursue the goals of the owners of the corporation for which they work. It is a view that is grounded on the assumption that human economic behaviour is motivated exclusively by self-interest defined as the desire to maximize financial wealth. It gives pride of place to property and liberty rights, essentially the right of people to advance their interests through the free and unfettered exchange of goods and services. Where this is allowed to occur, it is argued, the social interests and needs of people and communities will be efficiently and effectively, although unintentionally, satisfied and the moral aspirations of society effectively realized.

This cluster of theories is frequently characterized as the 'traditional or historical model' of the corporation, a description which, although inaccurate, highlights its influence on management thought both in the academy and in the corporate board rooms of industrialized societies.

Neither of these theories taken either together or apart explicitly condones corrupt practices. To the contrary, because conventional western morality routinely condemns such things as bribery, both theories imply that it is not an acceptable way of winning business in the industrialized world. Nevertheless, this cluster of theories does have striking implications for management whose focus is the global marketplace. First, they strip management of moral agency and therefore of personal moral constraints. Managers on this view are instruments whose sole moral obligation is to maximize profits for the benefit of owners or shareholders. All other constraints are external and relate to the exigencies of law and conventional morality. Respect for the letter of the law, as well as an awareness of local conventions, customs, and laws, and a willingness to work within their parameters are all that is required of corporations or their agents. Critical moral judgment or evaluation of the moral character of prevailing laws, conventions, or customs is irrelevant to fulfilling managerial responsibilities.

What is important about this moral framework for our immediate purposes is that its focus is entirely local and its moral content entirely conventional. Two things follow from this. First, managers have no obligation to carry western moral strictures into the global market-place. Second, what will count as corruption will be a function of the conventions and practices of the local cultures found in the geographi-cal locations where business is transacted. What we have then is an implicit theoretical justification for the popular maxim, 'When in Rome do as the Romans do.' The logic is clear and easy to follow. What is more important, the implications for the world of business are readily apparent.

The second cluster of theories of relevance for our purposes emanate from moral philosophy. They have been effectively articulated by lib-eral political and moral theorists for whom individual moral auton-omy and political liberty are core values. Two important principles underlie the thinking of these theorists. First, there is no one correct moral vision of the good life. It follows that there may well not be solu-tions to fundamental disagreements about how people should live and the principles that should guide their lives as individuals and groups. Second, individuals should be allowed to build their lives either alone or collectively without impediment and to the fullest extent compati-ble with an equal freedom on the part of others to do likewise.

Liberal political and moral theory has and continues to influence patterns of political argument and social policy in the industrialized world in profound ways. It is reflected in policies that seek to resist efforts on the part of individuals and groups to impose their moral views on the public, a moral perspective that has been decisive in shaping public policy with regard to such controversial issues as abor-tion. The recently rekindled euthanasia debate revolves around the appropriate application of these same principles to arguments about the extent to which the law should control end-of-life decision making. Arguments calling for the separation of church and state rest on these same liberal foundations as do attacks on any attempt to limit reading material in libraries and publicly funded schools and courses in accordance with concepts of decency or appropriate moral behaviour, however sincerely held.

In practice, what these kinds of theories appear to endorse is moral relativism, a view which now seems to be a deeply entrenched feature of popular culture.[13] On this view, judgments of right and wrong or good and evil are essentially manifestations of cultural patterns that vary from culture to culture and epoch to epoch. In our culture, this view is captured most visibly in attitudes towards sexual relationships. What is right for one individual or couple may not work for another. If there are to be rules, they are a matter of private not public decision and have to be fashioned by individuals in light of their own feelings and attitudes or those of the social groups to which they adhere.

One of the influential popular projections of these views on the political landscape concerns the notion of sovereignty. Nations, it is frequently argued, have the right to determine their own destiny free of external attempts to limit or dictate their choices. The sovereignty movement in Quebec has made these kinds of arguments familiar to Canadians.

It would be a mistake to underestimate the power of these theories in the popular mind or their implications for understanding and responding to the phenomenon of corruption. For they too would appear to lend credibility to the slogan, 'When in Rome do as the Romans do,' a view that often underlies the rationalization of behaviour that in a Canadian context, for example, would be rejected out of hand as morally unacceptable. Closely related is the view that for countries like Canada to impose their definition of bribery and corruption on the global marketplace constitutes moral imperialism. We have no right to impose moral values that define corruption for us on cultures where what we call immoral is thought to be commonplace and widely accepted, or so some would argue.

What I am proposing, then, is that these two distinct clusters of theories have had the effect, in western management circles of rationalizing contradictory standards and patterns of behaviour, namely, the rejection as entirely unacceptable at home of behaviour that is nevertheless tolerated and condoned abroad.

The Ethics of Corruption

The purpose of the analysis to this point in the argument has been first to underline the pervasive character of corruption in the global marketplace and second to lay bare the logical contours of that phenomenon. My task in this section of my chapter is to contrast logic with ethics. What then is corruption and why is it so widely thought to be unethical?

Let me begin by defining as corrupt any attempt whether successful or not to persuade someone in a position of responsibility to make a decision or recommendation on grounds other than the intrinsic merits of the case with a view to the advantage or advancement of herself or another person or group to which she is linked through personal commitment, obligation, or employment or individual, professional, or group loyalty. It should be clear that this definition is designed to be culturally neutral. It does not attempt to define what should constitute merit. It assumes only that people who are appointed to positions of responsibility have an obligation not to take advantage of their position to pursue objectives that prevent them from fulfilling to the best of their ability the function for which they are paid. This, I suggest, is the rule that lies at the heart of efforts on the part of western societies to identify and condemn corruption in its various guises. It is a rule which is entirely consistent with values such as efficiency, effectiveness, productivity, and competitiveness. Indeed, it would seem on the face of it to be essential to the realization of all of them.

What then are the ethical parameters of this quest? The ethical dimensions of practices can be evaluated against moral principles or values that are widely shared and consistent with critical morality. They can also be assessed in light of their consequences or impacts. Let us apply each of these tests to the issue of corruption taking bribery as the test case.

There are two moral principles that engage the issue. The first is the ethical obligation to be honest. The second is a principle of justice or fairness. Bribery fails on both counts. It is by its nature covert and deceitful. Payments intended as bribes are typically disguised. Double bookkeeping is often the strategy used to accomplish this objective. Second, whether it achieves its goal or not, bribery treats those who are deceived unfairly and unjustly, which is why deception is required. The reason is that the purpose of the bribe, as our definition makes clear, is to provide someone in a position of responsibility with an incentive to ensure that a decision is made that favours the briber, whether favoured treatment is justified on the merits of the case or not. Thus it provides the briber with an unwarranted or unfair advantage.

The significance and relevance of this moral test is borne out by examining the impact of bribery on those affected by it.

Let us examine first the impacts of bribery on corporations that accede to it in their efforts to compete successfully in global markets. For business, corruption increases uncertainty, reduces accountability, undermines control, and introduces what can turn out to be significant risks, risks that are easily overlooked and hard to quantify. Michael Mackenzie, former supervisor of Canadian Financial Institutions and a former treasurer of the Canadian chapter of Transparency International points out: 'Generally speaking, the making of bribes and the taking of favours puts one into a system of organizations, politicians, government officials and others, and once into the system it is usually very difficult to get out. For example, it is common practice of those who take bribes to set aside a portion for the person making the payment sometimes without even letting him know at the time!' He goes on to say: 'Without extremely good records, it may not be possible always to be sure that the employees of the payer are not themselves "on the take."'[14] This demonstrates that bribery can have damaging implications for companies that offer bribes.

Additional less tangible implications also attach to activities of the sort under examination. Corruption typically generates contempt for those being corrupted, since the acceptance of payments in exchange for favours implies a lack of moral integrity on their part. What is less obvious is the way in which contempt towards those receiving payment can turn into contempt and cynicism directed towards the company itself and its senior management. This potential impact on the way in which a company is perceived by its own employees is bound to be exacerbated if the company's public posture is one of denying any involvement in corrupt practices at home or abroad while at the same time engaging in them.

It is not uncommon for companies that engage in corrupt practices, particularly in developing countries, to assume that they can compartmentalize this kind of activity and the values associated with it and restrict its involvement to third world business transactions. What is too easily taken for granted, however, is that the people involved will be able to maintain the personal integrity required of them by the company in their dealings with the company itself and with the business world 'back home' while condoning or engaging in behaviour in foreign settings that they know would never be tolerated within the company itself. That is to say, although a transnational company may choose to condone corrupt practices in its foreign operations, it will nevertheless be seen as essential for its own welfare that its employees and agents retain their loyalty to 'first world values' when they come home and in all their internal dealings with the company.

The reasons are obvious. Internal corruption may not only impair, it can also cripple a corporation's capacity to compete effectively in a free market. For corruption by its nature undermines both the willingness and the ability of employees to advance the interests of the corporation as efficiently and effectively as their jobs and competition in the global market requires. This is because corruption distorts judgment; the right answer or the right decision is no longer what would best advance the interests of the corporation but rather what will best advance the interests of the decision maker.

Values are not easily compartmentalized. It is a serious mistake for companies to assume that management can easily move from third world to first world 'ways of doing things' when practices like bribery are involved. A little thought quickly indicates why this is the case. If the reason for engaging in corrupt activity in a third world setting is contracts and profits, it will be hard to reject similar reasoning should the need arise in first world settings. Furthermore, if advancing the interests of one's employer using unethical strategies is acceptable from a corporate or organizational perspective, why should the same strategies not be used where an employee's own interests are at stake? It is not surprising to learn, therefore, that reports of corrupt activities on the part of senior management in first world business settings are today quite common. In the global marketplace, Rome is as likely to be next door as halfway around the world.

The implications of corruption for the public sector in both the industrialized and developing world are even more striking. Where political culture and institutions are concerned, the effect of corruption both in the short and medium term is to strengthen and consolidate the political *status quo*. There are many reasons for this. First, corruption generates significant financial and other rewards for office holders. Where corrupt practices are tolerated by the regime in power, the illicit financial benefits that accrue to office holders generate both dependence on and indebtedness to the system and the people to whom they owe their appointments. Inevitably, the criteria of appointment shift from competence as well as commitment to fulfilling responsibilities efficiently and effectively, to patronage and loyalty to the regime conferring the benefit. The effect is to entrench the political *status quo*.

Corruption also tends to generate financial wealth for the governing elite both collectively and individually just because those in power inevitably demand 'a cut in the action.' Resulting personal wealth enhances the status of the political leaders. And their access to 'private' sources of financial wealth allows them to build a strong political apparatus which supports them in power. The end result is to strengthen both the appearance and the reality of political support for those in power.

Finally, corruption tends to strengthen the elite in power by undermining the rule of law. There are many reasons for this. Perhaps the most important is that no legal system anywhere formally condones practices like bribery. As a result, widespread corruption inevitably requires the connivance of law enforcement personnel as well as the courts. Respect for the law is an obvious casualty and with it public confidence in the law and legal institutions. This too serves to enhance the power of the governing elite, since where the law is not respected, those in power can use that power to protect and enhance their positions unrestrained by law.

Corruption also has significant economic repercussions, particularly for countries caught in its grip. It distorts economic policy making. Projects are undertaken not for their potential public benefits but because of their potential to advance the financial interests of those responsible for choosing them. Suppliers and contractors are chosen not on grounds of merit but because of their willingness to divert funds for the private benefit of officials or advisers in positions of influence. The result is distorted economic priorities and the diversion of resources from public projects and activities to private bank accounts.

These observations are illustrated by a 1994 report from Switzerland claiming that amounts in excess of $20 billion are currently held in Swiss banks for African leaders. In 1994, the vice-president of Ecuador estimated that as much as a third of third world debt may be a consequence of corruption and pointed out that even if only 10 per cent to 15 per cent of the debt of his own country were attributable to wasteful investment resulting from corruption together with the funds diverted from public use because of bribes, the sum would coincide with that part of its debt which at that time, Ecuador was unable to service.[15]

This effect is not unique to third world countries. Corruption in first world countries has similar results. However, it is particularly devastating in countries whose public resources are severely limited. What is at stake is more than just a few tax dollars. Rather, inefficient use of public funds undermines efforts to create an economic base that can provide the financial resources needed to build adequate health and educational systems and to ensure a minimally adequate standard of living for a country's citizens.

What often goes unacknowledged is the way in which complicity in corrupt practices on the part of foreign business enterprises adds to the problem. First world corporations frequently justify their complicity in corrupt practices in foreign settings with the observation that it is both necessary and appropriate that foreign business people adapt to local customs. This creates a business environment in which the perception that corruption is common is converted into a norm, which in turn supports the view that 'this is the way people do business over there.' As a result, the perception that 'this is the way people do business over there' feeds on itself. It becomes self-fulfilling.

We can see this process at work in another way. The perception on the part of a foreign corporation that corruption is widespread colours the interpretation of requests, refusals, interventions, and negotiations on the part of third world officials. The assumption of widespread corruption becomes an interpretive device that then undermines the position of the honest among those charged with public or business responsibilities, because their various interventions and initiatives are then assumed to be invitations to 'grease' the process. If the response is to offer a bribe, the corporation probably quite unintentionally has become engaged in a process of corrupting honest officials, thus further undermining whatever integrity the system still has.

Finally, corruption distorts social relationships and exacerbates social tensions. Where corruption is widespread, public status and privilege are not likely to be related to merit or contributions made to society or even to the capacity to contribute but rather to personal, tribal, or ethnic connections. Those individuals and groups disadvantaged by prevailing social arrangements will almost certainly regard their treatment and that of their family, friends, tribe, or ethnic group as unjust. Social tension or alternatively progressive alienation and disengagement is an obvious consequence. In the long term, the resulting social tensions provide the foundations for severe and violent social and political conflict.

The Paradox of Corruption Reconsidered

The practice of bribery by multinational corporations, as we have already noted, is paradoxical. It is obviously incompatible with moral norms that are deeply embedded in the management of virtually all multinational corporations. These norms also have wide public endorsement. Many of these same people, however, regard corrupt practices to be an essential part of doing business in foreign business transactions. In response to this phenomenon, I have attempted to show first, that the rationalization of corruption in global markets is just that, a rationalization. The evidence for this view lies in the fact that corrupt practices like bribery are fundamentally immoral judged by ethical standards that are widely accepted. When we test the morality of corruption by evaluating the costs it imposes on its victims, once again the evidence points clearly to its unethical character. It is not surprising therefore that there is no legal system in the world that tolerates bribery.

How then are we to reconcile this finding with the dominant shareholder model of the corporation and agency theories of management? Further, can the view that corruption is immoral wherever it occurs be endorsed without falling prey to the evils of moral imperialism, to which danger prevailing liberal moral and political theories have sensitized us?

Let us begin the discussion by recognizing that the shareholder model of the corporation is an abstraction that deviates in significant ways from the reality it purports to describe and explain. First, whatever the attractiveness of Milton Friedman's theory to some elements of the business and academic communities, even the most superficial review of business history will show that many corporations in the industrialized world have understood their social responsibilities to extend well beyond a single-minded focus on maximizing profits. To describe shareholders as people exclusively interested in share value is equally distorting. Progressive companies have traditionally undertaken to connect to the communities in which they were located in mutually beneficial ways, whether that meant the sponsorship of local events or philanthropic contributions to local or national charitable organizations and projects. This is in part because shareholders are also citizens whose welfare is affected not simply by the value of their investments but the quality of the communities in which they live. While shareholders might be capable in the short term of ignoring the long-term impacts of the corporations in which they invest on the communities in which they live, this stance is one that few can maintain for long in the face of such things as a deteriorating environment or disintegrating social systems. In short, it is widely accepted in the corporate community, although perhaps not always effectively communicated or argued, that corporations have social responsibilities that go well beyond maximizing shareholder financial wealth.

Agency theories of management, whatever their popularity in business schools, paint an equally distorted picture of management practice. Managers of corporations are not simply the agents of their owners. Indeed, any theory that implies that a manager's sole moral obligation is to facilitate the pursuit of the interests (narrowly defined as profit maximization) of the owners or shareholders is itself seriously deficient judged by the standards of liberal moral and political theory. For liberal moral theory projects moral agency on all individuals whatever their employment status. The agency theory of management, in contrast, has the opposite effect of stripping managers of their obligations as moral agents, picturing them not as morally autonomous individuals responsible for their actions to everyone affected by them, but as the mere instruments of property owners who are themselves described by such theories as amoral profit maximizers.

In fact, few managers would deny that they have ethical obligations to a wide range of corporate stakeholders including employees, customers, suppliers, and the public at large.

In short, management theories that appear to relieve managers of an obligation to evaluate corporate activities and policies from an ethical perspectives are themselves open to serious moral criticism.

Neither is liberal moral and political theory a serious obstacle to confronting corruption in the global market. It is true that accusations of corruption can be culturally insensitive. Patterns of behaviour do vary from culture to culture. Gift-giving at Christmas, for example, is widely practised by the business community in Canada. Gratuities for service are expected as a normal cost associated with restaurant dining throughout North America. Both practices would raise eyebrows in many countries in the world. But neither provide evidence of widespread corruption as the term is normally used.

It is true that evaluating the behaviour of people of one culture by the standards of another culture does suggest a form of imperialism. However, requiring that people fulfil their responsibilities honestly and fairly in accordance with culturally appropriate criteria of evaluation is not an act of moral imperialism. To the contrary, it is a standard for doing business on which a market economy ultimately depends. In its absence, there can be no genuinely free market. Deception subverts the free and voluntary exchange of goods and services and undermines the conditions for competition on which the market relies. In this sense, double standards in cross-cultural business dealings are as unpalatable from a moral perspective as double standards in culturally homogeneous settings.

Building an Ethical International Business Culture

It follows, therefore, that willing recourse to corrupt business practice is unethical in all corners of the global marketplace. But is unwilling acquiescence equally reprehensible? Does ethics require that corporations avoid corrupt practices like bribery whatever the prevailing standards of conduct in specific markets might be? The dilemma to which this question points is not easily resolved. Corruption is widespread. There are many corners of the global market from which an uncompromising corporation will thereby be excluded. Furthermore, accompanying that exclusion will be lost economic opportunities with all that implies for those likely to be negatively affected.

In a book entitled *Competing with Integrity in International Business*,[16] Richard De George points out that 'the ethical problems and dilemmas that arise from operating in a corrupt environment or from facing unethical competitors have no uniform or easy solutions.'[17] There are solutions, however. And they go well beyond simply not doing business in corrupt environments, or alternatively capitulating to the prevailing business norms. What some of those solutions are and the strategies available to corporations who encounter corrupt business environments is explored in some detail by De George. They include adherence to sound ethical principles, the use of moral imagination, patience, perseverance, publicity, honest reporting, and so on.

Exploring those strategies is not possible here. However, there is a remaining question that needs to be addressed. What kind of public leadership do we need and have a right to expect from defenders of free market economic principles and free trade? Perhaps the first and most fundamental need is ongoing and articulate public acknowledgment on the part of the business community that ethics does have a place in international business transactions. We also need explicit acknowledgment by business leaders and educators that the role of ethics is to ensure that international competition is governed by rules and that the wealth that results is fairly and equitably shared among those who contribute to its creation. This acknowledgment must be echoed by governments that increasingly are passing the responsibility for creating and sustaining economic activity to the private sector.

We need, second, broad acknowledgment on the part of the private sector that the problems posed by widespread corruption cannot be solved by individuals, individual companies, or individual governments acting on their own. This acknowledgment has two components. First, confronting corruption will require the active support and leadership of sector-wide associations. Mining companies must win the active involvement of national and international mining associations, financial services must address collectively problems in the financial services sector of the economy, and so on.

Third, we need a clear recognition on the part of the business community that there is a role here for governments acting nationally and internationally. Moving to curb corruption is unlikely to succeed while industrialized nations allow powerful corporations to deduct bribes for tax purposes as business expenses. Equally important, the criminalization of corruption within national boundaries must be extended to include international business transactions.

On all these fronts, there is reason for optimism. A growing number of Canadian multinational corporations now have codes of conduct. Increasingly, these codes incorporate rules prohibiting corrupt practices for both national and international business transactions. The International Chamber of Commerce has recently refocused its energies on the issue of bribery and corruption. Corporate support for Transparency International is growing. With all these developments has come an expanding public awareness of the problem, workshops designed to assist corporations to develop effective anti-corruption strategies, and increasingly effective research exploring the causes of corruption and evaluating alternative public and private sector responses.

Perhaps of more significance is a growing acceptance of the need for legislative responses particularly on the part of governments in the industrialized world. The widely accepted model for these purposes is the American Foreign Corrupt Practices Act. While not universally admired, there is recognition that criminalizing foreign corrupt practices in the pursuit of international business is a necessary step if the problem of corruption in international business transactions is to be effectively countered. This issue is now being actively addressed by international institutions such as the United Nations and the World Bank. The most recent indication that things are changing is the recently concluded OECD anti-corruption convention. Persuading the governments world wide to endorse the convention and implement its provisions should be a matter of priority for leaders in the private sector around the world.

Finally, along with institutions like the World Bank, international aid agencies like CIDA should be looking carefully at how the expenditures of aid funds can be rendered more transparent without intruding on the rights of those countries receiving aid to have their sovereignty and freedom to direct their own social and economic evolution respected.

In conclusion, the emergence of a global economy guided by free market principles has been welcomed by some as an opportunity to escape the restraints of local and national communities and national governments whose purpose it is to protect and advance the interests of their citizens. Supporters of this view fail to recognize the ethical imperatives that underlie free market competition. For those who hold these views, corruption is just another way of improving one's competitive position. If this view prevails, as many observers believe is possible, enthusiasm for the globalization of the free market system will surely be short-lived. The challenge is to identify the ethical values needed to ensure fair competition and the fair distribution of the wealth that market economies are capable of generating and then to mould national and international systems and institutions into effective systems of support for those values.

Notes

Earlier versions of this chapter were delivered as a public lecture in the Bank of Montreal, 'Ethics and Capitalism' Lecture Series at Trent University, 13 February 1997, and published in the *International Journal*, 53/4 (1998), 643–61.

1 Excepting, of course, a few countries like Cuba that continue to struggle to organize their economic and political systems around socialist principles.
2 'A Good Business Guide to Bribery: Grand Corruption in Third World Development' (Berlin: Transparency International, 1994).
3 Ibid., 3.

4 Ibid.
5 It is not irrelevant, here, that according to Transparency International's
   widely cited 'Corruption Perceptions Index,' Indonesia is widely perceived
   by those doing business around the world as one of the world's most corrupt countries. (The index is available from TI Canada, by writing the Business Ethics Program, Schulich School of Business, York University, 4700
   Keele St, North York, Ontario, Canada, Transparency International's Berlin
   headquarters, or visit the TI web site at www.transparency.de.)
6 The Canadian airbus scandal involved accusations that an Air Canada
   contract was won by the European manufacturers of the Airbus as a result
   of the payment of bribes to among others the prime minister of Canada.
   The accusations involved were never substantiated, and the Canadian
   government eventually was required to apologize to the then prime minister, Brian Mulroney, and to pay a very substantial out-of-court settlement
   for damages resulting from police investigations. Whatever the merits of
   the case, the fact that it was seriously entertained points to a widespread
   belief that bribery plays a significant role in at least some areas of the
   economies of the industrialized world.
7 This in spite of the fact that the International Chamber of Commerce has
   been recommending that companies resist the use of bribes in international
   business transactions since the 1970s, and the OECD has been urging that
   its member companies remove bribes as legitimate business expenses from
   tax regulations since 1994.
8 It is important to acknowledge that in the two years that have intervened
   since this article was first written there have been dramatic changes in this
   regard. In 1997, the twenty-nine OECD member countries plus five others
   signed a convention committing their governments to introducing legislation criminalizing the bribery of foreign public officials and removing
   bribes as legitimate business expenses for tax purposes. The convention
   came into force in 1999 with the enactment by Canada of Bill S-21, Canada's
   response to the OECD anti-bribery convention. At the time of writing, more
   than fifteen of the signatory countries have introduced legislation designed
   to meet the requirements of the OECD convention. It is now anticipated
   that within a very short period of time, most of the remaining OECD
   countries will have followed suit. While these developments are remarkable in their own right, sceptics will remain unconvinced that they mark a
   significant change of direction until there is clear evidence that the new
   laws are going to be vigorously enforced.
9 'Reframing the Debate between Agency and Stakeholder Theories of the
   Firm,' *Journal of Business Ethics*, 19/4, (1999), 319–34.

10 See, e.g., 'The Social Responsibility of Business is to Increase Profits,' in the *New York Times Magazine*, 13 September (1970).

11 Quoted by Patricia Hogue Werhane, in 'Formal Organizations, Economic Freedom and Moral Agency,' reprinted in *Business Ethics in Canada*, D.C. Poff and W.J. Waluchow, eds. (2nd ed.) (Scarborough, Ont.: Prentice Hall, 1998) 91.

12 Neil Shankman treats these as the same theory. The value of differentiating between them for my purposes is the shareholder focus of the one and the senior management focus of the other. Seen from a theoretical perspective, however, the two approaches generate one theory. (See note 9 above.)

13 Whether they actually do or do not will depend in part on the definition given to 'moral relativism' and partly to the theorist and specific theory under discussion. See, e.g., my discussion of 'Two Concepts of Community of Moral Theory and Canadian Culture,' *Dialogue*, Spring (1986) 31–52.

14 Quoted from the text of a speech made at the launch of the Canadian national section of Transparency International, 17 November (1996) in Toronto, Canada.

15 See 'TI Country Program in Ecuador: A Practical Approach for Building Islands of Integrity' (Berlin: Transparency International, 1994).

16 (New York and Oxford: Oxford University Press, 1993).

17 Ibid., 114.

6

Resistance Is Futile: Aboriginal Peoples Meet the Borg of Capitalism

DAVID R. NEWHOUSE

Over the past five years, I have had an extraordinary opportunity to observe and explore economic development as it is occurring in Aboriginal communities in Canada and to influence the policies of the Royal Commission on Aboriginal Peoples as a member of the RCAP policy team on economics. I have also had an opportunity to reflect upon what I have seen. I would like to share some of the issues and questions that I have begun to raise about economic development and Aboriginal peoples.

The value of a personal narrative and the knowledge that one gains from it seems out of place in a series of philosophical talks about ethics and capitalism. Personal experience and, more particularly, knowledge gained from personal experience are generally considered suspect as sources of knowledge within the academic environment. However, traditional Aboriginal epistemologies consider that personal experience and the reflection upon this personal experience to be essential to assembling a comprehensive understanding of something. It is in this tradition then that I offer these reflections.

Within the Aboriginal paradigm, it is also important that you know a bit about me, so that you can begin to understand the perspective I bring to this discussion. I am a member of the Onondaga Nation of the Six Nations of the Grand River. I grew up in a traditional Longhouse environment. My formal education has been in Canadian universities. The Onondaga are the philosophers of the Iroquois Confederacy, often looked at by others in a somewhat sceptical fashion for their long and esoteric dissertations and deliberations. I offer these reflections in the spirit at this cultural tradition as well.

I spent a decade working for the Canadian Department of Indian

Affairs and Northern Development in the 1980s. For most of that time, I was the Director of Housing. My job involved the allocation of resources for the construction of houses on Indian reserves across the county. The Indian housing policy of that time was a product of the 1960s. One of my main tasks was to produce a new policy that would be more appropriate for the 1980s and, more importantly, that would enable the production of more and better houses.

Housing is fundamental to human societies. We simply cannot exist without some form of shelter to shield us from the various elements of nature. The Indian housing policy recognized this and, recognizing that Indians were poor, provided an allotment to Indian bands for the construction of houses. This allotment of money was to cover somewhere between 50 per cent and 100 per cent of the total cost of a house. The size of grant depended on the economic circumstances of the band. The policy produced only a limited number of houses. What happened was that the Indian communities used the subsidies to provide a complete house for some community members rather than a partial subsidy. They simply took the money and built houses for those who needed them.

The officials of the department, up to the time that I arrived and even after I left, thought that this behaviour was highly irrational. They simply could not understand why Indian band councils did not use the grants as partial subsidies in the manner in which they were supposed to. What they wanted the councils to do was to provide each individual member a grant based upon his or her income and have the individual then complete the house using their own resources, using what they called sweat equity (i.e., their own labour) or their accumulated savings. They also wanted the councils to establish revolving loan funds. In these cases, the council would pool the grants, lend them out to members at low rates of interest, and in this way build more houses. Some of those communities which were in the southern part of Canada near large urban centres did establish loan funds, and these worked very well.

My colleagues in the Department of Indian Affairs at the time argued and believed that the behaviour of Indians was political. In some cases, band councils did indeed argue that as a result of treaties they were entitled to housing in return for having given up land. And they saw the behaviour as simply a way of getting the government to make good on its promise over the long term. And I must admit there was some of that.

If, however, you begin to explore beneath the surface of that explanation, you begin to see other things at work. My approach to the task of reviewing the housing policy was to see if I could create a market for housing. My belief at that time was if I could create a market, I could then cause more and better housing to be produced: more housing because there was indeed a huge unfulfilled demand for houses, and better housing because people would want to trade up or would want to demonstrate some pride of ownership. I reasoned that some houses would become available for sale from this process. After all, this was the way the vast majority of housing was provided for individuals in the rest of Canadian society. In cases where people were poor and unable to afford the marketplace, economic subsidies would be provided. There was plenty of experience with this approach.

As I began to explore what I had to do in order to create a housing market, I discovered that it was not a simple task: I had to create first of all some instrument of ownership. I had to create a regulatory environment which talked to the quality of the house. I had to create financial instruments that could be used to pay for houses. And I had to create within people a new view of a house and a desire to own a house.

So, in effect, I had to do two things: One was a technical task in creating all the mechanisms necessary to make a market work. The second was a social task – I had to change people's views about housing and the way in which they acquired it.

In effect, I began to see that if I were to make any changes at all in the housing situation of Indian people, I had to become a social engineer. Creating a market is a complex, difficult task that requires considerable effort across many fronts. Recent experience in creating a market society in the former Soviet Union, I think, bears out the difficulty involved. It requires a complete change in the way of life of a people. And it can be incredibly disruptive. At the time, however, we did not have the highly visible example of the Soviet Union in front of us.

Like a good bureaucrat, I made my findings known to my superiors. I can recall quite vividly my first meeting with the new deputy minister of Indian Affairs and Northern Development Canada. On a bright midwinter morning about ten years ago, I laid out what I have told you above. The deputy minister wanted to get out of the housing business as soon as possible, within five years if we could. I looked at him and said: 'We're in this business for at least a generation, i.e., for the next twenty years at least. That's the magnitude of the task that you want to undertake.' He looked at me and said: 'No, damn way are we staying in this business that long. I think that you're wrong. Go away and think about it some more. We need a new idea.'

So I did.

A few weeks later, he called me up to his office. I went up quite anxiously, wondering if I was going to have my job. What I had done was go away, think about it, and ship the same proposal back up again. When I walked into his office, the deputy minister's first words were: 'You're right. And I was wrong! So what do we do now?'

After I left his office, the housing review was completed. A new policy was devised. It looked a lot like the old one except that Indian councils now had a few more options and some degree of control over the use of resources. The resistance to the creation of a housing market as a way of providing housing on Indian reserves was too great to overcome.

We move forward in time a bit. I was called to a meeting in October 1997 of the Ontario Native Affairs Secretariat who wanted to hold a meeting with Aboriginal business people as background to the development of a new Aboriginal economic development policy for the government of Ontario. The meeting was uneventful. The participants all said the same thing: more business development, less government involvement, and improved access to capital and training.

One presentation struck me, however; it was made by members of a First Nations community near Sault Ste Marie, Ontario. They came and talked of a joint venture that they had entered into for the development of an industrial park on Indian land. They presented a video which they were using to attract firms to the park.

Picture, if you can, the video. Opening shot: man in canoe in the middle of lake, early morning, loons croon in the background, tranquillity and calm reign. All of this is designed to tell those who may wish to come that this is a land of calm, order, rationality. We move forward to the sales pitch: a shot of an industrial building. Voice over: 'Your company can be located here – there are no land taxes, no local improvement taxes, no business taxes. All you pay for is the building, and have we a deal for you. Need workers? Our well-trained workforce works for less than in any other place in the area. Talk to us about your labour needs. Our workers also work harder than all the rest.'

In 1994 the Royal Commission on Aboriginal Peoples was established by the federal government to examine and report on what should be done to improve the quality of lives of Aboriginal peoples in

Canada. One of the most persistent problems facing Aboriginal peoples throughout Canada has been low incomes and low participation in the labour force. It seems that, after almost two decades of consistent and concerted effort, incomes have not improved much. The analysis shows a complex problem and a multipart solution involving education, training, employment equity arrangements, anti-racism efforts, and local economic development.

The RCAP final report, released in November 1998, reflected the conventional and accepted wisdom that a major part of the solution to the problems facing Aboriginal peoples is economic development. In fact, the report links economic development to Aboriginal self-government on the grounds that the higher incomes that will come with economic development can help pay for self-government. It is now accepted by Aboriginal peoples, government officials, and business people that economic development is the key to the future. All that we have to do is figure out how to get more of it. And so, in the final report, we say the usual things: more training, more credit, more education, more business support, a national Aboriginal bank. The only difference between what we say today and what was said two decades ago is that today we say that these new institutions and processes should be under Aboriginal control. And no one questions us. We are talking the words of accepted wisdom. Economic development has become the Holy Grail of the Aboriginal community.

How do you go from the view of housing as a public good, to the blatantly market-oriented behaviour of the industrial park, to the strongly held view that economic development under the stewardship of Aboriginal peoples is of central and critical importance for the future of Aboriginal peoples? It appears to me that something has happened within Aboriginal societies in the past few decades. I want to talk about this transformation of Aboriginal societies that I see occurring around me. It is a transformation of a fundamentally moral kind, one that is fundamentally affecting the value-order of a society. This change is occurring almost without comment, although there are many who sense it and have offered prescriptions for mediating its worst effects.

As background to this transformation, I want to give you a sense of the times that Aboriginal peoples live in. The past two decades have been extraordinary for Aboriginal peoples. After the great pain of the past few hundred years and more importantly, the forced exile from the social, political, cultural, and economic space of Canada, a new society is emerging. Aboriginal peoples throughout Canada are determined to regain the stewardship of the structures and processes of their everyday lives. I call this effort 'Aboriginal governance' and see it as a much greater process than just Aboriginal government. It involves a whole range of societal actions being driven by Aboriginal ideas from Aboriginal thought.

Everywhere, we can see evidence of Aboriginal people beginning to govern themselves: most primary schools are now under Indian control, health care agreements are being negotiated, social welfare agreements and agencies are being established, communities are making agreements with community colleges and universities for higher levels of education, and some languages (e.g., Ojibway, Cree, Innuktitut) are becoming the language of work. There are at last count some 14,000 businesses, 40,000 students in colleges and universities, fifty financial institutions, including one trust company and one bank, and somewhere in the neighbourhood of 5,000 other organizations dealing with every need and issue that one can think of or invent.

All of this is occurring quietly and out of sight of most of us. Most of us only see the continuing poverty, social dysfunction, and political protests. This is what the media present to us. I will not deny that there is much poverty, violence at times, and political frustration and protest. One simply cannot ignore these. I do, however, want to set these aside for the time being because they mask some of the more important and fundamental changes occurring.

In the royal commission work, we argued very strongly for the centrality of economic development to the future of Aboriginal peoples' communities. Economic development if undertaken properly (i.e., if policy makers followed the ideas we were recommending), would provide higher individual incomes and higher revenues for local governments through either resource rents or some form of local or income taxes. The quality of Aboriginal peoples' material lives would improve over time, and, we hoped rise to the Canadian average.

And so we proposed the usual things: more education and training for the individual; more economic institutions like community economic development corporations, lending circles, capital corporations; more joint ventures between Aboriginal and non-Aboriginal firms; more control over land; and to prime the pump, more economic development agreements to provide starting capital. And being true to our own futures as academics, we also recommended more research to understand this whole system.

Economic development, as I said previously, has become the Holy

Grail of the Aboriginal community. There is much hope that is pinned on it. It is supposed to be that activity which provides people with control and allows them, indeed enables them, to preserve their culture and way of life. Every Aboriginal politician and most federal politicians repeat the mantra over and over again. At Trent University, we have a program devoted to Aboriginal economic development. This program was established at the behest of Aboriginal community leaders who want people who are educated and trained to develop their economies and manage the organizations which are formed within them. There are similar programs at other universities in Canada.

In the search for a better material life, however, we often forget to look around us. We do not see that as contemporary Aboriginal peoples, we now live within a capitalistic system, within a market economy. And that our economic development will occur within that system. We forget that we are only 1.0 million people, scattered in 600 or so isolated reserve communities across the country, and interwoven in some places in the rural and urban fabric. Like all people these days, we do not live in complete isolation from the world around us. Nor can we affect that world in any great way. In fact, we are more likely to be affected by it than the other way around.

And so in the quest for a better life within the context of contemporary North America, we encounter capitalism. We simply have no choice. This encounter, I contend, has profound effects for Aboriginal societies. It is fundamentally altering the moral order of Aboriginal society.

Most economists, anthropologists, and Aboriginal elders would describe traditional Aboriginal societies as non-market societies. The production, distribution, and consumption of goods was performed as a result of long-standing traditions. Most of the functions that we would describe as economic were embedded in the social roles of individuals. What was produced, how it was produced, how it was distributed, and how it was consumed would have evolved over time and become part of a shared history and way of doing things.

Max Weber defines 'traditional labour as work expended until reaching an accustomed level of livelihood.' Thereafter, the worker preferred leisure to any profits that might be gained from further exertion. This traditional or subsistence ethic, according to elders, economists, and anthropologists is the labour ethic that prevailed at the time of contact. People only accumulated what they needed or as Marshal Sahlins postulates, people only worked until they had enough, and then they stopped and contemplated the nature of the universe. Modern economists would say that there is a backward-sloping supply curve for goods.

This is not to say that Aboriginal peoples did not possess any desire to accumulate goods or were unfamiliar with trade. There were extensive trade networks throughout North America prior to the arrival of Columbus. These networks were used primarily for ceremonial or luxury goods. Most economic production was for subsistence or redistribution. Labour and resources would not have been primarily allocated to the demands of trade.

Some Aboriginal peoples did pursue the accumulation of goods. The accumulation of goods was a legitimate goal within the moral order provided that the goods were distributed and transformed into some form of social prestige, rank, or honour. A good example is the Potlatch that was common among many Aboriginal nations of the Pacific Northwest. For example, among the Tlingit, the primary way to earn social rank and honour was to acquire wealth and display industrious work habits. The Tinglit gave away their accumulated wealth in the Potlatch ceremony to honour their clan ancestors. Men gained new titles and social rank according to their Potlatch contributions. The host house or clan gained community prestige according to the wealth that it gave away. The giving away of wealth was viewed as an indication of their willingness to fulfil their moral duty to honour and remember their house and clan ancestors. In other societies, the distribution of goods was based upon need; one was simply expected to share the bounty of a hunting or fishing expedition.

These societies then developed and established a moral and social order which influenced the behaviour of individuals and institutions. The moral order indicated which goals were good and hence were supported, what type of social behaviour was acceptable and the nature, ends, and workings of social institutions. Moreover, it provided the glue that kept the society together. One could say that these societies had a moral commitment to this particular social/political/economic system. It was simply the right way to do things. The system they developed produced, in their view, the greatest good for the greatest number.

There is much literature which describes Aboriginal peoples' initial encounter with capitalism in various forms: the fur trade in Canada, the early settler economies, and the industrialization of the continent. This literature, especially over the past sixty to seventy years, has quite rightly described the devastating effects of this encounter upon Aboriginal societies. Indeed, we can see the effects of that encounter around us in the problems that are present and visible in Aboriginal communities today. In this initial encounter, Aboriginal peoples have been at the margins of capitalism, either as wage labourers or as consumers. This is the form that most of us encounter capitalism in our daily lives.

Yet there are an increasing number of Aboriginal people who want both to participate more fully in the capitalistic economy of Canada and to maintain some sense of traditional values and social order. In my work over the past two decades, I have found only a few Aboriginal people who want to reject capitalism. What I have seen is a headlong rush into it by young people and Aboriginal elites, with only some elders standing at the sides, urging caution and perhaps, in a few cases, outright rejection. Indeed, I can describe much of my own work as making capitalism work better in Aboriginal communities, developing, as it were, capitalism with a red face.

Capitalism requires us to think of the world around us in a different fashion. At its heart is a central process: the M-C-M^1 circle and an assumption about the proper ends of human behaviour. The M-C-M^1 circle which drives capitalism goes like this: start with a small amount of money (or capital); make or purchase commodities (goods) and sell them for more than was paid for them; then use this new and enlarged amount of money to do the same thing over and over again – each time, hopefully, increasing the capital.

This cycle, coupled with the emergence of a market where I can buy what I need and sell what I produce, and the emergence of money as a system of exchange, requires me to think much differently about my life, what is proper behaviour in that life, and the ends of that life. The emergence of the market as the dominant economic institution, replacing tradition and command as the method of provisioning means that I must begin to think about things in terms of the market, which is concerned with exchange value, and begin to value them in monetary terms. I can no longer think of them in social terms. And my behaviour begins to be labelled as productive or unproductive, according to its relation to the productive apparatus of society.

Another central idea linked with capitalism is the idea of progress. In simple terms, instead of the older European idea of the downward spiral of humanity from Eden or a golden age, the movement of humanity into the future has come to be conceptualized as an upward spiral of continual improvement: each day we are getting better and better, we are progressing, moving onward and upward to a better world. This better world has come to be defined in primarily material terms.

Central to our notions of capitalism is the idea that progress occurs through the continual striving of the individual to better his or her own position in the world. The idea that the happiness of all is the natural outcome of the self-regarding pursuit of the happiness of each has become intimately linked with capitalism.

Capitalism would also have not been possible without the means of production becoming private property, and the creation of a set of circumstances whereby most of the population must bargain to gain access to resources in order to live. The power of private property to organize and discipline social activity derives not so much from the ability of its owners to do whatever they want with it but with their power to deny access to it. Access to private property may be gained through a relationship which we have come to call employment: I will sell you a certain number of my hours in exchange for a wage. You retain ownership of what I produce with your private property. My labour (time, skill, knowledge) then becomes a commodity, liable to be bought and sold like any other.

Weber makes quite clear that capitalism requires a broad community moral consensus and commitment in its favour. One also needs to have this same consensus and commitment to its primary institutions: the market as the primary mechanism for the provisioning of society, the idea of private accumulation of wealth, the idea of defining progress only in economic terms, the idea that each of us in pursuit of our own economic interests improves our collective well-being, and the central idea of the capital cycle itself.

In my view, capitalism becomes more than an economic system. It becomes a world-view and a way of life. It postulates a way for the world to work and provides a somewhat complete view of the order of things. It has over the past 200 or so years developed a set of social institutions which support it and into which individuals are socialized. It also develops a social rhythm for society and defines social relationships.

What capitalism does ultimately is redefine the nature of society. It creates a moral system which is used for valuing ends and means. Society then becomes a collection of individuals; each of us is allowed to pursue our own needs on the basis that this will result in the greatest good for all. As a system of provisioning, it removes the system from the control of society. In the words of Karl Polanyi, it makes society serve the economy.

George Soros, the American billionaire, reflecting on the nature of capitalism in the *Atlantic Monthly* in February 1997 says that capitalism affects the values that guide people in their actions. As the market extends its sway across society, it progressively replaces traditional values. Marketing, advertising, packaging, the fundamentals which make the system work, begin to shape people's preferences and change their values. Unsure of what their values are as the traditional value-setting institutions of religion, spirituality, family, and local community lose their influence, they increasingly use money as the criterion of value. What is more expensive becomes better. Works of art are good because they are expensive. People are good because they are rich. And so on.

The nature of capitalism also forces the continued accumulation of wealth or its proxy – the continued consumption of what capitalists produce. The central calculus of capitalism regards wealth not just as a stock to be accumulated but as a stock capable of transformation into more wealth. In order to feed this cycle of ever-increasing wealth, capitalism creates a cycle of wants and needs which it then seeks to fulfil. Indeed, the capitalistic system attempts to tell us that we can become better people through the consumption of certain types of products and services. Our moral worth comes to be determined through the nature of our relationship to the M-C-M^1 calculus. All else becomes defined as an externality and hence not to be considered as a central factor in decision making within firms, and by extension within other organizations which do not have economic ends. Issues of spirituality and contribution to the common or collective good are not important.

This is the world that Aboriginal people are encountering. It is a world in which the central tenets are fundamentally different from those of traditional Aboriginal societies. The provisioning of Aboriginal societies, its economy so to speak, was embedded in its social structures. The working of this embedded economy was under the direction of tradition. And that tradition was maintained by elders.

The distribution of wealth within Aboriginal society was mediated by elders in accordance with some general principles of equity and need as I have stated before. Private property was not unknown, and there certainly were sets of laws to ensure its integrity. And there was trade, as we have discovered. Immense trade occurred throughout the

Americas, and goods moved everywhere. But the production of goods was mostly made in accordance with what Polanyi would call householding rather than for the market.

The central tenets of traditional Aboriginal life were harmony, balance, and reciprocity. Many Aboriginal peoples evolved social systems which attempted to live in cooperation with the natural world around them. That meant that the accumulation of material goods was somewhat limited. We should not, however, allow ourselves to think that material goods were not important, in Aboriginal societies. They were very important and in some places were used to determine prestige. What was not common, however, was the accumulation of wealth for its own sake in order to generate more wealth. In addition, material goods were used in order to establish and maintain relationships, both in the secular world and the spirit world.

Aboriginal people want to participate in the world of capitalism and hope that they can accomplish three things through that participation: improve their material standard of living; provide for the functioning of Aboriginal governments; and preserve traditional cultures with their value sets.

In the *Star Trek* series, the Federation meets the Borg. The Borg, as I have described, are a collectivist, humanoid-like race who are part machine and part human. They go about the universe absorbing cultures. They allow the absorbed peoples to maintain some semblance of themselves but they take over their minds. Individual thinking is not possible with the Borg. All thought and action are controlled from a central site: what one knows, all know. They are extremely quick to learn the weaknesses of their chosen candidates for absorption.

I think of our encounter as Aboriginal peoples meeting the Borg of capitalism. The Borg are an extremely powerful race and no one, except Captain Jean-Luc Picard and the *Starship Enterprise* has been able to defeat them. They absorb peoples at will. They are interested only in the technology of other peoples, not their thought or culture. Upon encountering a suitable candidate, they broadcast the following message: 'Your existence as you know it has come to an end. Resistance is futile.' That's how I see our encounter with capitalism.

The idea that we can somehow participate in capitalism without being changed by it is in my view wrongheaded. We already participate in the central institutions of capitalism within our own communities: we have private property, production for the market, institutions for access to credit, and local governments which pass by-laws to support the development of local business. We have a desire to accumulate wealth and to use that wealth to create more wealth, and we have accepted the idea, for the most part, that progress is measured in material terms.

More important, we are developing a broad community moral commitment to the institutions of capitalism. We argue for institutions which will give us easier access to capital, and we see the establishment of a network of almost fifty Aboriginal controlled credit institutions across the country. We argue for increased training so that we participate more effectively in the labour market. We argue for changes to the Indian Act to allow land to be privately held and to be used as collateral. And we argue for exclusive control over land through land claims and new treaties. And others agree. The Indian Act has been changed and we have gained exclusive control and ownership over land through the land claims settled to date.

In essence, this is the language of capitalism: land, labour, capital. This language is moving to the heart of the cultural agenda of Aboriginal peoples, although there are places of resistance that are springing up. New approaches like community economic development, new institutions like lending circles, adaptations like the use of elders in decision making, and preferences for small-scale enterprises over large-scale enterprises are being developed. These, however, are in my view mere adaptations or variations on a theme. The central tenets are still there. We can perhaps mediate the worst effects of capitalism, but even that will take much determined effort and the development of cultural and social institutions which remind us of our values.

Few Aboriginal people that I have encountered want to move back to a subsistence economy. Most want the material goods that capitalism brings. These material goods come with a cost. Many Aboriginal people believe that it is possible to escape the cost. I am not so sure that it is possible to play without paying.

It is possible to limit the effects of capitalism. There are those among us who manage to do it. The Amish and the Old Order Mennonites do it. They do it, however, through the creation of a closed society, strictly limiting the access of community members to the world outside. I do not hear any Aboriginal people saying that they want to do this.

We have participated at the edges of capitalism, as labourers, as small business people, as debtors. Now we seek to enter its heart. We will be transformed by it. Just as the Borg absorb cultures, capitalism will absorb Aboriginal cultures. And the moral order of Aboriginal societies will be changed.

Capitalism is an extremely adaptive, effective, efficient and seductive system. I compare it to Christianity in its ability to absorb new things and still retain its essence. Aboriginal peoples are also extremely adaptive. We have survived here, albeit in a diminished number, despite the attempts to assimilate us. Yet I am not convinced that we can survive the Borg of capitalism. We will be absorbed one way or another. What we can do is mediate the worst effects of capitalism through the continued use of our values and the transformation of these values into institutional actions. The world that we used to live in no longer exists.

The distance from the idea of the provision of housing as part of the basic human social contract to the corporate marketing behaviour of the Aboriginal industrial park in Northern Ontario is only a few years. It however represents a jump of 250 years or so in thinking.

Recently, I went to Kelowna in British Colmbia to attend the meeting of the National Aboriginal Economic Development Board. They had arranged for a luncheon speaker to come and talk about Aboriginal business. The speaker was the owner of the Native Investment and Trade Association. He was in his mid-thirties and a highly successful Aboriginal businessman. He currently owns a portion of a new TV network being started by Baton Broadcasting, is establishing the first mutual fund directed towards Aboriginal peoples, and is in the process of establishing a venture capital firm for Aboriginal enterprises. No one in the room blinked an eye when he talked of his plans to become an international financier.

The Borg have arrived and the absorption has already begun. Our existence as we have known it has come to an end. We need now to crete a way of living in the new world.

Notes

This chapter is a revised version of a paper presented at Trent University, on 20 March 1997, as part of the Bank of Montreal Distinguished Speaker Series.

The following books and articles were used in the preparation of this chapter: John Bagnell Bury, *The Idea of Progress: An Inquiry into its Origin and Growth* (New York: Macmillan, 1932). Jean Ensminger, *Making a Market: The Institutional Transformation of an African Society* (Cambridge: Cambridge University

Press, 1996). Robert L. Heilbroner, *The Making of Economic Society* (Englewood Cliffs, NJ: Prentice-Hall, 1962). Rolf Knight, *Indians at Work: An Informal History of Native Indian Labour in British Columbia 1858–1930* (Vancouver: New Star Books, 1978). David Newhouse, 'From the Tribal to the Modern: The Development of Modern Aboriginal Society,' Department of Native Studies Working Paper 4 (Peterborough: Trent University, 1995); and 'Modern Aboriginal Economies: Capitalism with a Red Face,' in *Sharing the Harvest*, Royal Commission on Aboriginal Peoples (Ottawa: Supply and Services Canada, 1995), 90–100. Karl Polanyi, *The Great Transformation: The Political and Economic Origins of Our Time* (Boston: Beacon Press, 1964). Royal Commission on Aboriginal Peoples, *The Report of the Royal Commission on Aboriginal Peoples* (Ottawa: Supply and Services Canada, 1997). Peter Saunders, *Capitalism* (Minneapolis: University of Minnesota Press, 1992). Marshall Sahlins, *Stone Age Economics* (Chicago: Aldine-Atherton, 1972). George Soros, 'The Capitalist Threat,' *Atlantic Monthly*, February (1997), 45–58. Frank Tough, *As Their Natural Resources Fail: Native People and the Economic History of Northern Manitoba, 1870–1930* (Vancouver: UBC Press, 1996). Max Weber, *The Protestant Ethic and the Spirit of Capitalism*, trans. Talcott Parsons (New York: Scribner, 1958). Fred Wein, *Rebuilding the Economic Base of Indian Communities: The Micmac in Nova Scotia* (Montreal: Institute for Research on Public Policy, 1986).

7

Capitalism, Ethics, and Ecology: The Tyranny of the Corporate Agenda

LIONEL RUBINOFF

The Ethic of Growth and the Domination of Nature

The most serious crisis facing the world economic and political order is the rapid depletion of natural resources and loss of biodiversity, which are occurring at a rate unprecedented in human and earth history – phenomena which are exacerbated by a startling disruption of global weather patterns brought about by ozone depletion and the accumulation of greenhouse gases in the upper atmosphere. Among the causes of what has been aptly described as a tragedy of the commons in the making, the obsessive pursuit of growth in both production and consumption, characteristic of capitalist industrial societies, may be singled out as a major contributing factor. Globalization, which is bringing the less-developed nations into the capitalist market place, is surely another contributing factor.

The foundational principle, and chief source of motivation, for the growth economy and the lifestyle of progressive consumption to which it gives rise, is the equation of welfare with affluence. This equation has sustained modern capitalism in much the same way that the Calvinist equation of salvation with worldly success, as measured by the accumulation of wealth, sustained the growth of capitalism in the early stages of its development. But although the pursuit of affluence has been promoted as the path to universal peace, prosperity, and justice in the secular world, it has fostered instead the very conditions which have brought us to the brink of a serious environmental crisis; or, in religious terms, to 'damnation' rather than 'salvation.' How did this come about?

One of the characteristic features of the growth economy is a generally misguided faith in the magic of the 'technological fix' which encourages and facilitates, almost without reservation, the implementation of policies that permit the substitution of an artificial for a natural environment.[1] Corporate capitalism, according to the economist Harry Johnson, explicitly rejects as 'naive and misleading' the Ricardian assumption that there is something special about the environment that requires keeping it intact in its existing form.[2] Another characteristic feature of capitalism is the equally misguided belief that nature has no value other than the uses to which it can be put by human industry. To the industrial entrepreneur, observes Thomas Berry, 'human possession and use is what activates the true value of any natural objects.'[3] Or, as Peter Drucker puts it, before it is possessed and used, 'every plant is a weed and every mineral just another rock.'[4] This is precisely the position argued by John Locke in his *Two Treatises of Government.*[5] For, writes Locke, 'God gave the world to mankind in common; but since he gave it to them for their benefit and the greatest convenience of life they were capable of ... It cannot be supposed He meant it should always remain common and uncultivated. He gave it to the use of the industrious and rational and labour was to be his title to it.'

So long as the pursuit of wealth was constrained by ethical and religious values the practice of capitalism was not incompatible with the improvement of mankind. But, as Max Weber points out, the practice of modern capitalism has divorced itself entirely from the ethical constraints associated with its religious roots. Max Weber writes:

> To-day the spirit of religious asceticism ... has escaped from the cage ... In the field of its highest development, in the United States, the pursuit of wealth, stripped of its religious and ethical meaning, tends to become associated with purely mundane passions, which often actually gives it the character of sport ... Of the last stage of this cultural development it might well be truly said: 'Specialists without Spirit, sensualists without heart.'[6]

As a result, the competition for wealth which may once have been subject to ethical constraints is now governed by the rule that, in the words of John Maynard Keynes, 'fair is foul and foul is fair; for foul is useful and fair is not. Avarice and usury and precaution must be our gods for a little longer still. For only they can lead us out of the tunnel of economic necessity into the daylight.'[7] Greed is not the only consideration, however. The driving imperative of the capitalist market, given the dehumanizing competition that now defines it, writes Murray Bookchin, 'is the need to grow, and to avoid dying at the hands of savage rivals. Important as greed and the power conferred by wealth may be, sheer survival requires that an entrepreneur must expand his or her productive apparatus to remain ahead of other entrepreneurs and try, in fact, to devour them. The key to this law of life – to survive – is expansion, and greater profit, to be invested in still further expansion. Indeed, the notion of progress, once identified by our ancestors as faith in the evolution of greater human cooperation and care, is now identified with economic growth.' As a result, according to Bookchin,

> However ecologically concerned an entrepreneur may be, the harsh fact is that his or her survival in the marketplace precludes a meaningful ecological orientation. To engage in ecologically sound practices places a morally concerned entrepreneur at a striking, and indeed, fatal disadvantage in a competitive relationship with a rival – notably one who lacks any ecological concerns and thus produces at lower costs and reaps higher profits for further capital expansion.[8]

Donald Worster agrees:

> The capitalists ... promised that, through the technological domination of the earth they could deliver a more fair, rational, efficient and productive life for everyone ... Their method was simply to free individual enterprise from the bonds of traditional hierarchy and community, whether the bondage derived from other humans or the earth. That meant teaching everyone to treat the earth, as well as each other, with a frank, energetic, self-assertiveness ... People must ... think constantly in terms of making money. They must regard everything around them – the land, its natural resources, their own labour – as potential commodities that might fetch a profit in the market. They must demand the right to produce, buy, and sell those commodities without outside regulation or interference ... As wants multiplied, as markets grew more and more far-flung, the bond between humans and the rest of nature was reduced to the barest instrumentalism.[9]

This is not the vision of capitalism that J.S. Mill had in mind when he recommended against allowing the appetite for growth to overwhelm the search for a political economy that would contribute to the improvement of mankind. For Mill the proper goal of the progressive state was what he called the 'stationary state.'

I cannot ... regard the stationary state of capital and wealth with the unaffected aversion so generally manifested towards it by political economists of the old school. I am inclined to believe that it would be, on the whole, a very considerable improvement on our present condition ... It is scarcely necessary to remark that a stationary condition of capital and population implies no stationary state of human improvement. There would be as much scope as ever for all kinds of mental culture, and moral and social progress; as much room for improving the Art of Living and much more likelihood of its being improved, when minds ceased to be engrossed by the art of getting on. Even the industrial arts might be as earnestly and as successfully cultivated, with this sole difference, that instead of serving no purpose but the increase of wealth, industrial improvements would produce their legitimate effect, that of abridging labour.[10]

Mill offered precisely the same advice on the goals of higher education. Rather than serving merely to equip students to earn their livelihood in a world in which citizens have been educated to be compulsive consumers, education should devote itself instead to the cultivation of civility. So far as the professional skills are concerned, writes Mill,

whether those whose speciality they are will learn them as a branch of intelligence or as a mere trade, and whether, having learnt them, they will make a wise and conscientious use of them or the reverse depends less on the manner in which they are taught their profession than upon what sort of minds they bring to it – what kind of intelligence and of conscience the general system of education has developed in them ... What professional men should carry away with them from a university is not professional knowledge, but that which should direct the use of their professional knowledge and bring the light of general culture to illuminate the technicalities of a special pursuit.[11]

It has become painfully evident, however, that in a society whose institutions and values have been shaped by the ethic of growth and its equation of welfare with affluence, citizens in search of consumer satisfaction will often turn a blind eye to the lack of civility that characterizes the indiscriminately consuming public. Such a public is also well practised in the art of self-deception, especially when it allows itself to tolerate the extent to which public policy has divorced itself from the ethics of ecological citizenship. There is no better example of this divorce than the willingness of politicians and policy makers to compromise environmental and ethical standards for the purpose of protecting their political agendas – which often depend upon catering to the corporate agenda.

Such compromises are often rationalized in the name of the so-called public interest and carry the promise of substantial economic benefits for the citizenry at large. In truth, however, the economic benefits are more likely to be enjoyed by the corporate elites (upon whom the politicians rely for their hold on power); and usually at the expense of the citizenry who are consistently misled by their political leaders into believing that the gross national product[12] is the ultimate index of economic health.

For the sake of holding onto the power which is the reward for their support of the corporate agenda, politicians are prepared not only to suppress any information that does not support their policies, but also to demonize those who speak out against corporates – whose purposes have been well served by the technological assault upon and reinvention of the environment so characteristic of capitalism. Environmentalists are thus branded as 'Luddites' and 'enemies' of the 'public interest.' The corporations, meanwhile, have cleverly conscripted the public into supporting their contempt for the agenda of environmentalists by sponsoring and helping to promote such pressure groups as 'The Wise Use Movement' in the United States and the 'Share Movement' in British Columbia – both of which have been inspired by the leadership of Ron Arnold, who has portrayed environmentalism as a conspiracy to 'kill jobs' and 'trash the economy.'[13]

A typical example of the attitude that favours jobs and the economy over protection of the environment is the advice of the economist Harry Johnson, when he considers the merits of building a factory in a town located on a river whose aquatic life and delicate ecology would be placed in jeopardy by the pollution caused by the factory. Johnson's approach to the economy versus ecology conflict takes the form of a cost-benefit analysis that would almost certainly favour the interests of the factory owners and developers over those of ecology. For, if the factory is built, there will be substantial economic benefits for the community which would otherwise not have 'materialized,' while everything that is lost by polluting the river can be regained by using some of the profits from the factory to, for example, build artificial swimming pools, water purification plants, and artificial fish ponds. In short, the price of progress in this instance is to replace original nature, the gift of natural selection, with a technologically engineered surrogate, the invention of human ingenuity.

> If a river is being polluted by paper-pulp production, prohibition of such production, or insistence that pulp manufacturers use an expensive non-polluting technology (a form of tax on them) may well be less socially efficient than a smaller tax on pulp mills used to provide free communal parking, swimming pools, and fish ponds, since the former remedy might well benefit the aesthetically sensitive rich while depriving the poor of employment opportunities, while the latter would compensate the poor for pollution by providing equivalent free facilities for recreation.[14]

Notice that in this analysis there is no mention of the 'rights' or 'well-being' or 'biotic integrity' of the river, or of the relative worth of exposure to *artificial* as compared with *natural* environments. Such considerations are ruled out by Johnson's dogmatic rejection of the assumption that there is something special about the environment that requires keeping it intact in its existing form – an assumption that he regards as 'naive and misleading.' 'Man's whole history,' writes Johnson,

> has been one of transforming his environment rather than accepting its limitations. He has domesticated and raised animals for his own use rather than relying on hunting them, and previously he invented weapons for hunting them made from pieces of the environment rather than relying on his original physical powers. He has cleared ground for the planting of crops rather than relying on what he could collect from nature's rather niggardly abundance. And he has steadily shifted his economic activities from an overt and direct reliance on using products made available by nature to organizing those products, or those sophisticated by human ingenuity, into an industrial productive system which, directly at least, is completely independent of nature's bounty.[15]

Such are the values which lie at the basis of the corporate agenda. As I was writing these words the CBC was broadcasting news of the Province of Alberta's reluctance to support Canada's position on the emission of greenhouse gases for the Kyoto climate conference held in December 1997, because it would conflict with the growth of Alberta's economy, which depends heavily upon the refining of oil. And indeed, Canadian climate change initiatives took a step backwards on 24 April

1998, when our energy and environment ministers agreed to yet another study of the economic implications of cutting greenhouse gas emissions before taking action.[16] The construction of mega-dams for the purpose of generating electricity for industrial use poses an equally serious threat to the environment. Yet governments worldwide persist in their willingness to support such projects, in spite of these projects' proven record of environmental degradation. The Canadian government has been particularly delinquent in this regard. Why, for example, is the Export Development Corporation helping to finance the Three Gorges Dam on China's Yangtze river, which violates every principle of ecology as well as the new International Code of Ethics which the Canadian government has recently urged Canadian corporations to voluntarily follow? And why is Ottawa preparing to sell $8 billion worth of CANDU nuclear reactors to China and Turkey without requiring any environmental reviews – in clear violation of Canadian law?[17]

The record of the Canadian government is no better when it comes to the financing of mining projects, such as the Lihir and Minima gold mines in Papua New Guinea, the Tapian copper mine in the Philippines, and the Oman gold mine in Guyana. Finally, the influence of the corporate agenda on the shaping of public policy is nowhere more evident than in the failure of the federal government to support a scientifically respectable Endangered Species Act. Instead, it has proposed an act which, while prohibiting the direct harming of endangered species, does not ensure legal protection of their habitats. This is a critical omission. Other deficiencies lie in the fact that the act only applies to a limited number of species, and allows the federal Cabinet, not the scientific community, to make decisions about the listing of species at risk. So significant are the deficiencies of this act that a group of leading Canadian scientists and environmentalists were prompted to write a letter of protest to Prime Minister Jean Chrétien in which they urged that the identification and protection of species at risk 'be made purely on considerations of conservation biology, not politics.'[18] Political interference, they warn, will undermine the credibility of the entire act. Precisely the same complaints have been made recently by scientists employed by the Department of Fisheries and Oceans (DFO) and Health Canada regarding the reluctance of government officials to accept scientific advice, on such matters as overfishing, habitat destruction, and the regulation of food additives and growth hormones, which conflicts with the interests of industry.[19] Is there any doubt that this kind of political interference, which marginalizes the advice of scientists, reflects a bias towards the interests of the corporate sector? Little wonder that there is widespread concern among environmentalists and social activists over the long-range implications of the recent attempt to negotiate the Multilateral Agreement on Investment which broke down in October 1998. If revived and implemented by the industrialized nations, this agreement will virtually transfer decision-making powers over culture, social programs, and the environment from elected politicians to non-elected and unaccountable executives of the multinationals. The agreement will ban governments from enacting any new environmental or labour legislation that could be deemed harmful to the business of a foreign or domestic investor and will also provide opportunities for foreign investors to seek compensation for any financial losses incurred as a result of the imposition of environmental regulations. Is there any greater conceivable threat to democracy?[20]

The bias of the corporate agenda is inherently anthropocentric. It is no secret that, under the influence of the politics of globalization, the economies of both the industrialized and developing worlds are heavily biased in favour of serving exclusively human needs. More than 40 per cent of the annual net primary production of the world's land now goes directly to meet human needs or is indirectly used or destroyed by human activity, leaving 60 per cent for the millions of other land-based species with which humans share the planet. While it took all of human history to reach this point, the human share of resources could double to 80 per cent by the year 2030 if current rates of population growth continue, and rising per capita consumption could shorten the doubling time considerably.[21] Contrary to what some policy advisers would have us believe, the consensus among most environmental scientists is that continuing growth in material consumption – the number of cars and air conditioners, the amount of paper used, and the like – will eventually overwhelm gains from efficiency, causing total resource use (and all corresponding environmental damage) to rise beyond the carrying capacity of the biosphere, as a result of which a 'tragedy of the commons' may be unavoidable.[22]

In the course of our industrial progress we have surrendered to a Faustian urge to transcend our natural limits and have become addicted to a dependency on a whole variety of 'exosomatic' technologies, all of which are anti-ecological, and in the end anti-economical. We may have convinced ourselves that the pursuit of the technologically possible is indispensable for our well-being. It is questionable, however, whether the conception of well-being that lends legitimacy to the growth society of consumerism has any moral authority. We have, it seems, surrendered to a kind of moral relativism for which 'anything goes,' and we are unable to distinguish between what we merely *desire*, which is a matter of psychological significance, and what is *desirable* because it has moral worth. In the words of E.F. Schumacher:

> present-day industrial society everywhere shows [the] evil characteristic of incessantly stimulating greed, envy, and avarice. It has produced a folklore of incentives which magnifies individual egotism in direct opposition to the teachings of the Gospel ... The modern industrial system has a built in tendency to grow; ... Whatever becomes technologically possible – within certain economic limits – must be done. Society must adapt itself to it. The question whether or not it does any good is ruled out on the specious argument that no one knows anyhow what is good or evil, wholesome or unwholesome, worthy of man or unworthy.[23]

There does indeed seem to be, as Thomas Berry suggests, a hidden rage in our tradition 'against those inner as well as outer forces that create a challenge or impose a limitation on our activities. Some ancient force in the Western Psyche seems to perceive limitation as a demonic obstacle to be eliminated rather than as a discipline to evoke creativity.'[24]

Not only does our pursuit of the possible ride roughshod over the distinction between the genuinely moral and the psychologically desirable, it is also anti-ecological, supporting a lifestyle pursued in arrogant defiance of the Second Law of Thermodynamics. There is no escaping the fact that the higher the degree of our economic development, and the more we surrender to our Faustian urges, the greater must be the annual depletion of low entropy, and the shorter becomes the expected life of both human and non-human life on this planet.

Here, according to Nicholas Georgesco-Roegen, is the dilemma. Every time we produce a Cadillac (or some other wasteful commodity that provides both employment and luxury for the wealthy) we do so at the expense of posterity. The same applies to the building of a tractor instead of making a plough or spade. In short, we cannot produce 'bigger' and 'better' refrigerators, automobiles, or jet planes without also producing bigger amounts of waste. Even attempts to recycle waste are entropic. Pollution control technology consumes an additional amount

) long term

of low entropy, which is actually much greater than the decrease in the entropy of what is recycled. There is no free recycling, just as there is no wasteless industry. We are thus forced to the conclusion that while economic development through industrial abundance may be a blessing for us now – albeit, a false blessing – it is definitely against the interest of the human species as a whole, if the species' interest is to have a life-span as long as is compatible with its dowry of low entropy.[25] Does this not raise serious questions about the ethics of our obligations to posterity?

It should be evident to any clear-thinking person that our craving for the extravagant has given birth to a pathological cult of commodity-fetishism, reinforced by a mass consumption economy that promotes a consume-now, pay-later, mentality. A mass consumption economy is one of rapid obsolescence and replacement, and it cannot but breed a throw away attitude towards human-made goods, irrespective of quality, while at the same time breeding a tolerance for replacing 'natural' trees with 'plastic' trees. In such a society, as the economist E.J. Mishan complains: 'There is no time [or inclination] to grow fond of anything, no matter how well it serves. And in any case, it will soon be superseded by a new model. In consequence, everything bought comes to be regarded as 'potential garbage,' and is treated as such.'[26]

The root cause of the pathology infecting the affluent, consuming society, in which affluence is equated with welfare, is an all-pervasive sense of 'permissiveness,' by which Mishan means, 'the apparent suspension of all norms of propriety and convention that is coming to make the question of what is decent and indecent, what is proper or improper, increasingly a matter of individual discretion.' Furthermore,

The emergence of a permissive ethic – itself an end product of the secularism that is entailed by the idea of progress – weakens the traditional safeguards against mass surrender to fashionable indulgence ... the continued expansion of modern industry as a whole depends directly on its success in whetting and enlarging the appetite of the consuming public so as to enable it to engorge the burgeoning variety and volume of goods. Clearly a discriminating public will not serve. Nor will a public whose demand for goods is restrained by considerations of propriety and good taste, or by accepted ideas of right and wrong. Promiscuity is the quality sought for, promiscuity coupled with insatiability ... This ideal public, is, of course, that found in the permissive society. For a society in which 'anything goes' is *ipso facto* a society in which anything sells.[27]

Needless to say, in such a society it would be virtually impossible to even understand, let along live by, the wisdom expressed by Socrates' remark that 'the unexamined life is not worth living.'

Symptomatic of the confusion infecting the permissive society is the practice of measuring economic well-being by the standard of the gross national product. The confusion lies in the manner in which the GNP is calculated. To begin with, the calculation ignores completely the deterioration of the natural assets which are consumed in the production of the income and wealth that is added into the total figure as income. At the same time, no recognition is made of the portion of the GNP representing the pollution and health costs that are incurred by the ways in which we generate wealth. In fact, a substantial proportion of the GNP represents expenditures aimed at relieving the stress and negative spin-off effects associated with the production of goods and services, or to provide lubricants, such as the consumption of alcohol and psychological counselling, which are necessary to keep the machinery of our industrial system well-oiled. Besides being blind to the destruction of natural wealth, the GNP, as currently calculated, gives a misleading interpretation of welfare by counting as income many of the expenditures made to combat pollution and its adverse effects.

The result is an inflated sense of both income and wealth, creating the illusion that a society is better off than it really is, and can sustain higher levels of resource extraction and consumption than is actually the case. Thus Robert Repetto, an economist with the World Resources Institute, warns: this failure to distinguish between natural asset destruction and income generation makes the GNP 'a false beacon, and can draw those who steer by it onto the rocks.'[28] A case in point, is the Alaska oil spill of March 1989. This accident, probably the most environmentally damaging in U.S. history, actually created a rise in the GNP, since much of the $2.2 billion spent on labour and equipment for the clean-up was added to income. Equally perverse is the fact that the medical care portion of the tens of billions of dollars in health costs incurred by North Americans annually as a result of air pollution, is counted on the plus side of the national income ledger. In the words of Jonathan Porritt:

> GNP measures the lot, all of the goods and services produced in the money economy. Many of these goods and services are not beneficial to people, but rather a measure of just how much is going wrong; increased

spending on crime, on pollution, on the many casualties of our society, increased spending because of growing bureaucracies: it's all counted.[29]

Yet, as E.F. Schumacher complains, the average economist simply takes it for granted that growth of GNP must be a good thing, irrespective of what has grown and who, if anyone, has benefited. 'The idea that there could be pathological growth, unhealthy growth, disruptive or destructive growth, is to him a perverse idea which must not be allowed to surface.'[30] This is precisely the theme explored so brilliantly in the well-known story by Dr Seuss about the Lorax and his struggle to 'speak for the trees' and save nature from the ravages of industry and the greed of entrepreneurs for whom nature is nothing more than a resource to be exploited for profit.

The Nuclear Liability Act and the Nuclear Lobby

A prime example of how the corporate agenda has influenced public policy is the little known and seldom discussed Nuclear Liability Act, which was passed into law by the Canadian government in October 1976. The Nuclear Liability Act exempts industries engaged in the manufacture of nuclear equipment from liability should there be a melt-down caused by one of their products. This means that even if these companies were clearly responsible for what happened, even if they falsified safety documents, deliberately cut corners in manufacturing the products, or knowingly shipped defective products, they would not be liable for any damages incurred by innocent victims. The government has also protected the utilities that operate our nuclear plants from bankruptcy by putting a cap of $75,000,000 on their liability, as well as negotiating insurance coverage at a minimum cost to the industry. And no municipal, provincial, or federal government is required by law to provide any guarantee of full or even partial compensation to victims of a nuclear accident. Additional funds for payment of claims may be authorized by Parliament, but this only means that in the event of an accident any compensation in excess of $75,000,000 will be covered by the taxpayers rather than the operators or insurance companies.[31]

In a critical review of the act published in August of 1987, Monique Hebert acknowledges the seriousness of this complaint.

By shielding the potentially negligent in this way, the legislation provides no incentive for them to uphold the high standard of care that must be observed by those associated with the nuclear industry. Consequently, the public's safety is at risk. Furthermore, the argument goes, by limiting the operator's liability, the legislation removes what could have been an effective safety valve against the substandard work of others. If the operator's liability were not limited, there would at least have been a strong incentive for them to exercise the utmost care in relation to the work done for them by others. But as their liability is limited, particularly to the extent that it is under the current legislation, even this safety valve is lacking.[32]

Monique Hebert's general conclusion is that 'the nuclear power industry in Canada is barely feeling the costs of having to insure itself against third-party liability,'[33] and she questions the justification for so shielding the parties who may actually be at fault should accidents occur.[34]

Is it fair for innocent victims to receive less consideration than those responsible for causing injury to them, in order to protect industries from excessive overhead costs and give them a competitive advantage on the world market? Would it not better serve the interests of justice to require that the nuclear industry be financially responsible for its actions, so that it would be forced to tighten safety standards, improve quality measures to detect defective parts, and provide better training to reduce the chance of human error leading to catastrophe? And if, in order to maintain the high standards expected of it, costs soar to the point where the industry is no longer cost effective, would this not provide an incentive to develop alternate sources of energy, such as appear possible in the area of solar technology, not to speak of the vast potential of pursuing conservation strategies?

A graphic example of how the nuclear industry has been shown favouritism in Canada is provided by Michael Clow in a study of nuclear coverage in four daily newspapers in Ontario and New Brunswick; the Toronto Globe and Mail, the Toronto Star, the Saint John Telegraph Journal, and the Fredericton Daily Gleaner. Clow's study, which covered sample periods during the 1970s and 1980s, concluded that the news coverage of the debate between the pro- and anti-nuclear camps 'favoured the pro-nuclear camp. Coverage was largely devoted to reproducing the press releases of the promoters of nuclear power. It is impossible to discern in these papers the case against nuclear power as the anti-nuclear movement argued it. The evidence indicates that these newspapers are not objective and impartial sources of information on the struggle that challenges business interests and government policies.'[35]

The pro-nuclear camp is a powerful alliance of certain business and government agencies which have pursued the construction of nuclear power stations since the late 1940s. The anti-nuclear camp is primarily a citizen's movement which has challenged the proponents of nuclear power over energy policy only since the mid-1970s, and which wants to put the nuclear industry out of business. But, according to Clow, the overwhelming weight of evidence from this and similar studies suggests that the news media has not been open to portraying serious challenges to business and government in Canada, the United States, or Britain.[36]

Biotechnology and Bovine Growth Hormone Controversy

A further example of the failure of public officials to safeguard the interests of Canadian citizens is provided by the current debate over the use of Recombinant Bovine Growth Hormone (rBGH), also known as bovine somatotropin (rBST). rBGH, which is designed to increase milk production, was approved by the U.S. Food and Drug Administration for use in the United States on 5 November 1993.[37] Since it went on the market in the United States an estimated 10,000 farmers have adopted its use, yet nine out of ten dairy farmers have opted not to use it, and some have gone to the expense of labelling their products 'No rBGH.'

rBGH is a synthetic hormone which increases milk production by 10 to 15 per cent. It is one of the first significant products of biotechnology to appear in our food supply. Its use has sparked a bitter controversy around the world which has now spilled over into Canada where rBGH has been reviewed by government drug regulators employed by the Bureau of Veterinary Drugs (BVD) who, like the Department of Fisheries and Oceans (DFO), who are mandated to speak for the fish, are supposed to represent the interests of animals.[38] In the beginning, the rBGH review by the BVD was assisted by a task force consisting of representatives of Agriculture and Agri-Food Canada, Industry Canada, the National Dairy Council of Canada, the Dairy Farmers of Canada, Monsanto Canada, Eli-Lilly, and the Consumers' Association of Canada.[39] Pending the outcome of this review, the manufacturers of rBGH agreed to a voluntary moratorium on the sale of rBGH in Canada which expired on 1 July 1995. Needless to say, the participation of Monsanto (who gave us Agent Orange and PCBs) and Eli-Lilly – the chief manufacturers of this hormone under the trade names Prosilac and Nutrilac – on the task force led opponents of rBGH to question the objectivity of this particular task force. This suspicion was reinforced by the replacement of the Consumers' Association representative, who had expressed serious reservations about rBGH, with a 'less opinionated' representative.

Another source of concern was the fact that the review process was made to rely primarily on data submitted by rBGH manufacturers and was conducted in secret because the data are deemed proprietary. And, based on what we now know about the review process leading to the settlement agreement with Alcan in August 1987 during the Kimano Completion Project controversy, this concern is not without foundation.[40] Eventually the review process was handed over to an internal review team consisting of scientists employed by Health Canada, whose conclusions were considerably more negative than those of previous reviews. Fortunately, it was this review which finally persuaded Health Canada against granting approval for the use of the hormone on 14 January 1999.

Added fuel for the rBGH controversy comes from a report on the CBC's *The Fifth Estate* report entitled 'Big Milk, Big Muscle, Big Money,' which was broadcast in November 1994. In the course of Lynden MacIntyre's interview with Bill Drennan, former division chief in the Bureau of Veterinary Drugs, allegations were revealed that Monsanto representatives offered Health Canada $1 to $2 million on the condition that the company receive approval to market their drug in Canada without being required to submit data from any further studies or trials.[41] It was also reported, on the same *The Fifth Estate* program, that Dr Margaret Haydon of the BVD has complained to the RCMP that files relating to rBGH applications have been tampered with.[42] *The Fifth Estate* also revealed that two British scientists, Dr Eric Bruner and Dr Eric Millstone, who were given permission by Monsanto to review data on rBGH, were prevented from releasing findings that showed a definite increase in mastitis in cows treated with the product. Not only did Monsanto claim that it would be improper for Bruner and Millstone to release their findings, they also delayed publication of the original material reviewed by Bruner and Millstone for five years. In his interview on *The Fifth Estate*, Dr Bruner expressed concern over the publication delay. 'I find it very curious,' he said, 'that Monsanto should object to our paper. Our paper is a relatively harmless analysis which shows some small negative effects of rBST. If they're seeking to suppress these data, as they have for the past three years, then it could be that there are other questions which we don't yet know about.'[43] Veterinarian David S. Kronfeld agrees. In a paper published in 1988 Kronfeld observed that 'favourable responses to rBST have been presented promptly, loudly and repeatedly. Unfavourable results have been delayed, subdued and obscured.'[44]

Notwithstanding the fact that there is some scientific evidence that this hormone is a potential health risk for both the cows and humans,[45] the manufacturers of this hormone lobbied aggressively to get it approved in the United States,[46] and the U.S. government, under the terms and authority of the North American Free Trade Agreement, has exerted considerable pressure on the Canadian government to approve its use in Canada. It is obvious that in the risk-benefit analysis that serves the corporate agenda, the anticipated $1 billion annual sales from this product are deemed to more than outweigh the potential health risks to humans. Opponents of rBGH, however, draw attention to the potential market risks for small dairy farmers because of the competitive advantage that will be gained by the large producers and are therefore pleased by the increasing opposition to its use among Europeans and many domestic consumers.[47]

There are several ethical issues raised by the rBGH controversy. There is first of all the suffering caused to the cows who are kept in a perpetual cycle of gestation and lactation which wears out their bodies quickly, thus cutting down a cow's normal life-span from twenty to twenty-five years to five years or less. And because their systems are overworked they must be fed a special diet of expensive high energy food. They are also more vulnerable to diseases, such as mastitis, a bacterial infection which leads to painful inflammation of the udder, thus requiring increased doses of antibiotics. There are a number of other concerns related to the effects of the added stress on cows resulting from the injections of rBGH and the treatments required to mitigate the side effects of this drug which ought to be sufficient to encourage a policy of caution with respect to its use. I do not think it would be an exaggeration to suggest that continued administration of rBGH to cows is a blatant case of inhumane treatment of animals for the sake of maximizing utilities for the exclusive benefit of humans – and in particular, the invested interests of powerful drug manufacturers. Such treatment of animals betrays the still pervasive influence of the Cartesian domination of nature ethic on the political economy of the industrialized world.

There are also legitimate concerns over the possibility that the effects of rBGH's impact on cows can be transmitted to humans.[48] It is possible, for example, that hormonal and antibiotic residues in milk and meat made from 'burned out' milk cows will have health implications for consumers of these products, especially children. There is also evidence that milk produced by rBST-supplemented cows contains an increased concentration of the IGF-1 protein, which results in an elevated level of this protein in the blood of humans. IGF-1 has been implicated in the establishment and maintenance of tumour growth. By protecting the tumour cells from apoptosis (programmed cell death), IGF-1 accelerates tumour growth. Increases in the levels of IGF-1 could thus stimulate a variety of indolent tumour cells which tend to appear in various organs with aging, resulting in the onset of clinical cancer decades before it would normally appear. It could also stimulate the progression and aggressiveness of childhood leukemias to a point where chemotherapy could not be effective, as well as generally inhibiting the treatment of cancer at various stages in its development. Although Monsanto has maintained vigorously that IGF-1 not destroyed by pasteurization would be completely broken down by digestive enzymes and therefore would have no biological activity in humans, this has been disputed by independent researchers. Indeed, researchers at the FDA reported in 1990 that IGF-1 is not destroyed by pasteurization and that pasteurization actually increases the concentration of IGF-1. They also confirmed that undigested protein could indeed cross the intestinal wall in humans. It seems, however, that in both the United States and Canada regulatory agencies are more influenced by scientific data supplied by the manufacturers of rBGH than by what has been learned through independent research, or even by government scientists. This verdict is confirmed by a recent and controversial 'Gaps Analysis' report by the 'rBST Internal Review Team' submitted to the Health Protection Branch, Health Canada, on 21 April 1998, which is critical of the failure by the manufacturers of rBST and previous reports sponsored by the BVD to consider and address all of the available evidence concerning not only the potential adverse effects of IGF-1 on human health, but a variety of other risks to both humans and dairy cows which may also be associated with the use of rBST.[49]

Approving the widespread consumption of BST supplemented milk thus appears to some critics as lending tacit approval to an experiment on an unsuspecting public that could have horrendous consequences and eventually overwhelm the health care system. In the opinion of Dr George Tritsch, a retired research scientist, 'The experiment would take one to three decades, when it would be difficult to dismantle a well-entrenched BST industry, and still have one to three decades worth of individuals in the pipeline. I can conceive of no animal experiments to test this and to provide hard data to predict the magnitude and time frame for this effect. The risk to benefit ratio of the experiment is clearly not in favour of the consumer.'[50]

It was, no doubt, precisely such concerns for animal and human welfare that have prompted Australia, New Zealand, and the European Community to ban the use of rBGH and rBGH-produced milk and meat products.[51] The moral issue at the centre of this controversy revolves around the apparent willingness of public officials and corporate executives to experiment with and compromise the health of consumers, not to speak of the animals, for the sake of the profits that will accrue from the widespread use of biotechnology. An equally pressing issue is the right of consumers to information with respect to which of the foods they put on their plates have been genetically engineered. The question has thus been raised whether all genetically engineered foods should be required by law to be appropriately labelled so that consumers can exercise their democratic right of choice with respect to the food they eat.[52]

Needless to say such a requirement has been fiercely opposed by the food and drug industries, and regrettably government bodies such as Health Canada and Agriculture Canada have been slow to respond to the growing expression of concern over the issue of genetically altered foods. On 1 December 1995, however, Agriculture and Agri-food Canada released a proposed guideline for the labelling of 'novel foods derived through genetic engineering.' The essence of this proposal is to allow the voluntary labelling of foods that have been genetically altered, and to allow the labelling of foods which have been produced without the use of genetic engineering, such as rBGH-free milk. But there would be no *requirement* that this be done. And, as in the United States where this is widely practised by dairy farmers, the costs of such labelling must be born by the producers, which will, of course, result in higher costs for the consumer.

In addition to the animal and human health issues that lie at the centre of the debate, there are a number of political and socioeconomic factors to contend with. For example, the economic analysis presented to the European Agricultural Council by its commission found that 'the widespread use of rBST would increase milk production enough to lead to the slaughter of 4% to 6% of dairy cattle in the EC, given current milk quotas – a development that would add to beef surpluses.'[53] There are additional concerns over the implications for small farmers of licensing the use of rBGH. One of the selling points for the use of rBGH is the promise that an increase in production will lead to a decrease in milk prices for the consumer. But this will lead to a decrease in dairy revenue for the producers, which in turn will affect the small producers more than the large ones and actually put some farmers out of business.[54] Then there will be further pressures on the system of subsidies. As well, it seems clear that only the agri-business companies would be able to absorb the combined costs of the hormone and the required 'high energy' feed, not to speak of the costs of the 'burning out' of cows. The critics of the use of rBGH who are concerned about the continued existence of small family farms believe that the issue is over what is socially desirable, not just what is economically efficient. A profile of what might be expected to happen to the Canadian dairy industry is suggested by the following report by Greta Gaard about what, according to Senator Russ Feingold of Wisconsin, is likely to happen in the United States.

> US dairy income will drop $1.3 (US) billion over the next six years due to the use of rBGH. The annual losses due to rBGH will climb to $546 (US) million by the year 1999, and up to 30 per cent of US dairy farmers may be forced out of business in the 36 months following the legalization of rBGH. The impact of this loss will be felt not only by dairy farmers, but also by entire rural communities, many of which are barely surviving. For each farmer who goes out of business, 25 other dairy-related jobs are lost.[55]

Senator Feingold also estimates that while the marketplace price of milk may drop, the 'hidden' costs to manage surpluses will rise by at least $65 million for 1994 and $116 million for the fiscal year 1995. In short, as in the case of the controversy over Alcan's Kimano Completion Project in British Columbia, the licensing of the use of drugs like rBGH amounts to just one more example of how large corporations work the system to their advantage, through arrangements in which taxpayers end up subsidizing their profits. And it is not only the animals and the taxpayers but the environment in general that are 'taxed'

and made to suffer the consequences of policies that favour the interests of transnational drug and chemical companies. As Greta Gaard
points out in her review of the rBGH controversy:[56]

> Current research does indicate that the kind of industrialized factory
> farming often used in conjunction with large-scale dairy production has
> severe implications for soil contamination and ground water pollution.
> The chemicals and antibiotics that are passed through the animal's waste
> leave residues in the land and water. Although some studies are giving
> attention to these issues the implications of these potential effects are not
> fully understood.
>
> Environmentalists and other activists continue to raise concerns about
> the use of rBGH which the promoting companies fail to address to their
> satisfaction. In this single issue, the costs of so many – the cows, the peo-
> ple, the farmers, the taxpayers, the world's hungry and the environment –
> must be balanced against the interests of some very powerful and multi-
> national drug and chemical companies. In the US, the scales have tipped
> towards the side of industry, and in Canada, the outcome remains to be
> seen.[57]

Finally, as Douglas Powell and William Leiss point out, recombinant
bovine somatotropin is one of the first products of molecular genetic
engineering, and the prospect of its commercial use has generated
unprecedented scientific analysis and public discussion. They are not
convinced that the risks are in fact such as to warrant a total ban on its
use. They do recognize, however, that an important theme in the history of resistance to technology is the question of public control over
technological decisions, challenging the authority of experts and questioning the motives of public officials. In this regard the rBST controversy offers itself as a classic example of how government, industry,
and the media have failed to act responsibly in making certain that
they have communicated the risks as well as benefits in the commercial use of biotechnology, with a full and informed understanding of
the nature of public concern. Quite apart from what the final verdict
might be, when all of the scientific data have been thoroughly analy-
sed, the rBST debate, particularly in Canada, demonstrates that what
constituted risk communication messages by the various social actors
were confusing, inadequate, and failed to recognize the broader social
context in which the rBST debate took place.[58]

Social Ecology and the Path to Sustainability

The foregoing examples of conflict between the values of corporate capitalism and environmental and community values are symptomatic of a spiritual sickness which has infected western culture throughout its long history of alienation from nature, as manifested in the arrogant view of western humanity that it has a divinely ordained mandate to exercise domination over inferior nature. Critics of western individualism and humanism, from Rousseau to E.F. Schumacher, Martin Heidegger, and Murray Bookchin, have profoundly questioned both the inferiorization of nature, that encourages replacing original nature with technological surrogates, and the equation of welfare with affluence, which prevents us from recognizing that the road to peace, permanence, and happiness is not the same as the road to riches.[59] On the one hand, as E.F. Schumacher complained, it should be evident to any clear-minded person that an attitude to life 'which seeks fulfilment in the single-minded pursuit of wealth – in short, materialism – does not fit into this world, because it contains within itself no limiting principle, while the [natural environment] in which it is placed is strictly limited.'[60] At the same time, Schumacher points out, materialism depends upon 'the cultivation of such drives in human nature as greed and envy, which destroy intelligence, happiness, serenity, and thereby the peacefulness of man,'[61] thus depriving persons of the satisfaction of their most basic needs, which Schumacher believes can only be achieved through an experience of 'health,' 'beauty,' and 'permanence.' Like John Stuart Mill, Schumacher favours a society in which the need for self-fulfilment can be satisfied through the pursuit of aesthetic and intellectual experiences; goals that will 'profit' persons in ways other than financial. A truly meaningful or becoming life is one which is at leisure from the mere pursuit of wealth and power.

Bertrand Russell shares the concerns of Mill and Schumacher over the uncritical pursuit of growth. In one of his more thought-provoking essays, Russell proposes that technological progress which is so uncritically revered in the modern world should be directed not towards commodity growth but towards growth in leisure time – not to be confused with unemployment – for workers. Alas, Russell laments, the pathology of growth dictates otherwise.

Suppose that, at a given moment, a certain number of people are engaged in the manufacture of pins. They make as many pins as the world needs, working (say) eight hours a day. Someone makes an invention by which the same number of men can make twice as many pins as before. But the world does not need twice as many pins. Pins are already so cheap that hardly any more will be bought at a lower price. In a sensible world, everybody concerned in the manufacture of pins would take to working four hours instead of eight, and everything else would go on as before. But in the actual world this would be thought demoralizing. The men still work eight hours, there are too many pins, some employers go bankrupt, and half the men previously concerned in making pins are thrown out of work. There is, in the end, just as much leisure as on the other plan, but half the men are totally idle while half are still overworked. In this way it is insured that the unavoidable leisure shall cause misery all round instead of being a universal source of happiness. Can anything more insane be imagined?[62]

Russell wrote this in 1935, during the height of the Great Depression. No doubt he would pass the same judgment on the insanity of the present method of dealing with technological change by a corporate sector which is prepared to sacrifice labour to the gods of technology and has responded globally to the opportunities provided by technology by adopting the practices commonly referred to as 'downsizing,' and 'outsizing,' all of which has the effect of reducing labour costs while increasing profits. Indeed, as Barnet and Cavanagh point out at the conclusion of *Global Dreams*,

> The surplus of gifted, skilled, undervalued, and unwanted human beings is the Achilles Heel of [the] emerging global system. The problem is starkly simple: An astonishingly large and increasing number of people are not needed or wanted to make the goods or to provide the services that the paying customers of the world can afford. The gathering pressures of global competition to cut costs threaten the vast majority of the 8 billion human beings expected to be living on earth in the first quarter of the next century with the prospect that they will be neither producers nor consumers.[63]

The motivation for adopting such practices does not lie in a desire for the improvement of mankind, as understood by Russell, Mill, and Schumacher. It is rather the increase of wealth and shareholder profits made possible by these practices that fuels this system of capitalism, supported by the illusion that affluence is the chief measure of welfare

✗ Cant go back

or well-being. Tolerance for disposable labour, meanwhile, has been cultivated by the long-standing tendency to accept a technologically engineered nature as an acceptable substitute for original nature. There is, in other words, as little reverence for the dignity of human labour as there is for pristine nature. The automated, voice-mailed, and cybernetic culture of contemporary industrial society is embraced enthusiastically in the corporate sector as a superior alternative to a labour-intensive industrial society, in much the same way that reason is believed to be superior to inferior nature. The inferiorization of nature and the inferiorization of labour-intensive technology, what E.F. Schumacher calls 'technology with a human face,' go hand in hand.

It was Schumacher's view that the tyranny of materialism and the expansion of so-called needs associated with it, which have given birth to *homo economicus* and 'growthamania,' has come about as a result of the exclusion of wisdom from economics, science, and technology, and its replacement by 'cleverness.'[64] In the language of Greek philosophy, materialism owes its vitality to the divorce between *techne* and *arete*. Under such conditions the real essence of human nature falls victim to a self-fulfilling prophecy in which humanity is defined as an accidental product of evolution, essentially competitive, and motivated exclusively by self-interest. In nature, survival is guaranteed by evolutionary 'fitness' as determined by those biological characteristics that give some species an advantage over others. In society, fitness is measured by wealth, and the power that wealth makes possible. It is by means of such power that the affluent societies have gained their advantage over the less affluent.

Thus has the equation of affluence with welfare given rise to a profit-oriented economy and system of technological, capital-intensive, mass production, as distinct from a system of production by the masses. This, as Schumacher laments, is the inevitable outcome of the divorce between 'cleverness' and 'wisdom' which has become a characteristic feature of the technological society. This is what happens, as Heidegger explains, whenever we substitute 'calculative' for 'meditative' thinking and measure the value of everything by 'what it is used for.'[65] In a truly just society, however, in which *techne* and functional rationality is under the firm control of wisdom and *arete*, the system of capital-intensive mass production will be replaced by a system of production by the masses, oriented towards the organic, the gentle, the non-violent, the elegant, and the beautiful.[66]

The transition from a society based on the maximization of profit (in which the ownership and consumption of goods is an end in itself) to a society in which consumption is moderated by genuine need, will, Schumacher argues, depend upon a system of education that recognizes and puts into practice a distinction between (a) the transmission of knowledge which is merely *techne* or 'know-how,' and (b) wisdom, which makes possible the transmission of ideas of value, of what to do with our lives; ideas or values which enable persons to choose between one thing and another, between mediocrity and excellence, between evil and good, between mere *desire*, which satisfies merely material needs, and the morally *desirable*, which contributes to a 'becoming existence.'

Such choices, explains Schumacher, require the cultivation of a kind of thinking that is capable of reconciling the demands of the economy with respect for nature and the dignity of humanity. This kind of thinking is quite different from that associated with either cost-benefit analysis or with the kind of thinking in which value is determined exclusively on the basis of a willingness to pay. It is precisely this kind of thinking which Aldo Leopold had in mind when he extolled the benefits of an ecological education, the kind of education which makes it possible for us to 'think like a mountain.' If such an education can inspire the adoption of a land ethic based on a conception of the economy oriented towards health, beauty, and permanence, productivity will be still be attainable, but as a by-product of these values. Productivity will now be ecological and sustainable. As the landscape architect Ian McHarg points out in *Design with Nature*, in everything – from farming to building human settlements – human activity must conform itself to the 'lay of the land' and its natural cycles and processes. For ultimately human productivity can only be sustained over time by a partnership with natural productivity: 'The farmer is the prototype. He prospers only insofar as he understands the land and by his management maintains his bounty. So too with the man who builds. If he is perceptive to the processes of nature, to materials and to forms, his creations will be appropriate to the place; they will satisfy the needs of social process and shelter, be expressive and endure.'[67]

Thus, for example, rather than view agriculture as essentially directed towards 'food-production,' as does the crude materialist, the ecological view sees agriculture as not only bringing forth the foodstuffs and other materials which are needed for a becoming life, but as keeping humanity in touch with living nature, of which we are and remain a highly vulnerable part, and thereby humanizing and ennobling humanity's wider habitat.[68] Heidegger draws attention to the archaic meaning of the word *denken* (to think),[68] which is a variation of the word *danken* (to thank). Thinking, Heidegger argues, is, in its most original and authentic mode, actually an act of thanking. In old English as well to think *(thencan)* is also to thank *(thancian)*. The relationship between 'thinking' and 'thanking' finds expression, according to Heidegger, in the ritual sowing of the seed, which is a donation, and the ritual thanksgiving in which the harvest or gift of nature is received in a mood of gratitude and humility.[69]

Consider in this regard, as a further example of how the mechanization of nature has alienated us from original thinking, Heidegger's well-known meditation on the Rhine, which was once a river about which poets wrote songs and poems, a river around which people fell in love, married, and gave birth. But alas, Heidegger laments, the Rhine is no longer 'full of gods'; it is now primarily a source of hydroelectric power. The multidimensional, heterogeneous reality once celebrated by poets has been reduced to a one-dimensional homogeneity. The river is now what it is used for, no more, no less. It is defined by utility.

> What the river is now, namely a water-power supplier, derives from the essence of the power station. In order that we may even remotely consider the monstrousness that reigns here, let us ponder for a moment the contrast that is spoken in the two titles: 'the Rhine,' as dammed up into the *power* works, and the 'Rhine,' as uttered by the *art* work, in Holderlin's hymn by that name. But, it will be replied, the Rhine is still a river in the landscape, is it not? Perhaps. But how? In no other way than an object on call for inspection by a tour group ordered there by the vacation industry.[70]

The river is now hydroelectric power, agriculture is transformed into 'the mechanized food industry,' and nature herself is pillaged as 'a gigantic gasoline station.' And 'everywhere everything is ordered to stand by, to be immediately at hand and, indeed to stand there just so that it may be on call for a further ordering.' The essence of technology *(techne)*, so long as it is under the guidance of *poesis* and *denken* (original thinking), lies in 'revealing.' But unlike this *techne*, by means of which the 'gods' are revealed, the revealing that holds sway in modern technology is a *challenging*, which puts to nature the unreasonable demand that it supply energy. Herein lies the difference between the old wooden bridge that joins the banks of the river, which allows the river to remain what it is and to run free and wild, and the hydroelectric plant, which brings the river under our command.[71] And so the poet, no longer able to commune directly with the gods within, must craft his language into a song in search of 'fugitive gods,' and failing this he must be content, as the poet Denis Lee laments, to sing to what is merely a 'trace' of the gods who have fled. Nor can we expect to find any trace of the gods or original thinking in the various voices of public policy which are currently shaping our political economy.

Heidegger's philosophy is thus a summons for the return of original thinking; a turning away from the technoculture, which is a 'provocation,' and return to mankind's original vocation as guardian of the earth.

It was Schumacher's and Heidegger's view that a civilization which regards agriculture as mere 'food production,' and which pursues it with such ruthlessness and violence – as in some applications of biotechnology – that the other dimensions of agriculture are not merely neglected but systematically counteracted, has very little chance of long-term survival. They would thus agree with Murray Bookchin's assertion that 'reconciliation of man with the natural world is no longer merely desirable, it has become a necessity.'[72]

The goals of an ecological society, such as envisaged by Schumacher, Bookchin, and Heidegger, are to keep persons in touch with living nature of which they are an integral part, to provide creative, useful work with hands and brain, to humanize and ennoble man's habitat, and to bring forth goods which are needed for a becoming existence.[73] Only a system of production that meets these goals is genuinely productive. The technology and economics of mass production based on profit and the accumulation of wealth is inherently violent, ecologically damaging, self-defeating in terms of non-renewable resources, and stultifying for the human person. The technology of production by the masses, what Schumacher calls 'intermediate technology,' or 'technology with a human face,' makes use of the best of modern knowledge and experience, is conducive to decentralization and participatory democracy, compatible with the laws of ecology, and gentle in its use of scarce resources. Most importantly, it is designed to enhance and ennoble the quality of all life and to serve the higher goals of human beings instead of making them servants of machines designed to maximize profits.

The task of education, in the ecological society, is thus to cultivate persons in the image of the classical ideas of the meaning of humanness, rather than persons intoxicated by the false promises of progress and the magic of the technological fix. The former – referred to by Schumacher as 'homecomers' – have developed the courage to say 'no' to the fashions and fascinations of the age and to question the presuppositions of a civilization which appears destined to conquer the whole world. The latter, the people of 'the forward stampede,' as Schumacher describes them, pursue goals not from any insight into our real human needs and aspirations (which technology is meant to serve) but solely on the grounds that the necessary technical means appear to be available.[74] Or, as Herman Daly puts it, such persons are possessed by 'a tendency to value the intermediate means according to the technical and physical possibilities for producing them. If it is possible, we must do it.'[75] And if it is both profitable and possible then our appetite for doing so is truly insatiable.

Finally, according to Schumacher, the great challenge facing education is to restore humanity's image of itself as more than a mere machine, accidentally thrown up by evolution between two ice ages, whose chief *raison d'etre* is to use knowledge for the sole purpose of manipulation. The classical image of humanity, as portrayed, for example, by Socrates, Plato, Aristotle, and St Augustine, is quite different. From the classical perspective, knowledge takes the form of not only *techne* but *arete* (wisdom). Etienne Gilson explains the difference as follows:

> The real difference which sets the one against the other derives from the nature of their objects. The object of wisdom is such that, by reason of its intelligibility alone, no evil use can be made of it; the object of science is such that it is in constant danger of falling into the clutches of cupidity, owing to its very materiality. Hence the double designation we may give science according as it is subservient to appetite, as it is whenever it chooses itself as an end, or is subservient to wisdom, as it is whenever it is directed towards the sovereign good.[76]

Science does not qua science contain any inherent propensity for serving one rather than another of these masters: mere desire or opportunity as distinct from the sovereign Good.

Unfortunately, according to Schumacher and Heidegger, western civilization, since the Renaissance, has witnessed the almost complete disappearance of knowledge as wisdom or *arete*, and the vacuum that has thus been created has been filled by an exaggerated emphasis on *techne*, with the result that Western humanity has become 'rich in means and poor in ends.' Indeed, Schumacher laments, we no longer even understand what it means to seek answers to the question, 'What ought I to do with my life? At what goals ought I to aim? What are my highest values?' 'A man's highest values are reached,' writes Schumacher,

> when he claims that something is good in itself, requiring no justification in terms of any higher good [the image of children dancing in the sun comes to mind.] But modern society prides itself on its 'pluralism,' which means that a large number of things are admissible as 'good in themselves,' as ends rather than means to an end. They are all of equal rank, all to be accorded *first priority* [which is, incidently, one of the cardinal doctrines of what has come to be known as the postmodern critique]. If something that requires no justification may be called an 'absolute,' the modern world, which *claims* that everything is relative, does, in fact, worship a very large number of 'absolutes' ... Not only power and wealth are treated as good in themselves – provided they are mine, and not someone else's – but also knowledge for its own sake, speed of movement, size of market, rapidity of change, quantity of education, number of hospitals, etc. In truth, none of these sacred cows is a genuine end; they are all means parading as ends.[77]

To this might be added the observation that the real tragedy in all of this is that genuine ends, such as Health, Beauty, and Permanence, because they are not recognized as such, find themselves competing with means, and whether they receive affirmation will depend not on their inherent worth but on a 'willingness to pay,' which in turn is measured by the criterion of instrumental value. This is the logic by which public expenditures in health care and education come to be regarded as investments in human capital rather than as necessary conditions for a 'becoming existence.'

It is precisely this logic that has been brought into existence through the pursuit of the corporate agenda. It is a condition in which the world has been divided into the 'rich' and successful, on the one hand, and the 'poor' and unsuccessful, on the other, and where the path to success is open only to those who live by Keynes's maxim, referred to at the outset, that 'fair is foul and foul is fair,' for, as Keynes points out, 'foul is useful and fair is not.' Unfortunately, and contrary to Keynes own expectations, capitalism is far from having outgrown this allegedly interim stage on the way to universal prosperity and is still driven by an ethic that prefers the expedient to the good.

Notes

1 See, e.g., H. Johnson, *Man and His Environment* (London: British North American Committee, 1973); Julian Simon, *The Ultimate Resource* (Princeton, NJ: Princeton University Press, 1981); and *Population Matters* (New Brunswick, NJ: Transaction Publishers, 1990); M. Krieger, 'What's Wrong with Plastic Trees?' *Science*, 179 (1973), 446–55; Laurence Tribe, 'Ways Not to Think about Plastic Trees,' *Yale Law Journal*, 83/7 (1974), 1315–46; and William Cronon, ed., *Uncommon Ground*, (New York: W.W. Norton, 1995); From the perspective of this attitude, 'plastic trees' are as good as 'natural ones.' Indeed, argues Kreiger, 'much more can be done with plastic trees and the like to give most people the feeling they are experiencing nature.' 'We have to realize,' he continues, 'that the way in which we experience nature is conditioned by our society – which more and more seems to be receptive to responsible interventions.' ('What's Wrong with Plastic Trees?' 453).

2 Johnson, *Man and His Environment*, 5. The physicist Eugene Rabinowitch lends support to this judgment when he deplores the fact that 'many rationally unjustifiable things have been written in recent years – some by very reputable scientists – about the sacredness of natural ecological systems, their inherent stability and the danger of human interference with them.' *Times*, 29 April, 1972. Cited by E.F. Schumacher, *Small Is Beautiful* (New York: Harper and Row, 1989), 110. In this article Rabinowitch argues that resource depletion and disappearing species do not pose a threat to human survival: 'for ... there is no convincing proof that mankind could not survive even as the only animal species on earth! If economical ways could be developed for synthesizing food from inorganic raw materials ... man may even be able to become independent of plants, on which he now depends as sources of his food.' Julian Simon agrees when he writes that there 'is no physical or economic reason why human resourcefulness and enterprise cannot forever continue to respond to impending shortages and existing problems with new expedients that, after an adjustment period, leaves us better off than before the problem arose.' *The Ultimate Resource*, 345.

3 'The Viable Human,' in *Environmental Philosophy: From Animal Rights to Radical Ecology*, M. Zimmerman and J.B. Callicott, eds. (Englewood Cliffs, NJ: Prentice-Hall, 1993), 176.

4 *Innovation and Entrepreneurship: Practice and Principles* (New York, Harper and Row, 1985), 30.

5 *First Treatise*, chap. IX, sect. IX; *Second Treatise*, chap. V, sects. 25, 27, 30, 34.

6 *The Protestant Ethic and the Spirit of Capitalism*, translated by Talcott Parsons (New York: Scribner's, 1958), 181–2.

7 Cited by Schumacher, *Small Is Beautiful*, 24.

8 'What Is Social Ecology?' in Zimmerman and Callicott, *Environmental Philosophy*, 368.

9 Donald Worster, ed., *The Ends of the Earth* (Cambridge: Cambridge University Press, 1988), 11–12.

10 *Principles of Political Economy*, book IV, chap. 6, *Collected Works of John Stuart Mill* (Toronto, University of Toronto Press, 1963), 753–6.

11 Inaugural Address,' in *John Stuart Mill on Education*, F.W. Garforth, ed. (New York: Teacher's College Columbia University, 1971), 156–7. Mill's advice is clearly at odds with the prevailing ideology of the present Conservative government of Ontario. In his address to *A Summit on the Future of Ontario Universities* (18 Nov. 1997) at the Metro Convention Centre in Toronto, Premier Mike Harris said that he sees little value in academic degrees in the humanities, geography, and sociology, in which 'the graduates have very little hope of contributing to society in any meaningful way'; by which he meant, in ways that are economically productive. (See the *Globe and Mail*, 21 Nov. and *Toronto Star*, 20 Nov.).

12 GDP has replaced GNP, but the issues raised about GNP by the authors quoted in this chapter all apply equally to the newer GDP.

13 This is the argument put forward in his book, *Trashing the Economy* (Bellevue, WA: Free Enterprise Press, 1993, 2nd ed., 1994). For further discussions of the significance of 'The Wise Use Movement,' see A.L. Rawe and Rick Field, 'Tug-O-War with the Wise Use Movement,' *Z Magazine*, Oct. (1992), 62–4, and Lorelei Hanson, 'Turning Rivals into Allies: Understanding the Wise Use Movement,' *Alternatives*, 21/3, (1995), 26–31. The Origins of the Share Movement in B.C. have been explored in a documentary prepared for the CBC's *Fifth Estate* and broadcast in 1993.

14 Johnson, *Man and His Environment*, 18; see also, 10–12.

15 Ibid., 5–6. This is a typical expression of the Baconian/Cartesian domination of nature ethic according to which the domination of nature, civilization, and freedom, go hand in hand. This equation is explicitly endorsed in the following statement by Rexford G. Tugwell, a former economic adviser to Franklin Delano Roosevelt: 'A part of the conspicuous victory over nature on this continent has been the power which has been exhibited in subduing natural material and forces to a will for well-being. Nature has been reduced to order, to regimentation. This is a process which should

have freed men as it enslaved nature.' *The Battle for Democracy* (New York: Columbia University Press, 1935), 195.

16 See Heather A. Smith's report on Canada's failure in recent years to provide credible leadership in the fight against climate change. 'Stopped Cold,' *Alternatives*, Fall, (1998), 10–16.

17 See the Sierra Club of Canada's bulletin on this matter, dated 29 April 1998.

18 Dated 14 Nov. 1996, and circulated throughout the Canadian academic community for signatures by Dr David W. Schindler of the University of Alberta. This is one of several letters sent to the federal minister of the environment by the scientific and academic community expressing support for strong federal legislation to protect endangered species and their habitats. On 31 July 1998 Drs David Schindler and Geoff Scudder circulated yet another letter for suggestions and signatures; a revised version of which was sent to Prime Minister Chrétien in November. In this we pointed out the deficiencies in the previously tabled bill (C-65) and stressed the importance of placing the responsibility for identifying which species and their habitats should be listed and protected by law with scientists rather than with politicians and bureaucrats who are more likely to fall under the influence of lobbyists for the corporate sector. In March 1999, those of us who had signed the letter were advised that the government had agreed to change the rules so that only government scientists could vote on species listing decisions. See also the *Globe and Mail*, 23 March 1999, A2. It is still not clear who will have the authority to make these decisions.

19 In May 1997 three leading marine biologists, Jeffrey Hutchings, Carl Walters, and Richard Haedrich, published a controversial article in the *Canadian Journal of Fisheries and Aquatic Sciences* (*CJFAS*, 5, 1198–1210), entitled 'Is Scientific Inquiry Compatible with Government Information Control?' in which they attempt to document the disastrous consequences that political interference with scientific research has had on the viability of the east and west coast fisheries. Among other things the authors condemn the Department of Fisheries and Oceans (DFO) for ignoring the advice of scientists and favouring instead policies favourable to the interests of government and corporations. Their complaints were endorsed by other leading scientists such as Ransom Myers, Killam Chair of Ocean Studies at Dalhousie University, and David Schindler of the University of Alberta – both of whom had previously been employed by the DFO. Media coverage of this controversy was quite extensive throughout June 1997. See, e.g., the coverage by the *Ottawa Citizen*, 23, 24, 27 June, 1997, on A1 and A2 of each day.

20 See Tony Clarke, *Silent Coup, Confronting the Big Business Takeover of Canada* (Toronto: Lorimer, 1997), and Linda McQuaig, *Shooting the Hippo* (Toronto:

Penguin, 1995), and *The Cult of Impotence* (Toronto: Penguin, 1998), as well as Tom Spears's report on the 'Friday Group,' in the *Ottawa Citizen*, 28 July (1997), C1. As reported by Spears, the Friday Group is an informal club consisting primarily of representatives of Canada's oil, gas, chemical, mining, forestry, and manufacturing industries, whose shared interests focus on strategies for opposing the strengthening of environmental regulations. It was no doubt pressure from such interest groups, as well as fall-out from the NAFTA treaty, that prompted the Treasury Board to send a directive to Environment Canada in February 1993 requesting that it determine whether its regulations 'impose barriers and disincentives to industry's development.' Instructions were given to 'look at existing regulations and identify those that significantly hinder Canadian competiveness or impose needless costs,' and to decide also 'whether environmental problems addressed by these regulations could be handled by another level of government.' See the *Globe and Mail*, 20 Feb. 1993. Following the election of the Harris government in Ontario in 1995, who then declared that 'Ontario was now open to business,' both the Ministry of the Environment and the Ministry of Natural Resources were downsized in keeping with the government's policy of business-friendly environmental deregulation, which leaves it up to business and industry to monitor itself.

21 For a more detailed analysis of the human impact on natural resources and wildlife habitats, see D.H. Meadows, D.L. Meadows, and J. Randers, *Beyond the Limits* (Toronto, McClelland and Stewart, 1992).

22 See, e.g., Nicholas Georgesco-Roegen, 'The Entropy Law and the Economic Problem,' in *Economics, Ecology, Ethics*, Herman Daly, ed. (San Francisco: W.H. Freeman, 1980).

23 *Good Work* (New York: Harper and Row, 1975), 27, 30–1.

24 'The Viable Human,' 179.

25 'The Entropy Law and the Economic Problem,' in Daly, *Economics, Ecology, Ethics*, 55–8.

26 'The Rise of Affluence and the Decline of Welfare,' in Daly, *Economics, Ecology, Ethics* 271. See Schumacher, *Small Is Beautiful*, 46.

27 Ibid., 278.

28 'No Accounting for Pollution: A New Means of Calculating Wealth Can Save the Environment,' *Washington Post*, 28 May 1989. Cited by Lester R. Brown, Christopher Flavin, and Sandra Postel, *Saving the Planet* (New York: W.W. Norton, 1991), 122. Chapter 9 of *Saving the Planet* is devoted to a detailed discussion of 'Better Indicators of Human Welfare' – a topic which is further explored in D.H. Meadows, D.L. Meadows, and J. Randers, *Beyond the Limits*.

29 *Seeing Green: The Politics of Ecology Explained* (New York: Oxford, 1984), 121.

30 *Small Is Beautiful*, 51.

31 For further information on this act, see 'Review of the Nuclear Liability Act' by the Interdepartmental Working Group to the Atomic Energy Control Board, Nov. (1991), and Alan Nixon, 'Nuclear Liability Act,' for the Science and Technology Division, Library of Parliament, 29 Jan. (1993).

32 'The Nuclear Liability Act,' Library of Parliament, Research Branch, 17 Aug. (1987), 24–5.

33 Ibid., 21.

34 Ibid., 25.

35 Michael Clow with Susan Machum, *Stifling Debate* (Halifax: Fernwood, 1993), 13.

36 Ibid., 13. It should be pointed out that an attempt by the Toronto-based Energy Probe, together with co-plaintiffs Dr Rosalie Bertell, a well-known environmental activist, and the City of Toronto, to initiate legal proceedings to strike down the Nuclear Liability Act was abandoned when the plaintiffs realized that they could not match the huge financial resources that the federal government and the nuclear establishment were prepared to spend to defend the act. Once again the corporate agenda takes precedence over the public interest.

37 It should be pointed out that the approval by the FDA was based almost entirely on evidence provided by reviews commissioned by Monsanto, the leading manufacturer of the hormone which goes by the trade names Prosilac and Nutrilac. For an apologia in favour of its use see David N. Harpp and Joseph A. Schwarz, 'The Straight Goods: Bovine Growth Hormone,' *Rapport*, 9/3, (1994), 6. A well-balanced discussion of this controversy can be found in Douglas Powell and William Leiss, *Mad Cows and Mother's Milk* (Montreal and Kingston: McGill-Queen's University Press, 1997), 123–52. The primary focus of this discussion is on the need for developing more effective means of communicating risk assessment to the public.

38 In addition to the FDA, the use of rBGH has the support of the World Health Organization, the U.N. Food and Agriculture Organization, and the American Medical Association. Groups in Canada that officially reject it include the National Dairy Council of Canada, the Animal Defence League of Canada, the Registered Nurses Association of Ontario, the Council of Canadians, the City of Toronto, and the Ukrainian Women's Association. In the course of a series of hearings conducted by the Canadian Senate's Standing Committee on Agriculture and Forestry, between June and December 1998, it was evident that several scientists employed by Health

Canada had serious reservations about the safety of rBGH for both humans and animals and that there was indeed a consensus among these scientists that the hormone should not be approved until further testing had been done. One prominent member of the research team, Dr Shiv Chopra, a senior scientist with the Bureau of Veterinary Drugs, has been particularly outspoken over what he perceived to be excessive political interference in the review process. He was only one of many scientists to complain about the pressures being exerted on scientists to approve the hormone.

39 It is worth noting that prior to the spring of 1998 neither the BVD, Health Canada, nor Agriculture Canada had conducted any studies of their own. Their decisions in this matter, like that of the FDA, were based primarily on data supplied by the manufacturers of rBGH, and by consultations with various experts and stakeholders. See 'Review of the Potential Impact of Recombinant Bovine Somatotropin (rBST) in Canada,' *Report of the rBST Task Force Presented to the Minister of Agriculture and Agri-Food Canada*, May (1995). However, the 'Gaps Analysis' Report by the 'rBST Internal Review Team,' which was submitted to the Health Protection Branch, Health Canada on 21 April 1998, drew attention to the fact that the manufacturers had not taken sufficient account of a growing body of evidence gathered by independent studies which questions the safety of this hormone for both animals and humans. (Shiv Chopra, Mark Feeley, Gerard Lambert, Thea Mueller, and Ian Alexander, *rBST (Nutrilac) 'Gaps Analysis' Report, by rBST Internal Review Team*. Ottawa: Health Protection Branch, Health Canada, 1998.) It is not likely that this report would have been commissioned had there not been pressure brought upon the government by the media attention provoked by community and public interest groups such as the Council of Canadians, and the National Farmers Union, who posted this report on their web site on 6 October 1998. It is worth noting that during the initial stages of the Senate Standing Committee on Agriculture and Forestry hearings on the safety of rBGH in June 1998 the 'Gaps Analysis' Report had not yet been made available. Its conclusions were dealt with by the Senate committee at its meetings on 22 and 29 October, during which the committee interviewed the scientists associated with the report. During the course of these hearings Senator Spivak raised questions about a report in the *Toronto Star* concerning memos from senior officials dated May 11 and 13 instructing committee members for the 'Gaps Analysis' Report to alter the report or harm their careers. At these same hearings Senator Whelan, a former federal minister of agriculture, who chairs the committee, complained about the extent to which multinationals are able to influence the decisions of both national and international regulatory agencies. As far as their deci-

sions go, Whelan exclaimed, 'I have as much respect for some of their decisions as hell would have for a snowball.'

40 For a detailed discussion of the controversy over Alcan's Kimano Completion Project see Bev Christensen, *Too Good to be True* (Vancouver: Talon Books, 1995), and Lionel Rubinoff, 'Politics, Ethics, and Ecology,' in *Canadian Issues in Environmental Ethics*, Alex Wellington, Allan Greenspan, and Wesley Cragg, eds. (Peterborough, Broadview Press, 1997, 133–53). See also Jeffrey A. Hutchings, Carl Walters, and Richard Haedrick, 'Is Scientific Inquiry Incompatible with Government Information Control?' 1204–6, and responses in the June issue, 54, 6, by William G. Doubleday, D.B. Atkinson, and J. Baird, 'Comment: Scientific Inquiry and Fish Stock Assessment in the Canadian Department of Fisheries and Oceans,' 1422–6; M.C. Healy, 'Comment: The Interplay of Policy, Politics and Science,' 1427–9; as well as the reply by Hutchings, Haedrich, and Walters, 1430–1.

41 As reported by the CBC's *The Fifth Estate*. The allegation was originally made by Dr Margaret Haydon in a memorandum to the RCMP. In this memo she claims that at a meeting with representatives from Monsanto at which they were discussing some deficiencies in Monsanto's research data, Monsanto offered to pay Health Canada a sum of 'one to two million dollars with the condition that the company receive approval to market their drug in Canada without being required to submit data from any further studies or trials.' When asked to comment on these allegations, Dr William Drennan of the BVD, who was present at the meeting, admitted that while it may have been perceived by those present as a 'bribe,' it was not taken seriously and would not be a factor in any decision that might be taken on the matter. Monsanto subsequently claimed, when they learned of the interview, that they had simply offered one to two million dollars to fund further research in the event that the drug was approved for use. These matters were also brought before the Senate Standing Committee on Agriculture and Forestry hearings conducted between June and December 1998.

42 See also Mary Pickering, 'The Canadian Review of rBGH: Confusion, Politics, and Alleged Bribery,' *Alternatives*, 21/3 (1995), 7. More recently, during an interview for a CBC series on biotechnology, Margaret Haydon repeated all of her allegations in a program which was broadcast on *Tuesday Morning*, 4 May, 1999.

43 Cited by Greta Gaard, 'Recombinant Bovine Growth Hormone Grows,' *Alternatives*, 21/3, 6.

44 'Biologic and Economic Risks Associated with the Use of Bovine Somatotropins.' *Journal of the American Veterinary Medical Association* 192 (1988), 1693–6.

45 Even Monsanto has admitted to there being risks associated with the use of its product and has actually listed twenty-one side effects that pose potential risks to cows in its promotional literature. It is convinced, however, and has managed to convince the FDA, that the benefits greatly outweigh the risks.

46 As reported by Lynden MacIntyre on the CBC's *The Fifth Estate,* supporters of Monsanto persuaded Tony Coehlo, senior adviser to the Democratic National Committee, to arrange a dinner with his friend Mike Espy, who was then the secretary of agriculture, for the purpose of soliciting Espy's help in reining in Senator Russ Finegold of Wisconsin, who was leading the lobby against the approval and use of rBGH. Among the 'talking points' provided to Coehlo by Monsanto in a memorandum dated 21 September 1993 was a reminder that 'Companies like Monsanto will likely pull out of the agriculture biotech area if the administration will not stand up to persons like Senator Finegold.' When a copy of Monsanto's notes to Coehlo was made public by Jeremy Rifkin, who was also leading a protest against the use of the hormone, the meeting between Coehlo and Espy was cancelled.

47 See the *Action Link Newsletter* issued by the Council of Canadians, dated August 1995, as well as Alex Boston, 'BGH Update,' *Alive: Canadian Journal of Health and Nutrition,* Sept. (1995), 62–3, and 'Index on Bovine Growth Hormone,' *Canadian Forum,* May (1995), 48; Brad and Julie Ovenell-Carter, 'Milky Solutions,' *Canadian Living,* May (1996), 41–8; Rhody Lake, 'Can We Call It Conspiracy?' *Alive,* July (1997), 6; David Ehrenfeld, 'A Techno-Pox upon the Land,' *Harper's,* Oct. 1997, 15–16; Hans R. Larsen, *'Milk and the Cancer Connection,' Alive,* Sept. (1998), 36–8; and Helen Forsey and Richard Lloyd, 'Still Kicking,' *Canadian Forum,* Dec. (1998), which reports on the efforts of Senator Eugene Whelan, a former federal minister of agriculture, and the current chair of the Senate Committee on Agriculture, to prevent the approval of rBGH, until further investigation and testing has proved it to be safe.

48 For more detailed discussions of the concerns raised by the use of rBGH, see Samuel Epstein, 'BST: The Public Health Hazards,' *Ecologist,* 19 (1989), 191–5; 'Udder Insanity,' *Consumer Reports,* May (1992), 330–2, and 'Setting a New Direction: Changing Canada's Agricultural Policy Making Process,' Toronto Food Policy Council Discussion Paper Series, #4, April (1995). The rBGH controversy is one of a number of case studies discussed in the latter paper.

49 Expressions of concern over IGF-1 were very much in evidence during the 4 June Senate hearings. On the matter of the public health impacts of IGF-1,

see p. 24 of the 'Gaps Analysis' Report. See also the previously referred to articles by Larsen, *Milk and the Cancer Connection*, 37, and Ehrenfeld, 'A Techno-Pox upon the Land,' 15–16. It should be pointed out that in spite of the apparent attempt by Health Canada bureaucrats to suppress the 'Gaps Analysis,' Report, it managed to find its way onto the National Farmer's Union web site and into the hands of the media and members of the Senate Agricultural Committee, thus forcing the government to give official recognition to its findings and recommendations. See, Helen Forsey and Richard Lloyd, 'Still Kicking,' *Canadian Forum*, Dec. (1998), 16, and a report by Nahlah Ayed in the Montreal *Gazette*, 6 Oct. 1998.

50 *Alive: Canadian Journal of Health and Nutrition*, Sept. (1995), 64.

51 In January 1992, the European Parliament agreed to extend a moratorium on BST, pending further evaluation of its safety in terms of animal welfare. As Michael W. Fox points out in his critique of biotechnology, the moratorium was triggered in part 'by evidence of a cover-up of Monsanto sponsored research on BST in dairy cows at the University of Vermont.' These cows apparently gave birth to stillborn and deformed calves, often retained the placenta after giving birth, and suffered more frequently from ketosis, a metabolic disease symptomatic of excess breakdown of fat. Veterinarian David Kronfield believes that BST may actually cause genetic damage to the offspring of treated calves. See Michael W. Fox, *Superpigs and Wondercorn* (New York: Lyons and Burford, 1992), 111, 123–4. See also, D. MacKenzie, 'Doubts over Animal Health Delay Milk Hormone,' *New Scientist*, 18 1992, 13. Notwithstanding such concerns as led to the European Community's ban on the use of growth hormones in beef production the World Trade Organization (WTO) ruled in August 1997 that this ban was illegal on the grounds that it contravened the rules of the 1994 General Agreement on Tariffs and Trade (GATT). This action by the WTO was in response to a complaint by the United States and Canada. See, in this regard, Michelle Swenarchuk, 'World Trade Organization Downs European Health Standards,' *Canadian Dimension*, Jan.–Feb. (1998), 21–2. For a detailed presentation and discussion of the evidence in support of allegations concerning Monsanto's 'checkered history' in the field of biotechnology, which includes reports about what appears to be Monsanto's persistent attempts to suppress unfavourable scientific research and criticisms of their products, see *Ecologist*, 28/5 (1998). The theme title for the entire issue is 'The Monsanto Files.' An investigative report on the Monsanto controversy was broadcast on CBC Radio One, as part of a series on biotechnology, on the morning of 4 May 1999.

52 Even such a conservative and pro-business newspaper like the *Globe and*

Mail has supported the mandatory labelling of all genetically altered food products. See editorial, 29 Jan. 1993.

53 Peter Aldhous, 'Thumbs Down for Cattle Hormone,' *Science*, 261 (1993), 418.

54 See Christopher L. Culp, 'Sacred Cows: The Bovine Somatotropin Controversy,' in *Environmental Politics: Public Costs, Private Rewards*, Michael S. Greve and Fred L. Smith, Jr., eds. (New York: Praeger, 1992), 52. Michael W. Fox points out that a 20 to 40 per cent increase in milk production in dairy cattle by using genetically engineered BST 'will have severe socioeconomic impact on the already overproductive dairy industry. It could mean even greater dairy surpluses and lower market prices, which will certainly put many smaller producers out of business. And dairy cows will suffer and burn out even faster than they do now ... the indirect costs to the farming community will far exceed the benefits, *which will accrue almost exclusively to the investors and manufacturers*' (my italics). As Fox points out, BST cows are more productive – forty BST cows may produce as much milk as fifty untreated cows. But they also require more feed for each cow, as well as an increase in the use of antibiotics to mitigate the increased risk of mastitis, thus offsetting the benefit of feeding fewer cows. At the same time they burn out faster and will have to be replaced at a faster rate. Taking all of these factors into account the so-called increased efficiency of this biotechnology is questionable, especially for small farmers. Fox, *Superpigs and Wondercorn*, 72–3. See also R.J. Kalter, 'The New Biotech Agriculture: Unforseen Economic Consequences,' *Issues in Science and Technology*, Fall (1985), 125–33, and R.J Kalter, R. Milligan, W. Lesser, W. Magrath, and D. Bauman, *Biotechnology and the Dairy Industry Production Costs and Commercial Potential of the Bovine Growth Hormone* (Ithaca: A.E. Research, Cornell University Department of Agricultural Economics, May 1985). A debate between Gary Comstock and Luther Tweeten on the costs and benefits of rBGH, including further references, may be found in the *Journal of Agricultural and Environmental Ethics*, 4/2 (1991), 101–30. This particular issue is devoted to opposing viewpoints on the ethics, economics, and politics of agricultural biotechnology.

55 Gaard 'Recombinant Bovine Growth Hormone Grows,' 8–9. Based on information supplied by a press release from Senator Russ Feingold, 5 Jan. (1994), and the Pure Food Campaign, Washington, DC (1993).

56 Gaard, 'Recombinant Bovine Growth Hormone Grows,' 9. See also *The Dairy Debate: Consequences of BGH and Rotational Raising Technologies*, William Liebhardt, ed. (Davis: University of California Sustainable Agricultural Research and Education Program, 1993).

57 Gaard, 'Recombinant Bovine Growth Hormone Grows,' 9. At the time of my beginning to research and prepare this chapter, the federal government had stalled off approving rBGH. However, as mentioned previously, on 14 January 1999, Health Canada finally decided not to approve it. Monsanto has made it clear that it intends to challenge this decision in the hope of convincing the Canadian government to reverse it. There is, in any case, little doubt that Health Canada's decision was prompted by the 'Gaps Analysis' Report, submitted to Health Canada in April 1998, as well as by the extensive media attention given to the Senate's Standing Committee on Agriculture and Forestry hearings which were held between June and December 1998. Both prior to and during the course of these hearings several prominent scientists employed by Health Canada spoke out about their concerns over the safety of rBGH, and about their concerns over what they perceived to be political interference with the conduct of scientific research. Several scientists complained about attempts by their supervisors to get scientists to interpret their data in ways that would support the interests of the pharmaceutical and biotech corporations, who, it seems, were paying for the research, and who were commonly regarded by officials at Health Canada as 'clients.' Explicit reference was made to these concerns during the Senate hearings on 4 June. When it is the pharmaceutical and biotech industry rather than the citizens of Canada who are regarded by Health Canada officials as clients, we are left with the very clear impression that public policy with respect to the approval and regulation of drugs and the application of biotechnology to agriculture is clearly biased in favour of the corporate agenda. Further evidence of the tyranny of the corporate agenda is disclosed in a recent front-page article by Laura Eggertson (*Toronto Star*, 3 April 1999) which examines the circumstances surrounding a serious outbreak of salmonella poisoning in March 1998. In this article questions are raised about the integrity of the Canadian Food Agency, responsible for inspecting companies that produce food and ensure they comply with standards set by Health Canada. For, as Eggertson points out, while the food inspection agency's foremost responsibility is to promote the health of Canadians, it is also responsible for working in partnership with industry to promote trade and agriculture. Predictably, this results in a conflict of interest and the suspicion that when push comes to shove its mandate as an agent of industry (which appears to be regarded as the primary client of the agency) seems to take precedence over its mandate as a federal watchdog for whom Canadian citizens ought to be regarded as the primary clients. Precisely this complaint was expressed by an irate citizen on a CBC *Fifth Estate* report on the cell phone industry (13 April 1999) when he ven-

tured the conclusion that rather than public watchdog agencies protecting Canadian citizens from industry, they seem more inclined to protect industry from citizens.

58 Powell and Leiss, *Mad Cows and Mother's Milk*, 124.

59 See Schumacher, *Small Is Beautiful*, 13–33.

60 Ibid., 30.

61 Ibid., 33.

62 Bertrand Russell, 'In Praise of Idleness,' in *In Praise of Idleness and Other Essays* (London: Allen and Unwin, 1935), 16–17.

63 (New York: Simon and Schuster, 1994), 425–6.

64 *Small Is Beautiful*, 39; *A Guide for the Perplexed* (New York: Harper and Row), 35–7.

65 See M. Heidegger, *A Discourse on Thinking* (New York: Harper and Row, 1966) and 'The Question of Technology,' in *Martin Heidegger: Basic Writings*, ed. by D.F. Krell (New York: Harper and Row, 1977), 283–317.

66 *Small Is Beautiful*, 35.

67 (Garden City, NY: Doubleday, 1971), 29.

68 *Small Is Beautiful*, 119.

69 See Martin Heidegger, *What Is Called Thinking?* (New York: Harper and Row, 1968), esp. Part II, Lecture III, 138–47, and *A Discourse on Thinking* (New York: Harper and Row, 1966).

70 'The Question Concerning Technology,' 297.

71 Ibid., 296–8.

72 Cited by E.F. Schumacher in *Small Is Beautiful*, 121.

73 Ibid., 119–20.

74 Ibid., 54.

75 *Economics, Ecology, Ethics*, 12.

76 *The Christian Philosophy of St Augustine* (London: Victor Gollanz, 1961), 122.

77 *A Guide for the Perplexed* (New York: Harper and Row, 1978), 58–9.

8

Can Capitalism Save Itself? Some Ruminations on the Fate of Capitalism

LEO GROARKE

One might begin a history of our present economic era with the collapse of the Soviet Union's communist experiment. It brings to a spectacularly abrupt end an epoch dominated by cold war rhetoric and two ideologically opposed superpowers – a communist Soviet Union and a capitalist United States. The history of the period can most readily be understood in terms of their ideological rivalry, which was manifest in a global competition for political influence and military, economic, scientific, and even artistic superiority.

At the beginning of a new millennium, American-style capitalism has emerged the victor. Soviet communism is, in marked contrast, of interest only to historians. In the wake of its demise, the world economy is characterized by frontier capitalism in the former Soviet states; by the rise (and sometimes fall) of free market economies in East Asia and the developing world; by global markets; and by increasingly powerful multinational corporations. Capital and investment flow around the world with an ease and speed which was previously unimaginable. Globally and nationally, capitalism has become the socioeconomic order of the day.[1]

Capitalism's proponents often treat its rise as a vindication of their own political perspective. To some extent this must be accepted – for the rise of capitalism does suggest that it can economically outperform communism. That said, history leaves no room for confidence in the permanence of the capitalist economy. Tribal societies, Greek city states, and feudalism in a multitude of forms all enjoyed their heydays. To many (perhaps most) who lived in their midst, their economic, social, and political structures seemed inevitable, permanent, and unassailable. But they all gave way to other forms of life that exposed their contradictions, their internal tensions, and their inability to accommodate new realities. It would be naive to think this is impossible in the case of capitalism.

Because capitalism has both strengths and weaknesses, its survival in the long term depends upon our ability to create a sociopolitical environment which can exploit its strengths and constrain its weaknesses. I will argue that a 'mitigated' capitalism can do both,[2] but that the weaknesses of capitalism will bring about its demise if they are not adequately addressed. I will therefore criticize capitalism's most enthusiastic supporters, for they ignore these weaknesses and in this way fail to recognize and address legitimate concerns about capitalist economies. As ironic as it may sound, it is the most strident defenders of capitalism who are most likely to sow the seeds of its demise.

The Strengths of Capitalism

Arguments for capitalism are sometimes founded on an inalienable right to private property. Such arguments maintain that individuals have a right to whatever private property they can accumulate (without resorting to violence, fraud, and the like) and, by implication, a right to trade such property in a free market.

Dan Usher has already noted that such arguments assume rather than justify the values inherent in capitalist economies. In answer to them, it can be said that a right to accumulate private property is not self-evident, but a source of constant and continuing controversy and debate. It follows that rights of this sort are an untenable basis for capitalism, especially as they are heavily biased in favour of the interests of those who own significant amounts of property (or have the opportunity to secure it). Those without such property can, in view of this, plausibly dismiss such rights as a covert attempt to rationalize a political point of view which is in reality designed to make the rich richer and the poor poorer.[3]

It does not follow that the property rights on which capitalism depends cannot be justified, but only that they must be justified in a less contentious way. As Usher has suggested, this can most plausibly be accomplished by arguing that private property and the exchange of goods and services in a free market contribute to the common good. Ironically from an ethical point of view, the benefits this makes possible are the result of a frank recognition that humans are motivated by self-interest rather than altruistic convictions of the sort which tend to be enshrined in principles of ethics.[4] The very success of capitalist economies thus shows that most humans are motivated by their own economic interests, which serve as a catalyst for the transactions which have made capitalist markets the economic engine of the world.[5]

Instead of bemoaning this aspect of human nature, capitalism harnesses it for the sake of economic prosperity and the common good. The exchange of goods in a free market is motivated by self-interest, but at the same time serves greater economic interests and benefits society at large. As Usher puts it, 'If there is any lesson to be learned from the discipline of economics, it is that, with certain qualifications, markets direct the usage of a multiplicity of resources to maximize the national income. Common greed is harnessed to the common good. Resources are utilized where their product is greatest. Lure of profit draws forth innovation.'[6]

In this way, competitive markets are the essential mechanism which provides the benefits that capitalism makes possible. In the best of circumstances, they let market players gain competitive advantages by producing goods or services which are innovative or more cost effective than alternatives. In sharp contrast, players lose competitive advantages (and their share of the market) when they produce goods and services which are substandard or not priced competitively. (Of course, it is more complicated than this, especially in real-life markets – but I leave a discussion of the complexities for later.) As the experience of the world's capitalist markets demonstrates, competitive self-interest can in this way create an exceptionally efficient system of production and exchange which generates wealth on a scale which was previously unimagined.

As many of capitalism's advocates emphasize, the market transactions it makes possible eliminate the need to plan a whole economy. This is an important point because planned economies have in practice proved to be unworkable.[7] The problems that attend them plagued the economy of the former Soviet Union, which could not match the performance of economies in the West. In the present context, it is enough to say that a successful attempt to plan a whole economy would require the ability to predict human needs, preferences, and behaviour to an extent that seems unattainable. In the process of eliminating planning of this sort, capitalism allows a pattern of production and distribution which is determined by the autonomous decisions of those who participate in the market and is as a result impressively sensitive to individual needs and preferences.

Hayek's defence of individual liberty in the market is to a great extent predicated on these kinds of considerations. He therefore stresses the limits of human knowledge, the extent of human ignorance, and the uncertainty which surrounds human actions. Hayek concludes that the liberty of the market is:

> essential in order to leave room for the unforeseeable and unpredictable; we want it because we have learned to expect from it the opportunity of realizing many of our aims. It is because every individual knows so little and, in particular, because we rarely know which of us knows best that we trust the independent and competitive efforts of many to induce the emergence of what we shall want when we see it.
>
> Humiliating to human pride as it may be, we must recognize that the advance and even the preservation of civilization are dependent upon a maximum of opportunity for accidents to happen. These accidents occur in the combination of knowledge and attitudes, skills and habits, acquired by individual men and also when qualified men are confronted with the particular circumstances which they are equipped to deal with. Our necessary ignorance of so much means that we have to deal largely with probabilities and chances.[8]

Freedom in the market accommodates these realities by allowing many different individuals (and groups of individuals) to explore different ways of doing things. The results of such experiments are judged by the market, which provides a mechanism for choosing which are most efficient.

As John Bishop and other contributors to this collection have already pointed out, it would be a mistake to think that capitalism as it is actually practised (and especially corporate capitalism) means the freedom to conduct and pursue business opportunities in any way whatsoever. This is a point to which we will return. For the moment, it is more important to emphasize that capitalism favours a market which is characterized by minimal constraint and regulation. This is a positive feature of the capitalist economy especially in cases in which regulation is difficult and problematic, and has unforseen consequences. As Bishop points out in the case of drugs, 'the intention of prohibiting the production and sale of narcotics in the United States was to reduce usage and addiction [but] the result has been increased usage, the targeting of children and others by pushers, and the domination of the "industry" by fabulously wealthy and extremely vicious drug barons.'[9]

By relying on the free market as the principle economic mechanism for determining the production and distribution of goods and services, capitalism reduces the need for administration and bureaucracy that would otherwise direct the running of the economy. A commitment to a fully planned economy requires, in contrast, an enormous, multilayered government which must have the power to control and intrude upon the lives of citizens. Especially as such power can easily be abused, capitalism in this way limits the government's ability to control the lives of individuals. In the process, it makes tyranny – either in the form of dictatorship or 'the tyranny of the majority' – more difficult to establish and sustain and can help secure the liberty of the individual. (Of course, there are other ways in which it can threaten the liberty of the individual. More of this anon.)

Many defenders of capitalism note that the limits it places on government creates a society which tolerates and encourages individual aspirations, eccentricity, and individually determined ways of doing things which need not be sanctioned by government or common prejudice. Within such a society, exceptional individuals have the opportunity to 'break the mould' established by past practice. This is in the best interests of society as well as themselves, for the benefits which result accrue to the common good as much as the exceptional individual. Hayek therefore argues that 'the freedom that will be used by only one man in a million may be more important to society and more beneficial to the majority than any freedom that we all use.'[10] At the very least it can be said that capitalism honestly recognizes that individuals are equal only in a moral sense, and not in the sense that they have equal abilities, drive, and intellect, and not in the sense that they can equally contribute to the common good.

According to many commentators, capitalism's rejection of regulation in the market is a manifestation of a deeper commitment to individual freedom. Liberty is, therefore, the basic value to which thinkers like Hayek appeal in propounding arguments for capitalism. While there is something to this, it is important not to exaggerate the freedom implied by capitalism's limits on the power of 'big government.' It would, in particular, be a mistake to equate market freedom and the political freedom we assume to be an essential feature of a just society. The existence of capitalist economies in many politically repressive states – Nazi Germany,[11] Chile under Pinochet, Singapore, and Hong Kong – shows that capitalism does not require democratic rights and freedoms. This should come as no surprise, for the freedom which characterizes capitalism is economic *rather* than political. It can best be described as the freedom to participate in market transactions. In most cases, it implies no more (and no less) than the freedom to exchange one's labour for goods and services in an open market.

The extent to which freedom of this sort is a strength of capitalism is open to debate, largely because its implications in the real world depend on conditions in the market. An uneducated man with few skills who is looking for work in a job market characterized by a handful of very powerful employers and an overabundance of labour may be free in the sense that he can participate in the market, but this is a freedom which is compatible with wages that force him to live in abject poverty without proper medical care, without schooling for his children, and without security for the future. That such a man in some sense enjoys economic 'freedom' seems of limited moral consequence, especially as he may live in a politically repressive state which denies him freedom of expression, the right to vote, and other democratic rights. It is on these grounds that many argue that the freedom capitalism guarantees does not necessarily contribute to the common good.

Whatever one thinks of such issues, capitalism is an impressive economic system. As I have already noted, its strengths include its ability to exploit individual self-interest for the sake of the greater good; its willingness to recognize frankly that different individuals are not equal; its ability to generate great prosperity and wealth through competition; its ability to coordinate the supply and distribution of goods and services without large-scale planning and regulation (without attempting to plan a whole economy); its tolerance for different ways of doing things; and (more controversially) the commitment to freedom implicit in its commitment to economic freedom. It goes without saying that these strengths make capitalism an attractive economic system. Looked at from the point of view of ethics, they raise the question whether capitalism might provide a basis for a prosperous economic order which could be the cornerstone of just and laudatory social and political relations.

The Weaknesses of Capitalism

As impressive as they are, the strengths of capitalism should not blind us to its weaknesses. From a moral point of view, one of its most serious failings is the profoundly negative effect it appears to have on the moral character of a society and the individuals whose lives it influences. In favour of capitalism it might be said that it leaves moral matters to the individual (and is in this sense amoral), and that it makes possible material prosperity which can be used in the pursuit of moral ends. While this is true to some extent, it must also be acknowledged that capitalist markets promote a consumer lifestyle which emphasizes the individual pursuit of wealth, to the detriment of things that matter more from a moral point of view.

Bishop has posed the questions that this raises in his Introduction to the present book. As he puts it:

> Many ... human activities that are of great moral value ... lie outside the market; examples include love, friendship, families, parenting, religion, artistic creativity, knowledge, and most self-fulfilment ... The material goods supplied by free markets seem morally insignificant compared with these non-market goods, even though material goods are necessary for all human activity. Perhaps then the market is only a means to pursue morally goods ends, most of which are outside the market. This would not be problematic if the market did not greatly impact these morally valuable activities, but does capitalism leave people with the time and energy for more morally worthwhile activities? Does the market tempt people into mere materialism? Does image advertising corrupt people's identities, preventing sincere relationships and self-fulfilment? Does the competition of free markets prevent the formation of friendships and communities?[12]

In his account of Aboriginal experience, David Newhouse similarly argues that life in a capitalist society makes us 'think about things in terms of the market, which is concerned with exchange value, and begin to value them in monetary terms.'[13] This fosters a notion of progress which is 'defined in primarily material terms,' and promotes 'the continual striving of the individual to better his or her own position in the world' on the basis of the assumption that 'the happiness of all is the natural outcome of the self-regarding pursuit of happiness of each.'[14] Capitalism is in this way 'more than an economic system ... It postulates a way for the world to work and provides a somewhat complete view of the order of things ... It develops a social rhythm for society and defines social relationships.'[15]

Usher argues that capitalism improves the character of citizens, but the independent attitudes he points to in the small-scale farmer or entrepreneur are not an obvious feature of corporate capitalism as we know it. In marked contrast, no one can reasonably doubt the extent to which capitalism has promoted a widespread commitment to a 'life-style of consumption' which is, in Bishop's words, 'centred on libidinal, impulsive, glamorous, gluttonous, and immediate hedonism.'[16] The attitudes that this implies are promoted by a trillion-dollar advertising and marketing industry which expounds, romanticizes, and advocates the materialistic (and frequently self-centred) values that motivate the quest for more and more consumer goods.

Capitalism's effect on personal values and attitudes corroborates Plato's view of human nature, which suggests that a preoccupation with material goods has negative repercussions for moral character, primarily because irrational appetites and desires expand rather than contract when we pay inordinate attention to them. In his *Republic*, Plato therefore argues that the good person uses reason and spirit to control appetite, 'which forms the largest part of each man's make-up and is by nature insatiable. He must [therefore] prevent it taking its fill of the physical pleasures, for otherwise it will get too large and strong to mind its own business and will try to subject and control the other elements ... and so wreck the life of them all.'[17] (One might thus compare a capitalist economy to Socrates' 'city in a fever,' which is propelled by the desire for a more luxurious lifestyle.)

In favour of Plato's view one might easily cite the lust for material possessions which tends to characterize contemporary capitalist societies. The rise in the ordinary person's standard of living which characterizes western Europe and North America in the past one hundred years is remarkable. In North America, a truck driver who works hard and is not wanton can enjoy material comforts which would have made a medieval nobleman giddy with excitement. But, the rise in standards of living this implies has failed to produce a satisfied populace which is no longer interested in material wealth (more money, more luxurious automobiles, bigger houses, new gadgets, and the like) and is eager to devote its energies to more important human goods. Instead, the result is an ever-escalating demand for comfort, luxury, and affluence which is encouraged by a popular culture which frequently equates social standing with wealth rather than moral, spiritual, artistic, or intellectual accomplishment. In the midst of such a culture, 'keeping up with the Joneses' has become an important way of maintaining self-esteem.

The consumptive lifestyles which have been fostered by capitalist economies are reflected in today's environmental problems, which threaten to drastically alter human (and non-human) life on planet earth. As Lionel Rubinoff writes:

> The most serious crisis facing the world economic and political order is the rapid depletion of natural resources and loss of biodiversity which is occurring at a rate unprecedented in human and earth history – a phenomenon which is exacerbated by a startling disruption of global weather patterns brought about by ozone depletion and the accumulation of greenhouse gases in the upper atmosphere. Among the causes of what has been aptly described as a tragedy of the commons in the making, the obsessive pursuit of growth in both production and consumption, characteristic of capitalist industrial societies, may be singled out as a major contributing factor.[18]

The environmental crisis this implies is bound to be exacerbated by the forces of globalization and development, which ensure the spread of capitalist economies and their consumer lifestyles.[19]

One might describe the consumerism which capitalism promotes as 'too much of a good thing,' for the material wealth that capitalism makes possible is, when it is not an obsession, a commendable achievement. Its moral worth will be immediately evident if one considers the lives of those who live in abject poverty in societies which do not enjoy material prosperity (in Indonesia, India, Peru, Romania, and so on). The problem is that capitalism achieves prosperity by promoting an obsession with material goods (so-called commodity-fetishism) which is objectionable on moral, social, and environmental grounds. Capitalism's ability to produce material things (what Rubinoff calls its *techne*) is thus a positive, but one which is reprehensible when it becomes an end in itself.

The obsessive materialism which capitalist economies promote is one of the weaknesses of capitalism when it is considered from an ethical point of view. Other ethical issues arise when one considers the workings of real (as opposed to theoretical) capitalist markets, for they frequently fall short of the ideals which are touted in popular defences of the capitalist economy. Consider Hayek's comment that 'Our faith in freedom does not rest on the foreseeable results in particular circumstances but on the belief that it will, on balance, release more forces for the good than for the bad.'[20] As long as one remains in the realm of hypothesis and theory it is easy to argue that this is so. In the real world the going is more difficult, for the ideal model of capitalism which Hayek and others assume often ignores the motivations and strategies that guide the accumulation of private property in real markets.

Julie Nelson discusses the problems with theoretical models of capitalism in her criticism of contemporary economics. As she argues, economic theory tends to treat players in the market as 'isolated' individuals whose actions are single-mindedly guided by the rational pursuit of their own self-interest. In the process, economic models ignore the extent to which human behaviour is driven by 'emotional motivations, related to such things as self-perception, prestige, envy, concern, and loyalty.'[21] Bishop similarly argues that the economic analysis of capitalist markets fails 'to recognize that people's lives are embedded in cultural, symbolic, and communicative systems.'[22] In morally assessing capitalism, the important point is that influences of this sort greatly complicate the workings of real markets, in many cases creating markets which fail to produce the benefits promised by theoretical accounts of capitalism.

One of the factors which frequently influences individual behaviour in the market is habit and convention. In many cases, this means that markets are driven, not by efficiency and an openness to innovation, but by past prejudice and by conventional 'wisdom' which precludes new efficiencies. Markets can to some extent compensate for these obstacles by disseminating information via normal market mechanisms. To this extent, one might say that one characteristic of an efficient market is the information which allows buyers to distinguish between superior and inferior (and more and less cost-effective) goods and services. The problem is that such information is very frequently absent from real markets, which are not ideal and typically operate on the basis of poor, incomplete, or misleading information. Misinformation is often explicitly fostered and sustained by seductive and intentionally misleading advertising which overwhelms more objective sources of information. To some extent the problems this creates are inevitable, for there will always be some market players whose interests are best served by attempts to purposely thwart the dissemination of relevant information which would compromise their success.

If I am someone who manufactures inefficient electrical appliances I may, for example, protect my share of the appliance market, not by improving my product, but by doing my best to ensure that the public is not aware of innovative, cost-effective alternatives. In the process of undermining such alternatives I may contribute to the environmental problems which we have already noted as one of the weaknesses of capitalism. If I have significant economic resources I may in this way have a profound effect on the market. Considered only from the point of view of my own interests, such a strategy may be more cost effective than the attempt to reorganize and reinvent the way that I do business. This is especially true if manufacturers who produce superior appliances are not able to compete with me because they lack the resources needed to disseminate information in the market. A number of commentators have argued that this is precisely what has happened in the energy market in North America, which possesses the technology needed to establish a sustainable economy from the point of view of energy efficiency, but has failed to move in this direction because of widespread prejudice and ignorance.[23]

The influences that often make markets irrational rather than efficient are exacerbated by the unequal concentrations of wealth and power that capitalist economies allow. Inequality is a necessary feature of the capitalist economy, for it provides the incentive which drives the market towards efficiency. The problem is that inequalities – and especially enormous inequalities of the sort that characterize free markets in the real world – can also have the opposite effect. This is an inevitable consequence of the fact that market players with great wealth can exert tremendous influence on the market, both through direct intervention (in the most extreme cases through monopoly and insider trading) and by (more subtly but often more significantly) influencing the legal, cultural, and political environment in which the market operates.

David Copp has already highlighted the ways in which economic power can influence political decisions in a capitalist economy. As Copp points out, it allows one to run for political office; makes economic threats and promises possible; and allows special access to, and control of, the mass media. (This both in virtue of direct ownership and sponsorship, and in virtue of quasi-legal mechanisms that produce phenomena like 'libel chill.') Though he does not discuss such matters in detail, Usher agrees that it is inevitable that in capitalism 'The rich enjoy a disproportionate access to politicians and a disproportionate influence on political decision making that compounds their initial economic advantages.'[24]

Especially as capitalism promotes the pursuit of self-interest, one must expect those who participate in markets to do what they can to further their own economic interests. In the context of vastly different economic resources, this means that real markets are often plagued by market strategies which promote regulatory favouritism, thoughtless buying rather than reflection, ignorance rather than informed choices, and morally and even legally objectionable market moves. This is to be expected in markets designed to reward strategies that promote economic advantage rather than right or wrong or the efficient working of the market. All the more so because success in the market can be achieved in many arbitrary ways – through inheritance or luck, for example, or through other means which have little to do with the provision of better goods and services.

This point is well made by Wes Cragg in his account of international corruption, which is a natural feature of unregulated global markets. The important point is that such corruption is objectionable not only on moral grounds – because it violates a basic moral duty to be honest – but also because it undermines those benefits which justify capitalist markets in the first place. It thus works to replace fair competition and efficiency with decisions made on the basis of unjustified patronage and which serve to entrench a political status quo, promote great and unjustified differences in wealth, and encourage (and justify) a pervasive suspicion of markets and the workings of capitalist economies.

Considered from the point of view of the common good, the problems with unregulated markets are further exacerbated by their failure to consider the interests of those who do not directly participate in the market and do not, therefore, influence its 'invisible hand.' The long-term consequences of market transactions will, for example, probably affect the lives of children and future generations *more* than the lives of those who actually participate in these transactions, but such groups have no way to ensure that their interests (in having a sustainable economy, for example) influence the direction of these transactions. Someone who suffers from the pollution produced by a papermill may be far removed from the market activities that guide its operation and so have little or no effect on its operations. More generally, the poor will have some influence on prices in the market, but relatively little influence in comparison with the rich, whose economic power allows them to influence the workings of the market much more significantly. As a decision-making mechanism, real markets therefore tend to favour, not the common good and those who need help most, but those who enjoy extensive private property and great economic power.

how to reg global markets ?

Mitigated Capitalism

One might easily elaborate the problems with unregulated capitalist markets in more detail. It is more important to consider what can be done about them. In the absence of attempts to constrain the weaknesses of capitalism, I think it likely that capitalism will in the long run be undermined by a combination of pressures which will be exacerbated by free markets marred by corruption, the trust–agency problem, and other practical impediments; the negative environmental impacts of consumerist economies;[25] the tremendous social pressures which are produced by great disparities in income and lifestyle;[26] and ethnic, religious, and other tensions which attempt to fill a moral vacuum which capitalism perpetuates. If particular capitalist economies do not wholly succumb to such forces, they may instead be forced to deal with them by evolving in a way that no longer guarantees democratic values like the right to free speech and political protest.

A democratic capitalism which is to persevere will, therefore, have to be bolstered by measures or conditions which mitigate its weaknesses. This suggests that market regulation has an important role to play in creating a sustainable capitalism. To many of those enamoured of capitalism, this will seem something of an anathema. Bishop has already pointed out that widespread scepticism about the effects and workability of government regulation is one of the hallmarks of capitalist politics today. As he puts it, 'The proponents of deregulation see themselves as championing a great cause against the forces of interfering governments, incompetent politicians, bungling bureaucrats, and socialism.'[27] The problem is that such views caricature legitimate regulation, both by romanticizing the workings of unregulated markets (which are treated as a panacea for all social problems) and demonizing regulation (which is treated as always corrupt, incompetent, and ineffectual). For though it must be granted that regulation can be incompetent and corrupt the market, it must also be said that capitalism can be justified only if it is guided by regulation which ensures that efficiency, competition, and reasonable social consequences are characteristics of the market. This is possible within a capitalist framework because such regulation need not deny that private property and the market have a primary role in establishing the production and distribution of goods and services.

The extent to which a justifiable capitalism needs a regulated market can be seen in the case of international corruption. As Cragg argues, there are useful things which private corporations can do to improve markets from this point of view, but 'the business community must clearly recognize that there is a role here for governments acting nationally and internationally.'[28] Without national (and perhaps international) regulation, corporations which make efforts to avoid corruption and 'play fair' are likely to suffer competitive disadvantages because they cannot employ effective market strategies which are available to their competitors. As Bookchin remarks in the context of ecological issues:

> However ecologically concerned an entrepreneur may be, the harsh fact is that his or her survival in the marketplace precludes a meaningful ecological orientation. To engage in ecologically sound practices places a morally concerned entrepreneur at a striking, and indeed, fatal disadvantage in a competitive relationship with a rival – notably one who lacks any ecological concerns and thus produces at lower costs and reaps higher profits for further capital expansion.[29]

It does not follow that capitalist managers and owners should not attempt to play fair in the market, but it does follow that their behaviour is likely to have a limited effect on behaviour in the market if it is not backed by external constraints imposed by government. Market players concerned to mitigate the negative aspects of unregulated markets need, therefore, to assert unapologetically the importance of government regulation, all the more so given that they often operate within a business culture in which it is politically incorrect to say such things. In answer to popular prejudices against 'big government,' it must be said that government needs significant powers in order to institute measures to ensure that capitalist markets are and remain free and competitive, and in order to mitigate the negative aspects of capitalism we have already noted.

This is especially true in the case of global corporate capitalism, for it creates a world economy in which large multinational corporations enjoy a degree of economic and political power which rivals that of nation states. A government charged with the responsibility of ensuring that Microsoft respects the principles of a competitive market cannot be a shrinking violet that lacks substantive powers.[30] The powers that it enjoys must be backed by a much broader appreciation of the extent to which market regulation is a necessary feature of a healthy capitalist economy.[31]

Because one of the prime functions of government in a capitalist

public /consumers fail too

society should be the regulation of capitalist markets, it is important that it operate in ways which ensures that its actions and decisions are not compromised by undue control or influence exerted by players in the market. As Copp puts it, political institutions need to be organized in a way that 'insulates political power and authority from economic power.'[32] Among many other things, this implies that proper regulation requires a vigilant attempt to separate public and private interests (one might compare an earlier need to separate the functions of the church and state). In practice, this is a constant problem which is evident in most capitalist economies, in which government and economic interests frequently collaborate in a way that compromises government's ability to act as an independent regulator of the market.

If this is correct, then the most defensible capitalism is a mitigated capitalism which is (contrary to popular prejudice) regulated by an independent government which has substantial regulatory powers. It is more difficult to say exactly what kinds of restrictions on the market are and are not defensible from this point of view. A detailed account of such regulation is beyond the scope of the present chapter, but it is important to end it with a general overview of justifiable and unjustifiable regulation. Our earlier discussion justifies (1) regulations which are designed to ensure that the market remains competitive and efficient, and (2) regulations designed to ensure that all players in the market respect the interests of those who do not have the ability to influence it significantly, even though they are significantly affected by its behaviour. In the latter case, it is essential that regulations affect different market players in an equitable way, as this is an important way to preserve fair competition in the market.

Many of the regulations which can in this way be justified are (at least to some extent) a standard feature of contemporary capitalism. They include measures to prevent monopoly, corruption, fraud, false advertising, insider trading, and so on. More substantive policy initiatives which can be justified in this way include measures designed to bolster the flow of relevant information in the market; environmental protection (to protect the interests of all of those effected by the negative impacts of market transactions on the environment); limits on inheritance (which increases the arbitrariness of success in the market); the redistribution of income and other mechanisms to prevent huge disparities in wealth and economic power (disparities which interfere with competitive markets and exclude the poor from the market); and public education to ensure the development of the intellectual capital needed to both establish an efficient market and guide government regulation (which in a democratic society depends on public opinion). As markets become increasingly global in their scope, such regulation needs to be globalized as well.

One might argue about the extent of such measures but it should be clear that they justify significant restrictions on the market. It follows that mitigated capitalism (i.e. justifiable capitalism) does not imply an unregulated market economy. To some extent, one might compare mitigated capitalism to capitalism as it exists in most capitalist economies today, for such economies often have many of the regulatory features I have already noted (among other things, this shows that mitigated capitalism can work in practice).[33] That said, there are ways in which the mitigated capitalism I propose implies an economy which is more radically capitalist than the economies of contemporary capitalist states. This is because the governments in such states regularly intervene in the market, not in order to ensure that markets are efficient or that all market players respect the interests of those affected by market transactions (i.e., not for the reasons justified by mitigated capitalism), but in order to introduce subsidies, regulations, grants, and other advantages intended (explicitly or implicitly) to favour particular market players. In the process, they disrupt and displace the proper workings of the market, denying it its proper role in determining the production and distribution of goods and services in a capitalist economy.

Some concrete examples can illustrate this point. Consider the City of Detroit's expropriation of 'Poletown' in 1981 – action it undertook in order to provide land for a GM cadillac assembly plant. Although this was the action of a municipal government it had tremendous implications for the neighbourhood, which contained some 1,400 homes, 16 churches, 144 local businesses, and a vigorous neighbourhood association which fought the move in a series of court challenges but lost in the Supreme Court. In making the move, the city favoured GM with regulatory action that was tantamount to an enormous economic subsidy. The extent of this favouritism can be better appreciated in the context of the fact that in the free market the acquisition of such land would have been impossible, for it is clear that no amount of compensation could convince the occupants to give up their homes and businesses and the more intangible roots, shared memories, relationships, and sense of place that accompanied them.[34]

In Canada, similar interventions in the market have been underscored in David Lewis's controversial book *Louder Voices: The Corporate Welfare Bums*.[35] On the basis of a number of examples, Lewis argued that the mechanisms of government are not used to create fair markets, but in order to establish a 'Corporate Welfare State' in which incentive grants, research grants, tax breaks, interest-free loans, and direct government investment support particular market players. In the present context, the important point is that government action of this sort fundamentally distorts the operation of the market and its ability to establish the efficiency which justifies it in the first place. Strangely, it creates capitalist enterprises which demand government interventions in the market which clearly violate capitalism's commitment to markets which are competitive, fair, and efficient.

Another example which can illustrate the ways in which governments regularly distort the workings of competitive markets is found in the transportation sector. Consider personal transportation. A commitment to competitive markets should imply that different modes of transportation – airlines, buses, personal automobiles, trains – compete against one another in an open market. Such competition can create a situation in which price properly reflects costs (and, in a mitigated capitalism, the negative externalities associated with smog, pollution, and noise). In such a situation real advantages properly accrue to more efficient means of transport. Yet transportation in capitalist countries typically contradicts the workings of such a market because governments provide hidden subsidies to less efficient means of transportation – most notably air and automobile transportation. This is done by government-funded infrastructures which mean that the price of these modes of transportation does not reflect their true cost. In 1990–1, Canada's National Transportation Act Review Commission found that roads annually enjoyed a hidden cash-flow subsidy of $2.224 billion, and a hidden book-value subsidy (which averages out depreciation costs) of $4.585 billion. In the United States, the subsidy to automobiles has been valued at $8 billion annually.[36]

As Rubinoff points out in his discussion of the Nuclear Liability Act, governments who indulge in these kinds of market transactions cannot be counted on to favour market players in ways that serve the common good. In the present context, the important point is that the mitigated capitalism I have proposed leaves no room for interventions of this sort. Rather, it rejects them on the grounds that they undermine competitive markets and in this way the efficiency that justifies free markets. Because such interventions are a frequent feature of economic activities in many contemporary capitalist economies, it follows that mitigated capitalism is, despite its commitment to regulation, committed to a very significant expansion of the free market's role in determining economic development. The capitalism I have proposed is in this way characterized by a profound commitment to the free market, although it is a commitment which expresses itself, not only in the rejection of many typical government interventions, but also in external constraints designed to ensure that the free market remains free and competitive for the sake of the common good.

Conclusion

If the account of capitalism I have proposed is correct, then popular attitudes to capitalism are simplistic. Those who support capitalism tend to be characterized by an unrestrained commitment to the free market which ignores its weaknesses and naively treats it as a panacea for all social ills. Those who reject capitalism condemn it on moral grounds without recognizing its great strengths. I believe that mitigated capitalism can provide a 'middle' way which both recognizes the ways in which capitalism is superior to alternative economic systems but also recognizes that it has weaknesses that need to be constrained if capitalism is to sustain itself.

In the end the greatest barrier to a reasonable capitalism may be common prejudices for and against it. Intellectually, it may be that our greatest need is for new metaphors which allow us to see beyond the simplistic picture of capitalism that portrays the market as an unmitigated good *or* evil. We might do better to compare the unregulated market to a spoiled child who lacks discipline or a fruit tree which must be pruned regularly if it is to bear good fruit. Left to their own devices with no guiding hand to direct them, there is no reason to believe that such a child or tree will turn out well. Something similar holds of capitalism, which can bring about substantial good, but only if it is disciplined, directed, and not allowed its natural excesses. Properly constrained, capitalism is our best hope for the future. But an unconstrained capitalism is, in the long run, likely to be the cause of its own undoing.

Notes

1 As David Newhouse suggests in his chapter herein, it is no longer possible

to underestimate the extent to which capitalism 'is an extremely adaptive, effective, efficient and seductive system' which is able 'to absorb new things.'

2 This might be contrasted with the 'unmitigated' capitalism which Copp criticizes.

3 Usher's use of a version of Rawls's original position and his veil of ignorance in deciding for or against private property is a useful mechanism insofar as it eliminates the role that vested interest easily plays in justifications of private property.

4 Of course, there are exceptional individuals who dedicate their lives to others – Mother Teresa and similar 'saints.' But they are saints precisely because their behaviour is so rare and exceptional (how much it is an exception to the suggested focus on self-interest depends on one's view of psychological egoism, but that is a matter beyond the scope of the present chapter).

5 In 'Famine, Affluence, and Morality,' *Philosophy and Public Affairs*, 1 (1972), 229–43, Peter Singer argues that famine in Africa obliges us to reduce our standard of living to that of famine victims. S. Kagan has argued that consequentialism requires that 'In a sense, neither my time, nor my goods, nor my plans would be my own. On this view, the demands of morality pervade every aspect and moment of our lives – and we all fail to meet its standards. This is why I suggested that few of us believe the claim, and that none of us live in accordance with it ... The claim is counter-intuitive. But it is true.' *The Limits of Morality*, (Oxford: Oxford University Press, 1989), 2. As laudable as such views may be (and whether they are laudable is open to debate), it is hard to see how the self-sacrifice they require can be the basis of a real social system.

6 Usher, herein, 104–5.

7 Though very large scale economic planning – in the Second World War, e.g. – has been successful in particular instances.

8 F.A. Hayek, *The Constitution of Liberty* (South Bend: Gateway Editions, 1960), 29.

9 Bishop, herein, 59.

10 Hayek, *The Constitution of Liberty*, 31.

11 For a fascinating look at the political thought that informs this aspect of Nazism, see Renato Cristi's recent study of Carl Schmitt, *Carl Schmitt and Authoritarian Liberalism: Strong State, Free Economy* (Cardiff: University of Wales Press, 1998).

12 Bishop, herein, 59.

13 Newhouse, herein, 286.

14 Ibid., 287.

15 Ibid., 287–8.

16 Bishop, herein, 38.

17 Plato, *Republic*, 442a–b.

18 Rubinoff, herein, 299.

19 Schumacher puts it more bluntly when he remarks that 'present-day industrial society everywhere shows [the] evil characteristic of incessantly stimulating greed, envy, and avarice.' Schumacher quoted in Rubinoff, herein 315.

20 Hayek, *Constitution of Liberty*, 31. One wonders how this belief (and this faith) can be reconciled with the human ignorance which he makes so much of in defending freedom (for if we really are ignorant to the extent that Hayek suggests, then how can we know that the results of freedom will be for the best?).

21 Nelson, herein, 220. There are two aspects of Nelson's thesis. One is the claim that economics has been characterized by an excessively narrow (and overly formal) conception of human nature. The second is the claim that this is tied to a patriarchal discipline which has been dominated by males. My own view is that the first thesis is correct. I am less sure of the second one. Among other things, because many men themselves have traditionally disagreed about the value of the kind of paradigm she rejects (both explicitly and implicitly, insofar as they favour one mode of intellectual inquiry over another). The nature of economics may not, therefore, be determined by men's preferences so much as the preferences of a particular group of men (to some extent, Nelson herself inclines in this direction when she suggests that both men and women can pursue economics in either way). However this may be, the question why economic models are the way they are is a secondary one in the present context. What is of real importance is the way their nature obscures important elements of human nature and their impact on human behaviour in and outside the market.

22 Bishop, herein, 14.

23 See, e.g., Kerri R. Blair and William A. Ross, 'Energy Efficiency at Home and Abroad,' in *Ethics and Climate Change: The Greenhouse Effect*, H. Coward and T. Hurka, eds. (Waterloo: Wilfrid Laurier University Press, 1993), 149–64.

24 Usher, herein, 99.

25 Contrary to popular belief, the ever-increasing complexity which characterizes capitalist economies as we know them makes them more rather than less susceptible to environmental catastrophe. As Dotto puts it, 'Complex, technologically-advanced societies are *more* vulnerable to rapid environmental and climatic change than so-called "primitive" societies, such as

hunter-gatherers ... Complex societies are characterized by centralized decision-making, a high rate of information flow, specialization among both individuals and institutions, pooling of resources, and a high degree of interconnectedness and dependency among the various elements of the society, resulting in a loss of local and individual self-sufficiency.' Lydia Dotto, *Thinking the Unthinkable: Civilization and Rapid Climate Change*, (Waterloo: Wilfrid Laurier University Press, 1988), 5.

26 Adam Smith recognized such tension as an intrinsic feature of any capitalist society, which he proposes as the principle reason it must have a civil magistrate. As Smith puts it: 'The affluence of the rich excites the indignation of the poor, who are often both driven by want and prompted by envy to invade his possessions. It is only under the shelter of the civil magistrate that the owner of the valuable property, which is acquired by the labour or many years, or perhaps of many successive generations, can sleep a single night in security. He is at all times surrounded by unknown enemies, whom, though he never provoked, he can never appease and from whose injustice he can be protected only by the powerful arm of the civil magistrate continually held up to chastise it. The acquisition of valuable and extensive property, therefore, necessarily requires the establishment of civil government. Where there is no property, or at least none that exceeds the value of two or three days' labour, civil government is not so necessary.' *The Wealth of Nations*, book V, pt. II, chap. 1.

Usher puts the problem very differently, writing that we cannot 'be sure that the inequalities of wealth and income in an unconstrained system of private property – in a society where the state protects property rights but lets the distribution of income develop as it may with no attempt to assist the poor or to redistribute property or income at all – will not grow to the point where private ownership of property becomes unacceptable to the great majority of the citizens.' Usher, herein, 112–13.

27 Bishop, herein, 54.

28 Cragg, herein, 264.

29 Book chin, quoted in Rubinoff, herein, 303.

30 Given the economic resources of multinational corporations, Mill's worry that intellectual as well as political power will be concentrated in the state (see Usher, herein, 107–8) is in our own times not as germane as the worry that intellectual power will be concentrated in capitalist enterprises which pursue their own self-interest. In a well-running capitalist society there is in view of this a pressing need to diffuse intelligence, activity, and public spirit *so that they are significantly represented in* government and outside the transactions of the market.

31 This is more important than is often realized, for the extent to which the regulation of any human behaviour is likely to be successful depends in large part on the extent to which this regulation is socially approved. A good example is action taken to curb drunken driving – action which has been largely successful because it is backed by a common consensus that this is a serious problem which needs to be addressed.

32 Copp, herein.

33 The difficulties of regulation deserve more comment than is possible in the present chapter. Suffice it to say that regulation has in many cases worked, but that the success of regulation depends on many factors which warrant further comment (the most neglected one is public opinion, which has the power to 'make or break' regulatory efforts in the criminal as well as the economic realm).

34 See Mary Ann Glendon, *Rights Talk: The Impoverishment of Political Discourse* (New York: Free Press, 1991), 29–30.

35 (Toronto: James Lewis and Samuel, 1972).

36 James MacKenzie, Roger C. Dower, and Donald D.T. Chen. *The Going Rate: What It Really Costs to Drive* (Washington: World Resources Institute, 1992).

Bibliography

Adams, Scott. 'Dilbert.' *Boston Globe*, 27 Oct. 1996, comic section 1.

Akerlof, George A., and Janet L. Yellen. 'Fairness and Unemployment.' *American Economic Review*, 78/2 (1988), 44–9.

Aldhous, Peter. 'Thumbs Down for Cattle Hormone.' *Science*, 23 July 1993, 418.

Anderson, Elizabeth. *Value in Ethics and Economics*. Cambridge, MA: Harvard University Press, 1993.

Arnold, Ron. *Trashing the Economy*. Bellevue, WA: Free Enterprise Press, 1993.

Atkinson, A.B. 'How Progressive Should the Income Tax Be?' In *Economic Justice*, E. Phelps, ed., 386–408. London: Penguin, 1973.

Barker, Ernest ed. *Social Contract*. London: Oxford University Press, 1947.

Barnet, Richard J., and John Cavanagh. *Global Dreams*. New York: Simon and Schuster, 1994.

Barry, Norman. 'What Moral Constraints for Business?' In *Market Capitalism and Moral Values*, S. Brittan and A. Hamlin, eds., 57–78. Aldershot: Edward Algar, 1995.

Becker, Gary Stanley. *A Treatise on the Family*. Cambridge, MA: Harvard University Press, 1981.

Becker, Lawrence C. *Property Rights: Philosophical Foundations*. London: Routledge and Kegan Paul, 1977.

Bell, Daniel. *The Cultural Contradictions of Capitalism*. New York: Basic Books, 1976, 1996.

Benhabib, Seyla. 'The Generalized and the Concrete Other: The Kohlberg-Gilligan Controversy and Moral Theory.' In *Women and Moral Theory*, D. Meyers and E.F. Kittay, eds., 154–77. Totowa, NJ: Rowman and Littlefield, 1987.

Berger, Peter. *The Capitalist Revolution: Fifty Propositions about Prosperity, Equality, and Liberty*. New York: Basic Books, 1986.

Bergmann, Barbara R. '"Measurement," or Finding Things Out in Economics.' *Journal of Economic Education*, 18/2 (1987), 191–203.

Berlin, Isaiah. *Four Essays on Liberty*. London: Oxford University Press, 1969.

Berry, Thomas. 'The Viable Human.' In *Environmental Philosophy: From Animal Rights to Radical Ecology*, M.E. Zimmerman and J.B. Callicott, eds., 171–81. Englewood Cliffs, NJ: Prentice-Hall, 1993.

Bishop, John Douglas. 'Adam Smith's Invisible Hand Argument.' *Journal of Business Ethics*, 14 (1995), 165–80.

– 'Moral Motivation and the Development of Francis Hutcheson's Philosophy.' *Journal of the History of Ideas*, 57/2 (1996), 277–295.

– 'Locke's Theory of Original Appropriation and the Right of Settlement in Iroquois Territory.' *Canadian Journal of Philosophy*, 27/3 (1997), 311–37.

Blair, Kerri R., and William A. Ross. 'Energy Efficiency at Home and Abroad.' In *Ethics and Climate Change: The Greenhouse Effect*, H. Coward and T. Hurka, eds., 149–64. Waterloo, Ont.: Wilfrid Laurier University Press, 1993.

Boadway, Robin, and Neil Bruce. *Welfare Economics*. Oxford: Basil Blackwell, 1984.

Bookchin, Murry. 'What Is Social Ecology?' In Zimmerman and Callicott, eds., *Environmental Philosophy*, 354–73.

Bork, R. *The Tempting of America*. New York: Free Press, 1990.

Boston, Alex. 'BGH Update.' *Alive: Canadian Journal of Health and Nutrition*, Sept. (1995), 62–3.

Brighouse, Harry. 'Political Equality and the Funding of Political Speech.' *Social Theory and Practice*, 21 (1995), 473–500.

– 'Egalitarianism and Equal Availability of Political Influence.' *Journal of Political Philosophy*, 4/2 (1996), 118–41.

Brittan, Samuel, and Alan Hamlin. *Market Capitalism and Moral Values*. Aldershot: Edward Elgar, 1995.

Brown, Lester R., Christopher Flavin, and Sandra Postal. *Saving the Planet*. New York: W.W. Norton, 1991.

Buchanan, Allen. *Ethics, Efficiency and the Market*. Totowa, NJ: Rowman and Allanhead, 1985.

Bury, John Bagnell. *The Idea of Progress: An Inquiry into Its Origin and Growth*. New York: Macmillan, 1932.

Chopra, Shiv, Mark Feeley, Gerard Lambert, Then Mueller, and Ian Alexander. *rBST (Nutrilac) 'Gaps Analysis' Report by rBST Internal Review Team*. Ottawa: Health Protection Branch, Health Canada, 1998.

Christensen, Bev. *Too Good to Be True*. Vancouver: Talon Books, 1995.

Christiano, Thomas. *The Role of the Many: Fundamental Issues in Democratic Theory*. Boulder, CO: Westview, 1996.

Clarke, Tony. *Silent Coup: Confronting the Big Business Tokeover of Canada.* Toronto: Lorimer, 1997.

Clow, Michael, and Susan Machum. *Stifling Debate.* Halifax: Fernwood, 1993.

Cobb, John B., and Herman E. Daly. *For the Common Good: Redirecting the Economy Toward Community, the Environment, and a Sustainable Future.* Boston: Beacon, 1989.

Cohen, Morris Raphael, 'Property and Sovereignty,' in *Property: Mainstream and Critical Positions*, C.B. MacPherson, ed., 153–75. Toronto: University of Toronto Press, 1978.

Cook, Thomas I., ed. *Two Treatises of Government.* New York: Hafner Press, 1947.

Coward, H., and T. Hurka eds. *Ethics and Climate Change: The Greenhouse Effect.* Waterloo: Ont: Wilfrid Laurier University Press, 1993.

Cragg, A.W. 'Two Concepts of Community of Moral Theory and Canadian Culture.' *Dialogue*, Spring, 1986, 31–52.

Cristi, Renato. *Carl Schmitt and Authoritarian Liberalism: Strong State, Free Economy.* Cardiff: University of Wales Press, 1998.

Cronon, William, ed. *Uncommon Ground.* New York: W.W. Norton, 1995.

Culp, Christopher L. 'Sacred Cows: The Bovine Somatotropin Controversy.' In *Environmental Politics: Public Costs, Private Rewards*, M.S. Greve and F.L. Smith, eds., 47–65. New York: Praeger, 1992.

Daly, Herman, ed. *Economics, Ecology, Ethics.* San Francisco: W.H. Freeman, 1980.

Dasgupta, Partha. *An Inquiry into Well-Being and Destitution.* Oxford: Clarendon Press, 1993.

D'Etreves, A.P. *Natural Law: An Introduction to Legal Philosophy.* London: Hutchinson's Universal Library, 1951.

De George, Richard T. *Competing with Integrity in International Business.* Oxford: Oxford University Press, 1993.

Dicey, A.V. *Lectures on the Relation between Law and Public Opinion in England in the Nineteenth Century*, 2nd ed. 1914. (Reprinted by New Brunswick, NJ: Transaction Books, 1981.)

– *Introduction to the Study of the Law of the Constitution*, 1915. (Reprinted by Indianapolis: Liberty Press, 1985.)

Dickenson, J. *Administrative Justice and the Supremacy of the Law in the United States.* Cambridge, MA: Harvard University Press, 1927.

Djilas, Milovan. *The New Class.* New York: Praeger, 1957.

Donaldson, Thomas. *Corporations and Morality.* Englewood Cliffs, NJ: Prentice Hall, 1982.

– *The Ethics of International Business.* Oxford: Oxford University Press, 1989.

– and Thomas W. Dunfee. 'Toward a Unified Conception of Business Ethics:

Integrated Social Contracts Theory.' *Academy of Management Review*, 19/2 (1994), 252–84.
– 'Integrative Social Contracts Theory: A Communitarian Conception of Economic Ethics.' *Economics and Philosophy*, 11 (1995), 85–112.
Donato, Katharine M. 'Keepers of the Corporate Image: Women in Public Relations.' In *Job Queues, Gender Queues*, B.J. Reskin andP.A. Roos, eds., 120–43. Philadelphia: Temple University Press, 1990.
Dotto, Lydia. *Thinking the Unthinkable: Civilization and Rapid Climate Change.* Waterloo, Ont.: Wilfrid Laurier University Press, 1988.
Drucker, Peter. *Innovation and Entrepreneurship: Practice and Principles.* New York: Harper and Row, 1985.
Dworkin, Ronald. 'What Is Equality? Part I: Equality of Welfare.' *Philosophy and Public Affairs*, 10/3 (1981), 185–246.
– 'What Is Equality? Part II: Equality of Resources.' *Philosophy and Public Affairs*, 10/4 (1981), 283–345.
– 'The Curse of American Politics.' *New York Review of Books*, 17 Oct. 1996, 19–24.
Ehrenberg, Ronald G., and Robert S. Smith. *Modern Labour Economics: Theory and Public Policy.* New York: Harper Collins, 1994.
Ehrenfeld, David. 'A Techno-Pox upon the Land.' *Harper's*, Oct. 1997, 13–17.
Elster, Jon. *Sour Grapes: Studies in the Subversion of Rationality.* Cambridge: Cambridge University Press, 1983.
England, Paula. 'The Separative Self: Androcentric Bias in Neoclassical Assumptions.' In *Beyond Economic Man: Feminist Theory and Economics*, M. Ferber and J. Nelson, eds., 37–53. Chicago: University of Chicago Press, 1993.
Ensminger, Jean. *Making a Market: The Institutional Transformation of an African Society.* Cambridge: Cambridge University Press, 1996.
Epstein, R. 'Possession as the Root of Title.' *Georgia Law Review* (1979), 121–43.
Epstein, R.A. *Takings: Private Property and the Power of Eminent Domain.* Cambridge, MA: Harvard University Press, 1985.
Epstein, Samuel. 'BST: The Public Health Hazards.' *Ecologist*, Sept./Oct., 1989, 191–5.
– 'Setting a New Direction: Changing Canada's Agricultural Policy Making Process.' *Toronto Food Policy Council Discussion Paper Series*, #4, April, 1995.
Fadiman, Jeffrey A. 'A Traveler's Guide to Gifts and Bribes.' *Harvard Business Review*, July–Aug., 1986, 122–36. Republished in *Ethics in the Workplace*, R.A. Larmer, ed., 315–25. Minneapolis: West, 1996.
Fairchild, Roy, ed. *The Federalist Papers.* Garden City, NY: Anchor Books, 1961.
Ferber, Marianne, and Julie Nelson, eds. *Beyond Economic Man: Feminist Theory and Economics.* Chicago: University of Chicago Press, 1993.

Fotheringham, Allan. 'One Day, Conrad Will Buy Me – and Fire Me.'
  MacLean's, 25 Nov. 1996, 132.
Fox, Michael W. *Superpigs and Wondercorn*. New York: Lyons and Burford,
  1992.
Frankel, Max. 'TV Remedy for a TV Malady.' *New York Times Magazine*, 8 Sept.
  1996, 36–8.
Freeman, R. Edward. *Strategic Management: A Stakeholder Approach*, Boston:
  Pitman, 1984.
Friedman, Milton. *Capitalism and Freedom*. Chicago: University of Chicago
  Press, 1962.
– 'The Social Responsibility of Business Is to Increase Its Profits.' *New York
  Times Magazine*, 13 Sept. 1970. Republished in *Business Ethics: Readings and
  Cases in Corporate Morality*. W.M. Hoffman and R.E. Frederick, eds., 137–41.
  New York: McGraw-Hill, 1995.
Fukuyama, Francis. *Trust*. New York: Macmillan, 1995.
Gaard, Greta. 'Recombinant Bovine Growth Hormone Grows.' *Alternatives*,
  21/3 (1995), 6–9.
Galbraith, John Kenneth. *The Affluent Society*. London: Hamish Hamilton, 1958.
Garforth, F.W., ed. *John Stuart Mill on Education*. New York: Teachers College
  Press, Columbia University, 1971.
Georgesco-Roegen, Nicholas. 'The Entropy Law and the Economic Problem.'
  In *Economy, Ecology, Ethics*, H. Daly, ed., 49–60. San Francisco: W.H. Freeman,
  1980.
– *The Entropy Law and the Economic Process*. Cambridge, MA: Harvard Univer-
  sity Press, 1971.
Gibbard, Allan. 'What's Morally Special about Free Exchange?' In *Ethics and
  Economics*, E.F. Paul et al., eds., 20–8. Oxford: Blackwell, 1985.
Gilligan, Carol. *In a Different Voice: Psychological Theory and Women's Develop-
  ment*. Cambridge, MA: Harvard University Press, 1982, 1993.
Gilson, Etienne. *The Christian Philosophy of St Augustine*. London: Victor
  Gollancz, 1961.
Girth, H.H., and C.W. Mill, eds. *From Max Weber*. New York: Oxford University
  Press, 1946.
Glendon, Mary Ann. *Rights Talk: The Impoverishment of Political Discourse*. New
  York: Free Press, 1991.
Goodin, Robert E. *Utilitarianism as a Public Philosophy*. New York: Cambridge
  University Press, 1995.
Greve, Michael S., and Fred L. Smith, eds. *Enviromental Politics: Public Costs,
  Private Rewards*. New York: Praeger, 1992.
Gwartney, James D., Richard Stroup, and J.R. Clark. *Essentials of Economics*.
  New York: Academic Press, 1985.

Hanson, Lorelie. 'Turning Rivals into Allies: Understanding the Wise Use Movement.' *Alternatives*, 21/3 (1995), 26–31.

Harding, Sandra. *The Science Question in Feminism*. Ithaca: Cornell University Press, 1986.

– 'Can Feminist Thought Make Economics More Objective.' *Feminist Economics*, 1/1 (1995), 7–32.

Harpp, David N., and Joseph A. Schwartz. 'The Straight Goods: Bovine Growth Hormone.' *Rapport*, 9/3 (1994), 6.

Harsanyi, J. 'Cardinal Welfare, Individualistic Ethics, and Interpersonal Comparisons of Utility.' *Journal of Political Economy*, 1955, 309–21.

Haslett, David W. *Capitalism with Morality*, Oxford: Clarendon, 1994.

Hasnas, John. 'The Normative Theories of Business Ethics: A Guide for the Perplexed.' *Business Ethics Quarterly*, 8/1 (1998), 19–42.

Hausman, Daniel M., and Michael S. McPherson. *Economic Analysis and Moral Philosophy*. Cambridge: Cambridge University Press, 1996.

Hayek, Friedrich A. *The Road to Serfdom*. Chicago: University of Chicago Press, 1944.

– 'The Use of Knowledge in Society.' *American Economic Review* (1945), 519–30.

– *The Constitution of Liberty*. South Bend: Gateway Editions, 1960.

– 'The Non Sequitor of the "Dependence Effect."' *Southern Economic Review*, April, 1961. Republished in Hoffman and Frederick, *Business Ethics*, 1995, 409–12.

Heidegger, Martin. *A Discourse on Thinking*. New York: Harper and Row, 1966.

– *What Is Called Thinking?* New York: Harper and Row, 1968.

Heilbroner, Robert L. *The Making of Economic Society*. Englewood Cliffs, NJ: Prentice Hall, 1962.

– *The Nature and Logic of Capitalism*. New York: W.W. Norton, 1985.

Hobbes, Thomas. *Leviathan or, the Matter, Form and Power of a Common-Wealth Ecclesiastical and Civil*. London: Andrew Crooke, 1651.

Hoffman, W. Michael, and Robert E. Frederick, eds. *Business Ethics: Readings and Cases in Corporate Morality*. New York: McGraw-Hill, 1995.

Hoffmann, Stanley. 'Look Back in Anger.' *New York Review of Books*, 17 July 1997, 45–50.

Hume, David. 'Of the Original Contract.' In *Social Contract*, E. Barker, ed., 207–36. London: Oxford University Press, 1947.

Hutchings, Jeffery, Carl Walters, and Richard Haedrich. 'Is Scientific Inquiry Compatible with Government Information Control?' *Canadian Journal of Fisheries and Aquatic Sciences*, 54/5 (1997), 1198–1210.

Jacobs, Jane. *Systems of Survival: A Dialogue on the Moral Foundations of Commerce and Politics*. New York: Random House, 1992.

Johnson, Harry G. *Man and His Environment*. London: British North America Committee, 1973.

Kagan, S. *The Limits of Morality*. Oxford: Oxford University Press, 1989.

Kalten, R.J. 'The New Biotech Agriculture: Unforseen Economic Consequences.' *Issues in Science and Technology* (Fall 1985), 125–33.

– R. Milligan, W. Lesser, W. Magrath, and D. Banman. *Biotechnology and the Diary Industry Production Costs and Commercial Potential of the Bovine Growth Hormone*. Ithaca, NY: Cornell University, Department of Agricultural Economics, 1985.

Keller, Evelyn Fox. *Reflections on Gender and Science*. New Haven: Yale University Press, 1985.

Knight, Rolf. *Indians at Work: An Informal History of Native Indian Labour in British Columbia, 1858–1930*. Vancouver: New Star Books, 1978.

Korten, David C. *When Corporations Rule the World*. West Hartford: Kumarian and Berrett-Koehler, 1995.

Koslowski, Peter. *Ethics of Capitalism and Critique of Sociobiology*. Berlin: Springer-Verlag, 1996.

Krell, D.F., ed. *Martin Heidegger: Basic Writings*. New York: Harper and Row, 1977.

Krieger, Martin H. 'What's Wrong with Plastic Trees.' *Science*, 179 (1973), 446–55.

Kronfeld, David S. 'Biologic and Economic Risks Associated with the Use of Bovine Somatotropins.' *Journal of the American Veterinary Medical Association*, 192 (1988), 1693–6.

Kuttner, Robert. *Everything for Sale: The Virtues and Limits of the Market*. New York: Knopf, 1997.

Kymlicka, Will. *Contemporary Political Philosophy: An Introduction*. Oxford: Clarendon, 1990.

Lake, Rhody. 'Can We Call It Conspiracy?' *Alive: Canadian Journal of Health and Nutrition* (July, 1997), 6.

Larmer, Robert A., ed. *Ethics in the Workplace*. Minneapolis: West, 1996.

Larsen, Hans R. 'Milk and the Cancer Connection.' *Alive: Canadian Journal of Health and Nutrition*, Sept., 1998, 36–8.

Lawson, Nigel. 'Some Reflections on Morality and Capitalism.' In *Market Capitalism and Moral Values*, S. Brittan and A. Hamlin. 35–44. Aldershot: Edward Elgar 1995.

Leone, Richard C. 'Foreword.' In *Everything for Sale*, Robert Kuttner, 1997.

Lewis, David. *Louder Voices: The Corporate Welfare Bums*. Toronto: James Lewis and Samuel, 1972.

Liebhardt, William, ed. *The Dairy Debate: Consequences of BGH and Rotational*

Raising Technologies. Davis: University of California Sustainable Agricultural Research and Education Program, 1993.

Little, I.M.D. *A Critique of Welfare Economics*. Oxford: Oxford University Press, 1950, 1957.

Locke, John. *Two Treatises of Government*. London: Whitmore and Fenn, 1688, 1821.

Longino, Helen. *Science as Social Knowledge: Values and Objectivity in Science Enquiry*. Princeton: Princeton University Press, 1990.

Lueck, D. 'The Rule of First Possession and the Design of Law.' *Journal of Law and Economics* (1995), 393–436.

Mackenzie, D. 'Doubts over Animal Health Delay Milk Hormone.' *New Scientist*, 18 Jan. 1992, 13.

MacKenzie, James, Roger C. Dower, and Donald D.T. Chen. *The Going Rate: What It Really Costs to Drive*. Washington: World Resources Institute, 1992.

Macpherson, C.B., ed. *Property: Mainstream and Critical Positions*. Toronto: University of Toronto Press, 1978.

Mandeville, Bernard. *The Fable of the Bees: Or Private Vices, Publick Benefits*, ed. F.B. Kaye. Oxford: Clarendon, 1714, 1924.

Marx, Karl. *The Revolutions of 1848: Political Writings*, vol. 1. London: Penguin, 1848, 1973.

McHarg, Ian. *Design with Nature*. Garden City, NY: Doubleday, 1971.

McLuhan, Marshall. *The Mechanical Bride: Folklore of Industrial Man*. New York: Vanguard, 1951, 1967.

McQuaig, Linda. *Shooting the Hippo*. New York: Penguin, 1995.

– *The Cult of Impotence*. New York: Penguin, 1998.

Meadows, D.H., D.L. Meadows, and J. Randers. *Beyond the Limits*. Toronto: McClelland and Stewart, 1992.

Menand, Louis. 'Inside the Billway.' *New York Review of Books*, 14 Aug. 1997, 4–7.

Meyers, Diana, and Eva Feder Kittay, eds. *Women and Moral Theory*. Totowa, NJ: Rowman and Littlefield, 1987.

Mill, John Stuart. *Principles of Political Economy*. Boston: Little Brown, 1848.

– *Principles of Political Economy*. Toronto: University of Toronto Press, 1963.

Mishan, E.J. 'The Rise of Affuence and the Decline of Welfare.' In Daly, *Economics, Ecology, and Ethics*, 267–81.

Moody-Stuart, George. *A Good Business Guide to Bribery: Grand Corruption in Third World Development*. Berlin: Transparency International, 1994.

Moog, Carol. *Are They Selling Her Lips? Advertising and Identity*. New York: William Morrow, 1990.

Mulligan, Thomas. 'A Critique of Milton Friedman's Essay "The Social

Responsibility of Business Is to Increase Its Profits.'" *Journal of Business Ethics*, 5 (1986), 265–9.

Narveson, Jan. *The Libertarian Idea*. Philadelphia: Temple University Press, 1988.

Nelson, Julie A. 'Gender, Metaphor and the Definition of Economics.' *Economics and Philosophy*, 8/1 (1992), 103–25.

– *Feminism, Objectivity and Economics*. London: Routledge, 1996.

– 'Feminism, Ecology, and the Philosphy of Economics.' *Ecological Economics*, 20 (1997), 155–62.

– 'For Love or Money – or Both?' Published in proceedings of the conference 'Out of the Margin,' Amsterdam, The Netherlands, 2–5 June 1998.

Newhouse, David. *From the Tribal to the Modern: The Development of Modern Aboriginal Society*, Department of Native Studies Working Paper 4. Peterborough: Trent University, 1995.

– 'Modern Aboriginal Economies: Capitalism with a Red Face.' Published in *Royal Commision on Aboriginal Peoples*, 90–100. Ottawa: Supply and Services Canada, 1995.

Notzke, Claudia. *Aboriginal Peoples and Natural Resources in Canada*. Toronto: Captus, 1994.

Nozick, Robert. *Anarchy, State and Utopia*. New York: Basic Books, 1974.

O'Neill, Onora. *Towards Justice and Virtue: A Constructive Account of Practical Reasoning*. Cambridge: Cambridge University Press, 1996.

Ovenell-Carter, Brad, and Julie Ovenell-Carter. 'Milky Solutions.' *Canadian Living*, May, 1996, 41–8.

Paul, Ellen Frankel, Jeffrey Paul, and Fred D. Miller. *Ethics and Economics*. Oxford: Blackwell, 1985.

Paul, Ellen Frankel, Fred D. Miller, Jeffrey Paul, and John Ahreus. *Capitalism*. Oxford: Blackwell, 1989.

Phelps, E., ed. *Economic Justice*. London: Penguin, 1973.

Phillips, Robert A. 'Stakeholder Theory and a Principle of Fairness.' *Business Ethics Quarterly*, 7/1 (1997), 51–66.

Plumwood, Val. *Feminism and Mastery of Nature*. London: Routledge, 1992.

Poff, Deborah C., and Wilfred J. Walchow, eds. *Business Ethics in Canada*. Scarborough, Ont.: Prentice Hall, 1998.

Polanyi, Karl. *The Great Transfromation: The Political and Economic Origins of Our Time*. Boston: Beacon Press, 1944.

Ponting, Clive. *A Green History of the World: The Environment and the Collapse of Great Civilizations*. New York: Penguin, 1991, 1993.

Porritt, Jonathan. *Seeing Green: The Politics of Ecology Explained*. New York: Oxford University Press, 1984.

Posner, R.A. 'Utilitarianism, Economics and Legal Theory.' *Journal of Legal Studies*, 8 (1979), 103–40.

Powell, Douglas, and William Leiss. *Mad Cows and Mother's Milk*. Montreal and Kingston: McGill-Queens University Press, 1997.

Rawe, A.L., and Rick Field. 'Tug-O-War with the Wise Use Movement.' *Z Magazine*. Oct. 1992, 62–4.

Rawls, John. *A Theory of Justice*. London: Oxford University Press, 1971.

Reich, Charles. 'The New Property.' *Yale Law Journal* (1961), 733–87.

Ridley, Matt. *The Origins of Virtue: Human Instincts and the Evolution of Coopera-tion*. New York: Viking, 1997.

Roemer, John E. *Theories of Distributed Justice*. Cambridge, MA: Harvard University Press, 1996.

Royal Commision on Aboriginal Peoples. *Sharing the Harvest*. Ottawa: Supply and Services Canada, 1995.

– *The Report of the Royal Commision on Aboriginal Peoples*. Ottawa: Supply and Services Canada, 1997.

Rubinoff, Lionel. 'Politics, Ethics and Ecology.' In *Canadian Issues in Environ-mental Ethics*, A. Wellington, A. Greenbaum, and W. Cragg, eds., 133–53. Peterborough: Broadview Press, 1997.

Russell, Betrand. *In Praise of Idleness and Other Essays*. London: Allen and Unwin, 1935.

Rutland, Peter. 'Capitalism and Socialism: How Can They Be Compared?' In *Capitalism*, E.F. Paul et al., eds., 197–227. Oxford: Blackwell, 1989.

Ryan, Alan. *Property and Political Theory*. Oxford: Blackwell, 1984.

Sahlins, Marshall. *Stone Age Economics*. Chicago: Aldine-Atherton, 1972.

Saunders, Douglas. 'Black's Citizen.' *Globe and Mail*, 1 March 1997, C1, C3.

Saunders, Peter. *Capitalism*. Minneapolis: University of Minnesota Press, 1992.

Schlatter, Richard Bulger. *Private Property: The History of an Idea*. London: George Allen and Unwin, 1951.

Schumacher, E.F. *Good Work*. New York: Harper and Row, 1975.

– *Small Is Beautiful*. New York: Harper and Row, 1989.

Sen, Amartya. *Poverty and Famines: An Essay on Entitlement and Deprivation*. Oxford: Clarendon, 1981.

– 'The Moral Standing of the Market.' In Paul et al., 1–19. *Capitalism*, 1985.

– *On Ethics and Economics*. Oxford: Blackwell, 1987.

– *Objectivity and Position*. The Lidley Lecture, University of Kansas, 1992.

Shankman, Neil. 'Reframing the Debate between Agency and Stakeholder Theories of the Firm.' *Journal of Business Ethics*, 19/4 (1998), 319–34.

Siebert, Horst, ed. *The Ethical Foundations of the Market Economy*. Tubingen: J.C.B. Mohr, 1994.

Silk, Leonard, and Mark Silk. *Making Capitalism Work*. New York: New York
    University Press, 1996.
Simon, Julian. *The Ultimate Resource*. Princeton: Princeton University Press,
    1981.
– *Population Matters*. New Brunswick, NJ: Transaction Publishers, 1990.
Singer, Peter. 'Famine, Affluence, and Morality.' *Philosophy and Public Affairs*,
    1 (1972), 229–43.
Smith, Adam. *The Theory of Moral Sentiments*. New York: Arlington House,
    1759, 1969.
– *An Inquiry into the Nature and Causes of the Wealth of Nations*. Indianapolis:
    Liberty Press, 1776, 1976.
Smith, Heather A. 'Stopped Cold.' *Alternatives*, Fall 1998, 10–16.
Soros, George. 'The Capitalist Threat.' *Atlantic Monthly*, February 1997, 45–58.
Strober, Myra. 'The Scope of Microeconomies: Implications for Economic
    Education.' *Journal of Economic Education*, 18 (1987), 135–49.
Sumner, L.W. *Welfare, Happiness and Ethics*. Oxford: Clarendon, 1996.
Swenarchuk, M. 'World Trade Organization Downs European Health Stan-
    dards.' *Canadian Dimension*, Jan.–Feb. 1998, 21–2.
Tawney, R.H. *The Acquisitive Society*. New York: Harcourt Brace, 1929.
Teeple, Gary. *Globalization and the Decline of Social Reform*. Toronto: Garamond,
    1995.
Tough, Frank. *As Their Natural Resources Fail: Native People and the Economic
    History of Northern Manitoba, 1870–1930*. Vancouver: UBC Press, 1996.
Transparency International. *TI Country Program in Ecuador: A Practical Approach
    for Building Islands of Integrity*. Berlin: Transparency International, 1994.
Tribe, Laurence. 'Ways Not to Think about Plastic Trees.' *Yale Law Review*, 83/7
    (1974), 1315–46.
Trigger, Bruce G. *The Huron: Farmers of the North*. Fort Worth: Holt, Rinehart
    and Winston, 1969, 1990.
Tritsch, George. 'More on BGH: IGF-1: The Human Experiment.' *Alive: Cana-
    dian Journal of Health and Nutrition*, Sept. 1995.
Tugwell, Rexford G. *The Battle for Democracy*. New York: Columbia University
    Press, 1935.
U.S. Department of Labor, Bureau of Labor Statistics. *Employment and Earnings*,
    43/1, (1996).
Usher, Dan. *The Economic Prerequisite to Democracy*. Oxford: Blackwell, 1981.
– 'Rawls, Rules and Objectives: A Critique of the Two Principles of Justice.'
    Constitutional Political Economy (1996), 103–26.
van Emmerik, Hetty. 'Gender, Paradigms, and Metaphors, and Some Implica-
    tions for Research in Business Administration.' Paper presented at the FENN

seminar 'Theoretical Concerns in Mainstream Economics,' The Hague, The Netherlands, Dec. 1995.

Waldron, Jeremy. *The Right to Private Property.* Oxford: Clarendon Press, 1988.

Warren, Karen J. 'Feminism and Ecology: Making Connections.' *Environmental Ethics*, 9/1 (1987), 3–20.

Wayne, Leslie. 'Hunting Cash, Candidates Follow the Bright Lights.' *New York Times*, 20 Oct. 1996, 5.

Weber, Max. *The Protestant Ethic and the Spirit of Capitalism.* London: Allen and Unwin, 1930.

– 'Bureaucracy,' in *From Max Weber*, ed. H.H. Girth and C.W. Mills, 196–244. New York: Oxford University Press, 1946.

Wein, Fred. *Rebuilding the Economic Base of Indian Communities: The Micmac in Nova Scotia.* Montreal: Institute for Research on Public Policy, 1986.

Wellington, Alex, Allan Greenbaum, and Wesley Cragg. *Canadian Issues in Environmental Ethics.* Peterborough: Broadview Press, 1997.

Wells, Jennifer. 'Winds of Change.' *Maclean's*, 11 Nov. 1996, 57–62. 'He Styles Himself as the Saviour of Papers, but Critics Label Conrad Black as an Editorial Storm Trooper.' *Maclean's*, 11 Nov. 1996, 56–61.

Werhane, Patricia Hogue. 'Formal Organizations, Economic Freedom and Moral Agency.' In *Business Ethics in Canada*, D.C. Poff and W.J. Waluchow, eds., 120–5. Scarborough, Ont.: Prentice Hall, 1998.

Wolf, Naomi. *The Beauty Myth.* Toronto: Random House, 1990.

Worster, Donald, ed. *The Ends of the Earth.* Cambridge: Cambridge University Press, 1988.

Yakabuski, Konrad. 'Quebec Unshaken by Exodus.' *Globe and Mail*, 17 March 1997, B1–B4.

Zimmerman, David. 'Coercive Wage Offers.' *Philosophy and Public Affairs*, 10 (1981), 121–45.

Zimmerman, Michael E., and J. Baird Callicott, eds. *Environmental Philosophy: From Animal Rights to Radical Ecology.* Englewoood Cliffs, NJ: Prentice Hall, 1993.

Contributors

John Douglas Bishop obtained a PhD in moral philosophy from the University of Edinburgh in Scotland (1979) and an MBA in finance from McMaster University (1985). He then worked for two multinational computer corporations in Toronto while reading widely and writing in the area of business ethics. In 1991 he accepted a position at Trent University in Peterborough, Ontario, teaching business ethics, advertising, and marketing. His research interests include making ethical theory practical for use in corporations, the moral justification of the free market economy, and Adam Smith. He has published in the *Journal of Business Ethics, Journal of the History of Ideas, Business and Society,* and the *Canadian Journal of Philosophy.*

David Copp is Professor of Philosophy at Bowling Green State University. He taught previously at Simon Fraser University, the University of Illinois at Chicago, and the University of California at Davis. He is author of many articles in meta-ethics and in normative moral and political philosophy. In 1995 he published *Morality, Normativity, and Society* (Oxford University Press).

Wesley Cragg, a Rhodes Scholar, obtained both BPhil and DPhil degrees from Oxford University. In July 1992 he was appointed George R. Gardiner Professor of Business Ethics at York University in Toronto. He has published widely in Canadian and international journals on topics in business ethics, occupational ethics, moral education, applied ethics, moral, political, and social philosophy, and philosophy of law. He is a former president of the Canadian Philosophical Association, a member of the Executive Committees of the International Society for Philosophy of Law and the York Centre for Practical Ethics. He is currently chair and president of Transparency International (Canada).

Leo Groarke is Professor of Philosophy at Wilfrid Laurier University. He has taught and researched in the areas of ethics, logic, and the history of ideas for almost twenty years. His publications include many articles in scholarly journals, anthologies, and the popular media. His books include *Nuclear War: Philosophical Perspectives* (Peter Lang, 1985), *Greek Scepticism* (McGill-Queen's, 1990), *Good Reasoning Matters!* (co-authored with C. Tindale and L. Fisher; Oxford, 1997), and *The Ethics of the New Economy: Restructuring and Beyond* (WLU Press, 1998).

Julie A. Nelson has a number of research interests including exploration of the relation of feminist theory to the definition and methodology of the discipline of economics as well as the empirical analysis of household demand behaviour. She is the author of *Feminism, Objectivity, and Economics* (Routledge, 1996), and co-editor (with Marianne A. Ferber) of *Beyond Economic Man: Feminist Theory and Economics* (University of Chicago Press, 1993). She is the author of numerous articles, including 'Feminism and Economics' (*Journal of Economic Perspectives*, 1995) and 'On Testing for Full Insurance Using Consumer Expenditure Survey Data' (*Journal of Political Economy*, 1994).

David R. Newhouse is working on a project entitled 'From the Tribal to the Modern: The Development of Modern Aboriginal Society,' in which he explores issues surrounding the encounter between Aboriginal thought and western knowledge and how this encounter is playing out in the ongoing move towards Aboriginal self-governance. He is the editor, along with Professors Peter Kulchyski and Don McCaskill, of *In the Words of Elders: Aboriginal Cultures in Transitions* (University of Toronto Press, 1999). Professor Newhouse is Onondaga and from the Six Nations of the Grand River Community near Brantford, Ontario.

Lionel Rubinoff is Professor Emeritus of Trent University. He studied at Queen's University and the University of Toronto. In a long and distinguished career he has taught at the University of Toronto, York University, and Trent University. He has published many books including *The Pornography of Power* (1968); *Faith and Reason: Essays in the Philosophy of Religion by R.G. Collingwood* (1968); *The Presuppositions of*

Critical History by F.H. Bradley: With Introduction and Commentary (1968); *Tradition and Revolution*, ed. with an introduction (1970); *Collingwood and the Reform of Metaphysics* (1970); and *Objectivity, Method and Point of View*, with J. Van Der Dussen (1991). He has contributed chapters and articles to many books and scholarly journals. He is currently completing a book on the moral foundations of environmentalism.

Dan Usher was an undergraduate at McGill University, did his graduate studies at the University of Chicago, worked briefly with the United Nations in Bangkok, was for five years a research fellow at Manchester and Nuffield College in Oxford, spent a year at the Business School of Columbia University, and has been at Queen's University since 1967. He is the author of *The Price Mechanism and the Meaning of National Income Statistics*, *The Measurement of Economic Growth*, *The Economic Prerequisite to Democracy*, and *The Welfare Economics of Markets, Voting and Predation*.

SHORT CUTS

INTRODUCTIONS TO FILM STUDIES

OTHER TITLES IN THE SHORT CUTS SERIES